THE
WORLD
OF
THE
CELTS

THE
WORLD
OF
THE
CELTS

SIMON JAMES

With over 300 illustrations, 59 in color

Thames & Hudson

To my parents

Author's note
I would like to express particular thanks to Martin Millett and Ian Stead, who read much of the text in draft (but bear no responsibility for what I have made of their help and comments). Thanks also to Timothy Potter, Ralph Jackson, Catherine Johns, Valerie Rigby and many other colleagues at the British Museum and elsewhere for information and discussion. I am also grateful to Patricia James, Steve Trow, Simon Keay, Colin Haselgrove, Barry Cunliffe and Anthony Harding for information and other assistance, and to Pete Horne for illustrations and comments. Special thanks to Peter Connolly for allowing me to reproduce some of his excellent paintings. I gratefully acknowledge the Society of Antiquaries, London for allowing me to reproduce plates from the Ramsauer Protokoll, and the Trustees of the British Museum who kindly gave permission to reproduce drawings by Steve Crummy and myself.

Finally I would like to acknowledge a particular debt to the staff at Thames and Hudson for their support, great professionalism and good humour throughout this project.

Half-title: Face of an Iron Age Celt, from a gold coin of the Gaulish Parisii.
Title-page: Bronze statuette of a god (?), 42 cm tall, from Bouray, France, first century BC or first century AD.

Copyright © 1993 Thames & Hudson Ltd, London

First published in 1993 in hardcover in the United States of America by Thames & Hudson Inc., 500 Fifth Avenue, New York, New York 10110

thamesandhudsonusa.com

First paperback edition 2005
Reprinted 2012

Library of Congress Catalog Card Number 92-80340

ISBN 978-0-500-27998-4

Printed and bound in Hong Kong
by Paramount Printing Company Limited

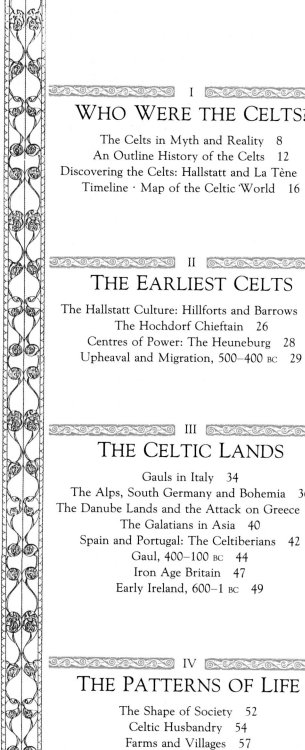

CONTENTS

WHO WERE
THE CELTS?

'This, then, is what I have to say about the people who inhabit the dominion of Gallia Narbonensis [southern France], whom the men of former times named 'Celtae'; and it was from the Celtae, I think, that the Galatae as a whole were by the Greeks called Keltoi – on account of the fame of the Celtae ...'

Strabo 4,1,14

THE CELTS are among the greatest peoples of European history, and indeed prehistory; long before Rome conquered the known world, Celtic speakers shared many common bonds – of language, customs, art and culture – across a vast area. They dwelt not just in Britain and Ireland, but from Spain and France to southern Germany and the Alpine lands, Bohemia, and later in Italy, the Balkans and even central Turkey.

Portrayed by the Greeks and Romans as fearsome and dangerous barbarians, the non-literate ancient Celts bequeathed no texts to redress the biased picture left by the Classical authors. Today, however, archaeology has given them a voice, through the physical traces they left behind. Modern archaeology has revealed much about Celtic society, economy and religious practices not mentioned in the surviving Classical texts. Celtic metalwork in particular shows a technical and artistic brilliance unsurpassed in prehistoric Europe. Survey and excavation reveal that many of their lands were populous and well-farmed, dotted with settlements and gathering-places, and often forts and shrines.

This new material evidence, combined with reassessments of the fascinating details that Caesar, Polybius, Strabo and other Classical writers *did* record, has permitted a fresh understanding of the world of the ancient Celts. They can now be seen as an intelligent, complex, wealthy and accomplished family of societies, who came to play a pivotal role in the making of Europe.

Gauls, having plundered an Italian sanctuary, flee the wrath of the vengeful gods. Detail of a terracotta relief from Civitalba, Italy, second century BC.

THE CELTS IN MYTH AND REALITY

CELTIC ICONS, CELTIC CARICATURES

The Celtic past is enshrined in France, where schoolchildren learn about 'our ancestors the Gauls'. Vercingetorix, leader of the revolt against Caesar's conquest of Gaul, has long been venerated as a hero of French history. A great bronze statue of him was erected at Alesia, the site of his last stand (below left). It embodies the romantic nineteenth-century view of the Celts as noble barbarian heroes.

Public familiarity with the Gallic past was essential to the huge popularity in France of the cartoon character Asterix the Gaul, the irrepressible little warrior who carries on the fight against the Romans after the fall of Alesia. The books have now been translated into many languages. (Below right) Asterix chats with Getafix the Druid, appropriately in a Celtic tongue; from a Welsh edition.

THE PEOPLE WE CALL CELTS have deep roots in European history, and can be traced back for at least twenty-five centuries, to beyond the very beginnings of literate civilization north of the Alps. The word 'Celtic' means something to most people, but the images it conjures up are very varied. To some it may mean little more than the name of a soccer or baseball team; but to others it suggests Irish monks in chilly *scriptoria* creating dazzling illuminated manuscripts, or kilted Scots, a Welsh eisteddfod or ancient warrior heroes charging into battle in chariots.

Some images are more contemporary, associated with the cultural heritage and national consciousness of the modern Irish and other western European peoples who speak – or once spoke – Celtic tongues. The French in particular, although paradoxically not normally thought of as Celts (except the Bretons), are infused with a romanticized sense of their Celtic or Gallic ancestry. Other images are rooted in the most distant past, and centre on the gorgeous, elaborate decoration of swirls and abstract designs of late prehistoric 'Celtic art'; or on the Druids and their supposed association with ancient stone circles and alignments.

So 'Celtic' has for many people come to reflect a continuity with the remote past. But how have our ideas of the ancient Celts come to us, and to what extent do they represent reality? And who actually were the Celts, and where and when did they live?

The Celts: discovery or invention?

People have never been quite sure where the term 'Celtic' came from. The earliest surviving references are to be found in the writings of ancient Classical authors. With inconsistency and inexactitude they described and speculated about the peoples whom the Greeks called *Keltoi* and *Galatae*, and whom the Romans called *Celtae* and *Galli*. In contradiction to today's popular conceptions, it might come as some surprise to discover that no Classical writer referred to the ancient British or Irish as Celts. For, 2,000 years ago, the term 'Celt' strictly referred to people living in continental Europe. Indeed, the idea that inhabitants of Iron Age Ireland or Britain could be referred to as Celtic only came into common currency during the seventeenth and eighteenth centuries – as a result of early work in the field of linguistics.

During the Renaissance, renewed study of the writings of Classical authors revived interest in both the Graeco-Roman world and in the aboriginal cultures of lands such as England and France. Later, work on these texts by scholars such as the Scot, George Buchanan (1506–82) and the Welshman Edward Lhwyd (1660–1709) led to the conclusion that Gaulish – spoken by the ancient Gauls of France – was related to contemporary Irish, Scots Gaelic, Welsh and other languages. The term 'Celtic' was chosen, resurrected from *Celtae* – Caesar's ill-defined name for the people of central Gaul – but now it was understood to refer to this *group of related languages*.

During the eighteenth century this linguistic classification was extended to become a general ethnic label for *all* the peoples of Britain, Ireland and the continent who were thought to have spoken Celtic tongues in pre-Roman and later times. This very broad definition of the Celts as an ethnic group is still popular today. But it is highly unlikely that all the ancient peoples now known as Celts referred to themselves by that name, or indeed had any concept of a 'pan-Celtic' identity. Beyond their related speech, the ancient Celts as widely conceived today were no more an ethnic unity than, say, modern Argentinians, French and Romanians who all speak Romance languages (derived from Latin), but do not see themselves as uniquely related and distinct.

The Celts were not a homogeneous family of peoples possessing a single, self-conscious ethnic identity. Nor can we speak of a Celtic empire or even a universal and exclusively Celtic material culture. The Celts may have had much in common in terms of social structure, religion, and material culture, but there was also enormous variability. For instance, political structures in the last few centuries BC ranged from small tribal chiefdoms to highly centralized states, and even 'regional superpowers' such as the Arverni and Aedui in Gaul and the Catuvellauni in Britain. And, contrary to popular belief, Druidism was probably not a general feature across the Celtic world, but was confined to the northwest. In fact, it is in many ways the sheer *diversity* of evidence that makes the study of these peoples so fascinating. We return, therefore, to the most satisfactory definition of the Celts – as peoples speaking languages of the Celtic family.

The first 'real' Celts in history

The name *Keltoi* first appears in Greek texts dating to about 500 BC, and was used to refer to societies on the northern fringes of the Classical Mediterranean world. People

(Above) Modern self-styled Druids celebrating the autumn equinox in a ceremony at Primrose Hill in central London, 1991.

COUNTERFEITING THE CELTS: THE CASE OF THE ROMANTIC HIGHLANDER

During the later eighteenth and early nineteenth centuries the 'discovery' (or virtual invention) of the Celts as an ethnic entity was seized upon by the Romantic movement, which was fascinated with concepts of the noble savage, nature, primitivism and mysticism. The so-called Celts, ancient and recent, were reinterpreted and even deliberately falsified to create the powerful romantic images we have today, personified for instance by the modern orders of the Druids.

The romantic reinvention of the Celtic past was particularly notable in Scotland. It is possible to trace in detail the creation of the image of the Gaelic-speaking kilted Highlander, a cultural icon with the most tenuous links with the reality of earlier times. For example, the kilt itself is known to have been invented

as late as about 1730 by an English industrialist, Thomas Rawlinson, while he was running an iron smelter at Invergarry. He wanted a more practical version of the contemporary Highland dress for his Scots workmen, who wore a belted cloak or plaid arranged into pleated skirts and slung over the shoulders. Rawlinson removed the upper part, sewed in the pleats, and the kilt was born (see right).

The kilt was not widely worn until the ban on Highland dress was lifted following the Scots rebellion of 1745 (p. 179). Ironically, it was not the common men who thankfully returned to 'traditional' garb, but the (increasingly Anglicized) aristocracy, who eagerly adopted an attire only recently considered by the Lowland Scots to be the dress of miserable cattle-thieves (rich

Highlanders had worn trews).

One of the most celebrated episodes in the reinvention of the Scottish Celts was the so-called discovery of the works of 'Ossian'. Supposedly the compositions of an ancient Highland bard, the whole text was an elaborate forgery, based on Irish material and a vivid imagination, written by James Macpherson in the 1760s. He hoodwinked an entire generation – including the great historian Edward Gibbon.

First created by the Romantic movement, and further embedded in the popular imagination by the novels of Sir Walter Scott, the image of the Highlander remains an obstacle to a true understanding of Scottish history. Yet 'Ossian' and the other romantic reinventions helped to foster a genuine interest in the past.

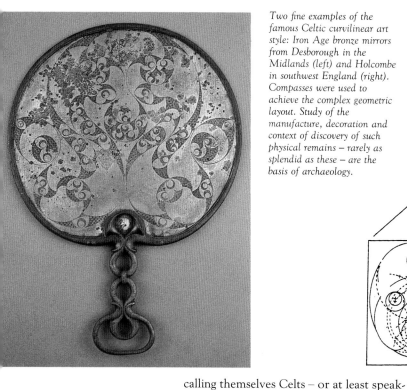

Two fine examples of the famous Celtic curvilinear art style: Iron Age bronze mirrors from Desborough in the Midlands (left) and Holcombe in southwest England (right). Compasses were used to achieve the complex geometric layout. Study of the manufacture, decoration and context of discovery of such physical remains – rarely as splendid as these – are the basis of archaeology.

calling themselves Celts – or at least speaking languages we would consider to be Celtic – may have existed earlier, but since no one north of the Alps was literate at this time, we have no definitive evidence. (It is, therefore, a nonsense to use the term 'Celtic' for the broad sweep of European prehistory from the Stone Age to the Bronze Age, as is still sometimes done.) Strictly speaking, then, we can justifiably use the term 'Celt' only for the period following its first mention in surviving

(Left) A large bronze tablet from Botoritta, the ancient site of Contrebia Belaisca, near Saragossa in Spain. It bears a text in Hispano-Celtic, apparently a legal document of about 200 words long. Another long text has recently been recovered at the site.

THE AFFILIATIONS OF CELTIC LANGUAGES

The diagram here shows the Celtic languages as part of the wider Indo-European family. The exact relationships between the Celtic tongues are often uncertain, since extinct members (such as Hispano-Celtic and Gallic) are only partially known from tiny fragments.

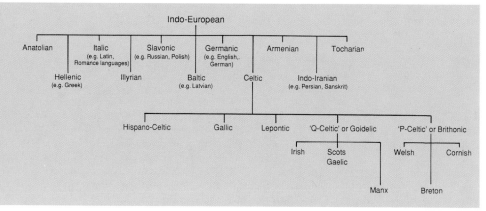

documents. There is, however, a growing quantity of spectacular archaeological evidence for the silent centuries before the coming of literacy to the Celtic north.

How do we know? Sources of evidence

There are three main classes of evidence regarding the ancient Celts during the Iron Age and through the Roman period: documentary, linguistic and archaeological. Each gives us a range of complementary information with which to build up our picture of early Celtic societies.

Documentary sources. These comprise all written material relating to the Celts, from texts on coins to stone inscriptions, and especially histories and other texts by Greek and Roman writers. It is only through such written documents that language, and concepts such as ethnic identity and belief, can reach us today, since they leave no direct physical trace.

Linguistics. The ancient Celts left us few written records of their languages, so we must rely on alternative sources, such as the Celtic names and words in Classical texts, or surviving Celtic place-names. Building on the work of early linguists (p. 8), philologists now group the Celtic tongues as one branch of the much broader Indo-European linguistic family.

Some ancient Celtic languages are now extinct (such as those of Spain or the dialects of Gaul), but six distinct Celtic languages do still exist, or existed in recent times. Scholars divide these into two families: 'Q-Celtic' or Goidelic and 'P-Celtic' or Brithonic (see table). The basic distinction lies in the replacement of the apparently earlier *q-* sound of Q-Celtic by a *p-* sound (for example, the Old Irish word for 'son' is *mac*, but in Old Welsh it is *map*). There are three Q-Celtic languages (modern Irish, Scots Gaelic and Manx), all derived from Old Irish, and three P-Celtic languages (Welsh, Breton and Cornish), thought to originate from the ancient British tongue. It is not terribly clear how the extinct Celtic languages relate to these modern families, although Gaulish seems to have been essentially P-Celtic.

Traditionally, scholars believed that Q- and P-Celtic represented the languages of two waves of Celtic migrants across

Europe. But this theory is no longer thought to be very likely: it now seems that Celtic languages evolved gradually, across a large area, rather than spreading from one small region.

Archaeological evidence. Archaeological methods of tracing the lives of ancient people now extend from the laboratory analysis of the composition of metals to the survey of patterns of settlement and land-use. In between are the more familiar techniques of excavation of individual farms, forts, sanctuaries and cemeteries, and the study of pots, tools, the physical remains of the people themselves, the crops they cultivated, and the animals they ate.

Archaeology has great strengths. For although on its own it can give us only a partial picture (not all materials survive), the evidence is free from the distorting lens of the prejudices of Graeco-Roman authors – although archaeologists too have their own biases! It is also particularly good at identifying patterns, such as the geographical distribution of coins or types of pottery which may reveal economic and trade contacts.

So, putting all these sources of evidence together, we are able to build a plausible portrait of life in the Celtic world.

The moment of discovery: a hoard of gold torcs lies as it was found in the pit where it was buried 2,000 years ago. Excavated in 1990, this was one of several such hoards found at Snettisham in Norfolk, England, over the last forty years. Such discoveries certainly make headlines, and give a striking impression of the wealth, technological skill and artistic sophistication of Celtic communities. However, most archaeological evidence is much more mundane, consisting for instance of pits and post-sockets, pollen, pot sherds and bone fragments; these often shed more light on the lives of earlier people than do such rare finds of gold.

AN OUTLINE HISTORY OF THE CELTS

ANCIENT HISTORIANS OF THE EARLY CELTS

Polybius (c. 200–after 118 BC). This Greek politician published in about 150 BC a history of Rome's rise to world power, from the time of Hannibal to the Battle of Pydna in 168 BC – which marked the end of Greek resistance and Polybius' own exile to Rome. He dealt at length with the Gauls of Italy and their conflict with Rome.

Poseidonius (c. 135–50 BC). A Syrian Greek philosopher and teacher of Cicero, Poseidonius travelled extensively in the western Mediterranean, including at least the southern parts of Gaul. His extensive Histories have been mostly lost except for fragments, which include precious eyewitness descriptions of the Gauls soon after 100 BC. Poseidonius appears to have been a valued but sometimes uncredited source for many other Graeco-Roman writers; his work has been quoted, for instance, by writers such as Strabo, whose works have survived.

Diodorus Siculus (died 21 BC or after). Between c. 60 and 30 BC, Diodorus the Sicilian wrote a world history in forty books, ending with Caesar's Gallic wars, much of which survives. Britain and Gaul are dealt with in the fifth book.

WHEN THE CELTS FIRST APPEAR on the historical stage around 500 BC, they seem already to have been spread over much of the Alpine region and the areas immediately to the north, in central France, and in parts of Spain. Traditionally these early Celts are broadly associated with part of the archaeologically-attested Hallstatt culture of the European Iron Age. Excavations have revealed richly adorned tombs, assumed to be those of chieftainly or royal classes, associated with a number of major defended centres. These 'princedoms' furnish evidence for trade with the Classical Mediterranean, especially the Greek colony of Massalia (Marseilles).

Beginning in the fifth century BC, in a zone stretching from eastern France to Bohemia, a new Celtic culture arose, named after the archaeological site of La Tène in Switzerland where it was first identified (pp. 14–15). This too was characterized by splendidly furnished graves containing evidence of Classical contacts (with Etruscan cities via the Alps). Soon after 400 BC, these La Tène Celts erupted over the Alps, seizing and settling the Po Valley and sacking Rome in about 390 BC. They were known to the Romans as *Galli*, Gauls – a term later used particularly of the Celts of France. Others migrated through the Balkans, attacking Greece and perhaps sacking Delphi in 279 BC. Known to the Greeks as *Keltoi* or *Galatae*, some burst across the Hellespont and carved out a kingdom in central Turkey (Galatia).

While the documentary sources tell us nothing of events in distant northern France or the British Isles, archaeology reveals the spread of La Tène culture (especially decorated metalwork) to those areas in the fifth and fourth centuries BC. It has often been assumed that this reflects the migration northwards of Celtic-speaking groups, paralleling the clearly recorded movements south and east from a supposed Celtic homeland in and north of the Alps, where La Tène art arose. But it now seems likely that Celtic speakers already populated much of northwestern Europe and the British Isles, perhaps from far earlier times. The expansion of La Tène art may

simply reflect the spread of a new fashion which arose in one part of the Celtic-speaking region.

In the third century BC, the Celtic world consisted of a shifting mosaic of autonomous tribes and states stretching from Ireland to Hungary, with isolated pockets and partly Celtic populations from Portugal to Turkey. But during the later third and second centuries BC the Celtic lands were beginning to come under pressure from the Germans and to fall under the sway of Rome, which conquered first northern Italy, then parts of Spain and, in the second century BC, southern France. In Turkey, the Romans crushed the power of the Galatians, who were almost annihilated by the kingdom of Pontus in the 80s BC. The greatest blow Rome dealt the Celtic-speaking world was the conquest of Gaul in the 50s BC. Spain was entirely conquered before the turn of the millennium, by which time the Celts of the Danube had all but vanished.

This left only the British Isles. Claudius invaded southeastern Britain in AD 43, and by the early 80s the Romans had conquered as far as the Highlands of Scotland (Caledonia). However, the legions proved unable to hold the north, which remained a largely free zone of at least partly Celtic stock.

Ireland was the only part of the Celtic world entirely to escape the colonial ambitions of Rome, and she sat out the centuries of the Roman empire largely undisturbed – until her tribes took part in the dismemberment of the provinces in the later fourth and fifth centuries AD.

Roman rule seems to have virtually extinguished the culture and, very slowly, the language of the continental Celts – although the Gauls adapted well to Roman ways, Gaul becoming the linchpin of the Roman west. After Rome fell in the fifth century AD, and the old Celtic lands came under Germanic rule, even the name of Gaul disappeared, to be replaced by France (derived from the Germanic tribe of the Franks).

Celtic language and social structure seems to have survived quite well in the west and north of Britain until Roman rule collapsed, probably because Britain was never as thoroughly Romanized as Gaul. Following the appearance in the sixth century of the proto-Welsh and other British kingdoms, there was a resurgence in Celtic culture – perhaps in response to the establishment of the early Anglo-Saxon realms by Germanic invaders in the east of the country. La Tène style art made something of a comeback, largely due to the vigour and influence of newly-Christian Ireland. Western Britons crossed the Channel to Armorica in Gaul, and so established Brittany.

Ireland experienced a cultural golden age during the sixth to eighth centuries AD. Many groups of Irish raided and settled the western seaboard of Roman Britain (where Christianity had been established by the fourth century); some of these returned to their native country – resulting in the evangelization of the Irish kingdoms. With astonishing speed, Ireland became one of the greatest centres of European Christianity, and Irish monks and clerics worked to evangelize the largely-pagan British and English, establishing famous monasteries such as those at Iona (a small island off the west coast of Scotland) and Lindisfarne in Northumbria. Some of the Irish sea-rovers, who were known as *Scotti*, founded a kingdom in western Caledonia; this was the genesis of the medieval kingdom of Scotland.

The Celtic revival of the early Middle Ages was halted by the appearance of the Vikings at the end of the eighth century. The Norse ravaged Europe, and invaded Ireland, beginning the long and troubled history of foreign intervention there.

From the eleventh century, the Celtic nations of the British Isles were under constant pressure from their large neighbour, England, as the Bretons were similarly threatened by the developing kingdom of France. The story of the Celts in the later Middle Ages is one of gradual absorption and partial assimilation. Wales lost her independence in the thirteenth century, by which time the Celtic identity of Cornwall was being rapidly eroded. Brittany was subsumed within France in 1532. Ireland only fell fully under English rule during the reign of Elizabeth I. Her death in 1603 also began the final unification of England with Scotland; the two countries were formally unified in 1707. The Gaelic-speaking clan society of Scotland's Highlands and Islands was effectively destroyed after the rebellion of 1745. Ireland was also incorporated into the United Kingdom, in 1801.

The Celtic parts of the British Isles underwent severe economic difficulties in the eighteenth and nineteenth centuries, especially in Scotland – with the systematic depopulation of the Highlands – and in Ireland, where rural distress culminated in the Potato Famine of the 1840s and appalling loss of life. Together with these agricultural difficulties, the growing demand for industrial labour and the new opportunities overseas engendered a new wave of migration, as Scots and Irish in particular flooded into the expanding industrial cities, or emigrated to America and Australasia.

During the nineteenth and twentieth centuries the Celtic languages experienced steep decline, even being actively suppressed. Yet at the same time, the rediscovery of the past contributed to developing national self-awareness in modern Celtic Europe, and was essential to the final rebirth of Irish statehood in 1921. Vigorous nationalist movements also exist in Scotland, Wales and Brittany.

Today Celtic tongues are still spoken as first languages, and the development of Welsh and Gaelic television and radio has done much to promote their survival. Although facing an uncertain future, Celtic speech will certainly survive for generations to come.

ANCIENT HISTORIANS OF THE EARLY CELTS

Strabo (c. 64 BC–AD 21 or later). An Asiatic Greek, a geographer and historian, Strabo was personally acquainted with Poseidonius. Book Four of his surviving seventeen-book Geography deals with Gaul and Britain: he also describes Spain, Italy and Galatia.

Caesar (100–44 BC). Gaius Julius Caesar, perhaps the most famous Roman of all, was the most audacious politician of the last days of the Roman republic; indeed, it was he who ultimately destroyed it, leading – after the wars following his assassination – to the rise of the emperors. His conquest of Gaul (58–51 BC) provided him with the military prestige, soldiers, and wealth he needed to seize supreme power at Rome. His Commentaries (better known as the Gallic War) were works of propaganda to advertise and explain his actions, which were strictly illegal. The texts are consequently politically biased, but the scale and detail of the account make them invaluable – and fascinating to read.

Characteristic moustached Celtic faces on flagons from (left to right) Waldalgesheim, Germany, c. 350 BC; Basse-Yutz, France, c. 400 BC; Dürrnberg, Austria, 400–350 BC.

DISCOVERING THE CELTS: HALLSTATT AND LA TÈNE

(Right) By contemporary standards, Johann Georg Ramsauer's excavations at Hallstatt (1846–63) were meticulously recorded, witness these vivid watercolours of the graves and some of the objects from them.

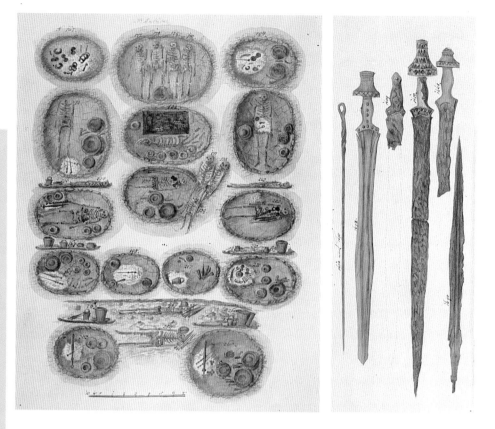

HISTORICAL SOCIETIES AND ARCHAEOLOGICAL CULTURES

Archaeology emerged in the nineteenth century as a scientific discipline, and archaeologists thus sought to apply scientific methods of classification and analysis to the past. Scholars adapted the idea of evolution to develop a concept of human technological progress, through the 'Three Ages' of Stone, Bronze and Iron and thence to the rise of historical civilizations. Subsequently archaeologists further categorized the debris left by earlier peoples into archaeological 'cultures' with shared attributes such as types of tools, methods of building and pot-making, rites of burial, and artistic styles. But such archaeological cultures rarely correspond simply to ethnic groups, and the case of the Celts is no exception. It is an attractive idea to assume that all Celts adopted the quintessentially 'Celtic' La Tène art style and material culture: indeed it is found in most of the territories where other evidence suggests Celtic was spoken – but not in all. La Tène-style objects are virtually absent from Spain, which had a very important Celtic element in its population. Neither was La Tène culture confined solely to Celtic speakers, moreover, for aspects of it were incorporated into other cultures, such as those in Dacia, Germany, Thrace and the Roman empire.

INTEREST IN THINGS CELTIC really started to blossom in the mid-nineteenth century following the discovery of two spectacular sites at Hallstatt in Austria and La Tène in Switzerland. Identified as the relics of the ancient Celts, the finds fed into the more general curiosity in Europe's past that had been kindled by the new, scientific approach to the excavation and documentation of antiquities. Changes were afoot in the field of Celtic studies, for scholars began to broaden their definition of the Celts from the (eighteenth-century) focus on the documents and linguistics, and now started to search for their actual physical remains. Thus began the exploration of Celtic archaeology.

Hallstatt

Artifacts were first unearthed at Hallstatt in Upper Austria early in the nineteenth century, and excavations continued at the site from 1846 to 1863. These revealed a cemetery of an astonishing one thousand graves – many containing sumptuous funerary offerings. The individuals buried came from an early Iron Age community, whose livelihood depended on mining the nearby deposits of rock-salt. Investigations of the mines themselves yielded clothing, equipment and even the body of a miner, perfectly preserved by the salt.

The cemetery mostly dates to the seventh and sixth centuries BC, and includes some splendid 'chieftains' graves'. It remains one of the richest known cemeteries of its kind, with a wide range of weapons, brooches, pins and pottery, as well as imported Italian bronze vessels which have been used to date the cemetery. Few graves date to the fifth century, because the site was eclipsed by more convenient deposits of salt at Dürrnberg. In the fourth century BC, Hallstatt was devastated by a vast landslide.

La Tène

Situated on the northern edge of Lake Neuchâtel in Switzerland, La Tène was identified as an archaeological site in 1857 when an archaeology enthusiast discovered a series of ancient timber piles driven into the bed of the lake. His interest aroused, he then found iron weapons and tools hidden in the mud among the piles. Drainage and dredging operations carried out during the 1860s and 1880s brought many additional discoveries, including human remains and, early in the twentieth century, well-preserved wooden items including shields. A total of 166 swords, 269 spearheads, 29 shields, 382 fibulae, plus belt clasps, razors, tools, bronze cauldrons, wooden yokes, iron ingots and other objects, were salvaged. Excavations ceased in 1917, but the nature of the site is still discussed. Variously thought to be a trading emporium or frontier station, more recent research suggests that La Tène may have been a religious sanctuary. Whatever its true role, La Tène remains a key site to the understanding of Iron Age chronology, art and technology.

The Hallstatt and La Tène 'cultures'

Celtic studies took a new turn in the later nineteenth century when scholars began to identify Celtic artifacts at many sites across Europe. In 1872, the archaeologist Hans Hildebrand proposed that the objects recovered from Hallstatt and La Tène were the product of two separate periods of the pre-Roman Iron Age. Adopting the names of the two sites, he suggested that the earlier 'Hallstatt culture' was followed by the 'La Tène culture'.

The Hallstatt culture is now thought to span a period from c. 1200 to 475 BC. We have no way of ascertaining exactly who was responsible for the earlier, Bronze Age Hallstatt material, because we have no written records from this epoch; indeed it is very likely that the remains of peoples other than Celtic-speakers are included under the Hallstatt label. But we can be fairly sure that some artifacts from the later, Iron Age, part of the Hallstatt period represent the relics of the earliest Celts as defined by their first mention in the Classical texts. Indeed, the Celts can be credited with many of the greatest developments of the Hallstatt period, such as the fine hillforts constructed during the sixth century BC or the rich tombs from the 'princedoms' of the western Hallstatt lands.

Whereas the Hallstatt culture probably extended to other language groups, the La Tène culture is identified very closely with the Celts. The La Tène culture evolved during the fifth century BC in part of the Hallstatt area, when Rome was an infant republic and Athens was beating off the Persians and making her own bid for empire. Characterized in particular by the famous curvilinear ('curving line') art – a largely abstract style of decoration applied especially to metalwork – La Tène culture is more broadly defined by a wide repertoire of pottery and metalwork styles, burial rites, and settlement types. The original La Tène heartland lay during the fifth century BC in an area covering eastern France, southern Germany, Austria and Switzerland, from where it subsequently spread. La Tène is the culture of the Celts who featured so prominently in the history of the ancient world.

(Below) The location of La Tène. (Bottom) Part of Paul Vouga's excavations at La Tène in the early decades of this century, showing in plan and section a pile-built 'bridge' across the watercourse, and some of the many items – including weapons and human remains – deposited around it.

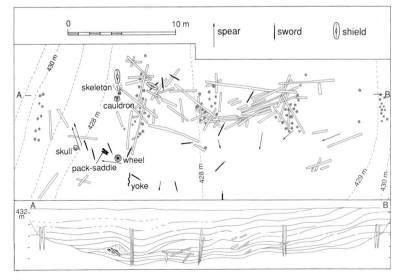

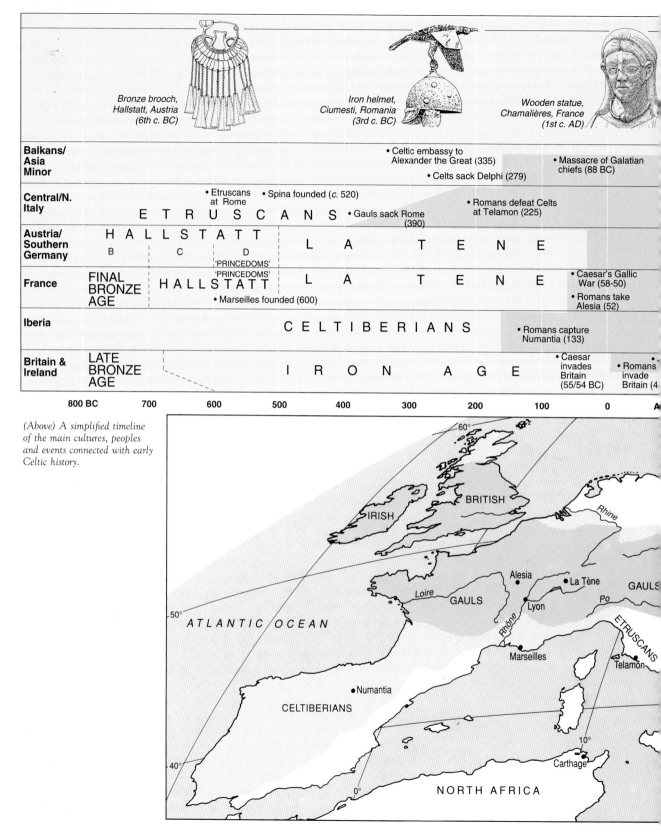

Bronze brooch,
Hallstatt, Austria
(6th c. BC)

Iron helmet,
Ciumesti, Romania
(3rd c. BC)

Wooden statue,
Chamalières, France
(1st c. AD)

	800 BC	700	600	500	400	300	200	100	0	AD
Balkans/ Asia Minor					• Celtic embassy to Alexander the Great (335)	• Celts sack Delphi (279)		• Massacre of Galatian chiefs (88 BC)		
Central/N. Italy	E T R U S	• Etruscans at Rome	• Spina founded (c. 520) C A N	S	• Gauls sack Rome (390)		• Romans defeat Celts at Telamon (225)			
Austria/ Southern Germany	H A L L S T A T T	B	C	D	L A	T	E N	E		
France	FINAL BRONZE AGE	H A L L 'PRINCEDOMS' S T A T T	'PRINCEDOMS' • Marseilles founded (600)	L A	T	E N	E	• Caesar's Gallic War (58–50) • Romans take Alesia (52)		
Iberia			C E L T I B E R I A N S				• Romans capture Numantia (133)			
Britain & Ireland	LATE BRONZE AGE		I R O N	A G	E			• Caesar invades Britain (55/54 BC)	• Romans invade Britain (4...)	

(Above) A simplified timeline of the main cultures, peoples and events connected with early Celtic history.

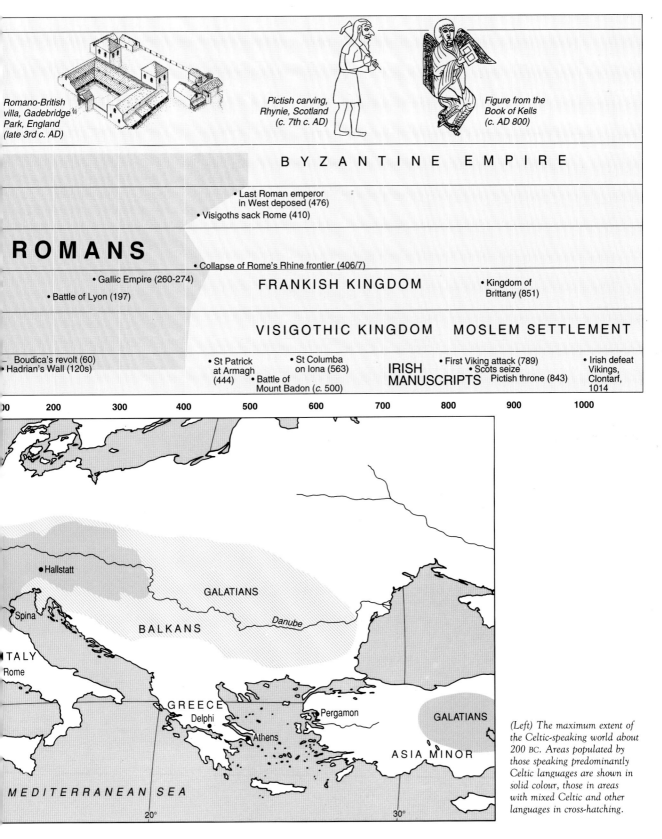

Romano-British
villa, Gadebridge
Park, England
(late 3rd c. AD)

Pictish carving,
Rhynie, Scotland
(c. 7th c. AD)

Figure from the
Book of Kells
(c. AD 800)

BYZANTINE EMPIRE

• Last Roman emperor
in West deposed (476)
• Visigoths sack Rome (410)

ROMANS

• Collapse of Rome's Rhine frontier (406/7)

• Gallic Empire (260-274)   FRANKISH KINGDOM   • Kingdom of
                                                              Brittany (851)
• Battle of Lyon (197)

VISIGOTHIC KINGDOM   MOSLEM SETTLEMENT

Boudica's revolt (60)   • St Patrick   • St Columba   • First Viking attack (789)   • Irish defeat
• Hadrian's Wall (120s)   at Armagh   on Iona (563)   IRISH   • Scots seize   Vikings,
                               (444)   • Battle of   MANUSCRIPTS   Pictish throne (843)   Clontarf,
                               Mount Badon (c. 500)   1014

| 200 | 300 | 400 | 500 | 600 | 700 | 800 | 900 | 1000 |

Hallstatt

GALATIANS

Danube

Spina

BALKANS

ITALY
Rome

GREECE
Delphi

Pergamon

GALATIANS

Athens

ASIA MINOR

MEDITERRANEAN SEA

20°   30°

(Left) The maximum extent of
the Celtic-speaking world about
200 BC. Areas populated by
those speaking predominantly
Celtic languages are shown in
solid colour, those in areas
with mixed Celtic and other
languages in cross-hatching.

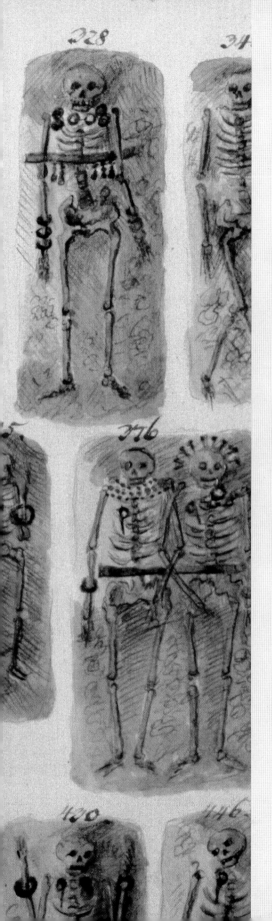

THE EARLIEST CELTS

'The Danube traverses the whole of Europe, rising among the Celts ... [who] dwell beyond the Pillars of Hercules, being the neighbours of the Cynesii, who are the westernmost of all nations inhabiting Europe.'

Herodotus, *Histories*, 4, 49 and 2, 33

BOTH DOCUMENTARY and archaeological evidence suggest that the Celts occupied, in the sixth century BC, a vast swathe of land from the Iberian peninsula to the Upper Danube. While we know little of their very early history, it is clear that by this time the Celts had established defended settlements, mastered the art of ironworking and mining, and had begun to trade with the Classical world.

One of the earliest Celtic achievements we can trace was the establishment of the so-called chiefdoms of the unromantically named Western Hallstatt culture. The dry archaeological label does not convey the richness of their hillforts nor the lavishness of their burials. Such settlements were scattered near the headwaters of the major rivers of Europe from the Loire to the Danube, and it is almost certainly their occupants to whom Herodotus is referring above. These Hallstatt princedoms were responsible for some spectacular cultural developments and are thought to be the first distinctive and detectable flowering of Celtic culture.

Watercolours of some of the graves excavated by Johann Georg Ramsauer at the cemetery of Hallstatt in Austria between 1846 and 1863.

THE HALLSTATT CULTURE: HILLFORTS AND BARROWS

(Opposite) Map to show the westward shift in the distribution of vehicle burials between Hallstatt C and D, and the location of the 'princely' centres. Note the proximity of these settlements to routes along major river valleys, and the access to the Greek port of Massalia.

THE CELTS, as we have seen, had their roots in the Hallstatt culture that extended right across central Europe. Spanning a period from *c.* 1200 to 475 BC, the Hallstatt era is divided by archaeologists into four phases: A, B, C and D. Roughly speaking, Hallstatt A and B correspond to the late Bronze Age, *c.* 1200–800 BC; C belongs to the very early Iron Age, *c.* 800–600 BC; and Hallstatt D ranges from *c.* 600 to 475 BC.

Hallstatt Europe

Late Bronze Age northern Europe apparently lacked large-scale political organization: there were no major centres of power. But long-distance exchange was already well established, notably of copper and tin, which were used to make bronze. At Hallstatt in Austria, another vital commodity was being mined as early as 1000 BC for transport to distant regions: this was salt, a food preservative essential in a world without refrigeration. During the eighth century BC, iron, a revolutionary new commodity, was also introduced to central Europe. Control of these products and their means of distribution may have been the key stimulus to the appearance of centres of power in the Iron Age.

Until the eighth century, the known settlements (farms, villages and a few hillforts) suggest no more complex organiz-

(Right) Stone figure which is thought to have stood on the Hirschlanden burial mound, Baden-Württemburg, Germany (reconstructed below). The naked man sports a dagger, neckring and conical hat, similar to those discovered buried with the Hochdorf 'prince' (pp. 26–27). Later sixth century BC.

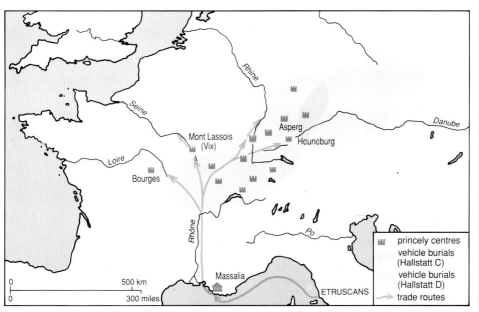

THE ORIGINS AND
SPREAD OF CELTIC
LANGUAGES

*Traditionally, many scholars
identified Celtic origins with
the appearance in the fifth
century BC of La Tène culture
in parts of Germany, eastern
France and some adjacent
areas; Celtic speech was
supposedly spread from these
regions by the migrations
starting c.400 BC. Almost
certainly, however, Celtic
languages existed much earlier.*

*Firstly, archaeological finds
seem to indicate a strong
continuity with native Bronze
Age traditions in areas such as
Britain and Ireland. Here there
is no evidence that large-scale
Celtic migrations took place.
Secondly, we have already seen
that Celtic-speakers were
probably spread across a wide
part of Europe as early as the
sixth century BC. Stone
inscriptions, for instance,
suggest that the 'Golaseccan
culture' (on the Alpine fringe
of Italy, and dating from the
ninth to fifth centuries BC) was
Celtic-speaking.*

*So, were Celtic tongues
disseminated by an even
earlier, prehistoric wave of
migrations? In reality, Celtic
languages need not have
started and spread from one
small area at all; they could
have evolved gradually and
simultaneously over a large
area, hand in hand with
shared social, political and
religious practices.*

*This sort of common heritage
may help to explain the spread
of La Tène culture to, say, the
British Isles: close links of
outlook and kinship already
existed, which would
predispose people to adopt new
artistic styles. The idea is
controversial, and it does not
explain why these peoples –
and not others – became Celts.
But the theory fits much more
plausibly with the
archaeological evidence, which
provides little support for
westward migrations of Celtic
peoples matching the
historically known movements
south and east.*

ation than petty chiefdoms. Around this time, however, some richer burials appear among the mass of ordinary graves with few offerings. Found from southern Germany to Bohemia and western Hungary, the more affluent graves include those of warriors (sometimes with prestigious iron swords), and a small number even with four-wheeled wagons.

Between 800 and 600 BC (the Hallstatt C period), the early Celts – as many surely were – began to build fortified settlements on hilltops with increasing frequency north of the Alps. Attendant clusters of burial mounds mark the graves of the rising noble classes, who no doubt had the hillforts built and certainly wished to symbolize their distinctiveness from the rest of society in ever richer grave goods. The burial mounds include spectacular contents, such as fine funerary carts. Here again the increasing volume of trade seems to have been the major factor in the appearance of these nobilities. It is not hard to imagine how a lord might gain status and influence through the control of a precious commodity such as iron or salt.

The chiefdoms of the later Western Hallstatt

In the last phase of the Hallstatt period (Hallstatt D, c. 600–475 BC), the richest graves – notably those with vehicles and costly imports – are more concentrated to the west (in eastern France, southwest Germany and adjacent areas) than previously. They tend to be clustered around a handful of major hillforts, probably the seats of princes or chiefs whose graves they mark. Why the westward shift? The answer seems to be connected with the establishment in c. 600 BC of a new Greek trading colony at Massalia (Marseilles), near the mouth of the Rhône. The new chiefdoms or 'princedoms' lie close to the major routes connecting the Rhine, Seine, Loire and Upper Danube with the Rhône corridor. Like the minor aristocracies of the preceding period, the Hallstatt D princes derived much of their wealth from trade. The lucky appearance of the Greek entrepôt at Massalia not only provided the western Celtic lords with the chance to make spectacular new profits, but it also gave them access to new classes of luxury goods from Greece and the Mediterranean with which to display their power. Greek imports are indeed found buried in the Western Hallstatt D graves.

Reaching the Greek world via Massalia, stories about these 'barbarian' chiefdoms (where Celtic was probably spoken) were in all likelihood one of the earliest sources for tales of the people called *Keltoi*.

Seats of power and 'princely' burials

The seats of these chiefdoms or 'princedoms' were a small number of very rich, fortified, hilltop settlements. The most

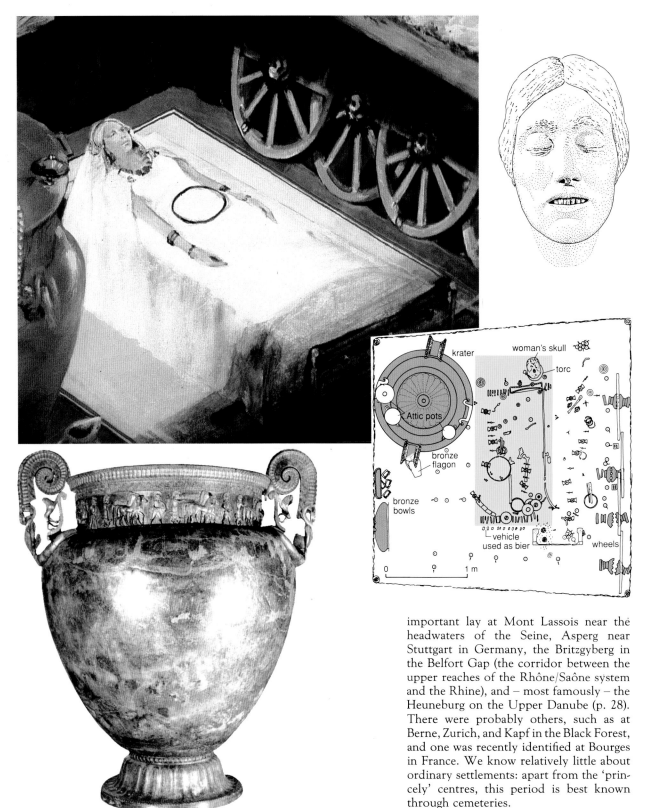

krater

woman's skull

torc

Attic pots

bronze
flagon

bronze
bowls

vehicle
used as bier

wheels

0   1 m

important lay at Mont Lassois near the headwaters of the Seine, Asperg near Stuttgart in Germany, the Britzgyberg in the Belfort Gap (the corridor between the upper reaches of the Rhône/Saône system and the Rhine), and – most famously – the Heuneburg on the Upper Danube (p. 28). There were probably others, such as at Berne, Zurich, and Kapf in the Black Forest, and one was recently identified at Bourges in France. We know relatively little about ordinary settlements: apart from the 'princely' centres, this period is best known through cemeteries.

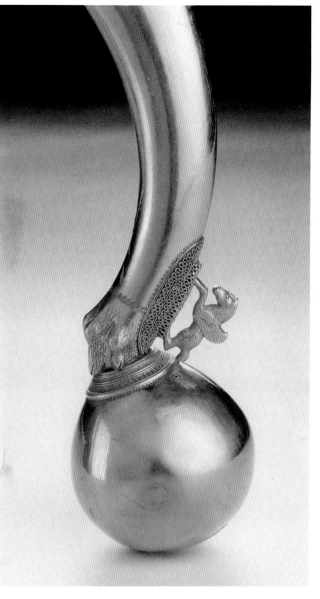

Opposite:
In 1953, the burial of a noblewoman was excavated beneath a stone cairn at Vix, near Mont Lassois in France. Dating to the end of the sixth century BC, the tomb consisted of a 10-ft (3-m) square chamber: see plan (centre right).

The body belonged to a woman, about 35 years old, whose skull was sufficiently complete to reconstruct her probable appearance (above right). She lay on the chassis of a vehicle which served as a bier. The wheels had been removed and leant against a wall of the timber burial chamber (reconstruction, above left). With the skull was a beautiful gold torc (see right).

The other half of the chamber was filled with wine-drinking gear, including an Etruscan flagon and Attic cups. The grave was dominated by an enormous bronze krater, the largest ever found (below left). Decorated with gorgons, Greek warriors and chariots, and surmounted by a lid with a statuette of a woman, it stands 5 ft 4 in (1.64 m) high. Made in Sparta or in Greek southern Italy, there are signs that the vessel travelled north in pieces, and was reassembled – possibly by Greek artisans – at its destination, attesting the close links between Mont Lassois and the Greeks.

(Above and left) The Vix torc. Originally thought to be a diadem, it is much more likely to have been worn around the neck. Made from a pound (480 g) of gold, it is an exquisite piece of artisanship, its simple and elegant shape embellished by fine filigree work and tiny Greek Pegasus figurines. Although an object of northern conception, it is so Greek in style and technique that scholars continue to argue about its manufacture: was it made in a Mediterranean workshop, or more locally – by a resident Greek or a Greek-trained native smith?

The hillforts were not merely centres of high-quality manufacture. Nearby graves reveal that luxury goods were frequently imported (mostly from the Classical south, but occasionally from further afield – even silk from China). It is noteworthy that the finest burials, under large mounds, cluster within a few kilometres of the major 'prince-ly' centres. Some of these extraordinary tombs show new levels of prosperity, as at Vix and Hochdorf. They generally housed a single central burial with a timber-lined chamber, and offerings included gold objects, Classical imports and four-wheeled vehicles (hearses? travelling carts?), all reflecting the high rank of the deceased.

Classical contacts

The Greek and Etruscan imports consist of a limited range of items, almost entirely connected with wine, its transportation, preparation (it had to be strained and diluted from the jar) and drinking. Mont Lassois has produced wine jars or *amphorae* from Massalia, Attic (Athenian) black-fig-ure pottery and bronze vessels. The famous tomb of a noblewoman, found at nearby Vix, contained an enormous bronze wine vessel or *krater*. Grapes were not yet grown north of the Alps: wine was clearly a greatly prized novelty, and the paraphernalia and ritual with which Greeks and Etruscans surrounded wine drinking were adopted by the Celts. Hallstatt aristocrats and their craftsmen also appreciated aspects of Classical art: the humanoid heads on the handles of Etruscan wine buckets were imitated at the Heuneburg.

But Classical imports were actually remarkably localized, and are almost unknown outside these few hillforts and the richest of their satellite burials. This suggests that the goods were controlled by a small section of society, an idea supported by the high quality of the pieces (the Vix *krater*, for example, is more spectacular than anything surviving from Greece itself). Were these diplomatic gifts rather than trade items? And was there also larger-scale trade in materials going on which have left no trace? Clues lie in the structure of Hallstatt society.

How did the Hallstatt chiefdoms work?

The Hallstatt D chiefdoms may just be the archaeologically detectable heart of a much larger system of exchange connecting northern Europe with the Classical world, via the Rhône. Their wealth derived from controlling the trade passing north and south through their territories.

Scholars have suggested that booty, minerals, and trading goods were procured in the north, from as far away as Britain and the Baltic. We may imagine that gold, tin, amber, furs, honey, and slaves made their way south. But what flowed north is less clear: there are few Classical imports in this northern area. The Hallstatt chiefs evidently profited hugely as middlemen, and they procured the finest luxuries for themselves. They adopted foreign ways and indulged in ostentatious consumption through feasting and burial rites (see box). To the wagons which already marked aristocratic funerary ritual the ruling groups added the wine, the special vessels and perhaps also the furniture and ceremony of the Greek drinking-party or *symposion*.

Fierce rivalry within the nobility of each chiefdom must lie behind such spectacular expressions of material wealth. At a higher level, there will have been a similar rivalry *between* the chiefdoms, as each jockeyed with its neighbour for power and lavishness of lifestyle. The rapid development of social complexity through internal competition may be seen in the later Celtic world, and in other societies (pp. 118–21).

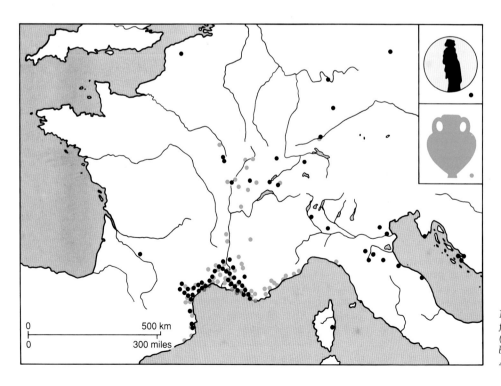

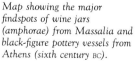

Map showing the major findspots of wine jars (amphorae) from Massalia and black-figure pottery vessels from Athens (sixth century BC).

0   500 km

0   300 miles

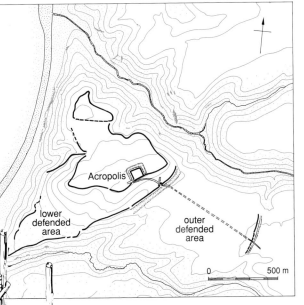

(Right) The enormous complex at Závist in Bohemia sprawled over several hilltops; the naturally steep slopes are supplemented by defensive earthworks. The central 'Acropolis', apparently a major cult centre, had especially elaborate defences (reconstructed below).

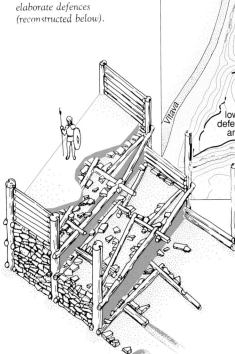

Inspired from without or driven from within?

There is a common assumption that it was economic and perhaps political contact with the 'superior' Classical world that precipitated change among the 'barbarian' Celts. The main source of evidence for such a Classically-centred world view is the presence of Greek pots, Etruscan flagons and, much later, Roman amphorae among the funerary items of the Celtic nobles. Yet if Classical culture was so obviously superior, why was its influence confined to a few chiefdoms, quite distant from Classical centres? And what happened in the Rhône Valley, *between* Massalia and the Hallstatt centres, where Classical imports have been found on sites and in graves, but without major centres or spectacular burials? Were these people immune to Classical influence because they had not yet developed their own aristocracy, hungry for distinction?

The idea of a Classical stimulus similarly fails to explain contemporary developments elsewhere – for example in Bohemia (possibly already a Celtic-speaking area, but certainly part of the Hallstatt world) – where Etruscan and Greek imports are unknown. During the sixth century at Závist near Prague, a large settlement developed with strong defences and an acropolis-like centre with an altar. Was it the focus of some kingdom or proto-state built on the agricultural wealth of Bohemia? If so, this was seemingly entirely due to local factors, for there is no evidence of contact with the Classical world. The Závist evidence thus suggests that some of the northern 'barbarians' developed complex societies in response to *internal* pressures.

In conclusion, the Hallstatt D chiefdoms are better seen as the culmination of long-term internal changes than as the product of Classical influence. Thus the importing of Classical goods represents not so much the arrival of the 'light of civilization' as the fact that some northern societies were sufficiently sophisticated to have use for such luxury items. Classical imports may indeed have acted as a catalyst to speed the growth of the centralized 'chiefdoms', but the process was already well under way. The connection with Greek Massalia was not the sole cause of the appearance of the princedoms of the Western Hallstatt D, the first great flowering of Celtic culture; but it did fuel it and help shape it.

GIVING AND TAKING: THE CEMENT OF SOCIETY

In many 'primitive' societies no distinction is made between social and economic affairs: there may be no commercial exchange as we conceive it, or even barter. Yet goods are exchanged and services given, frequently on a large scale. Relations up and down the social pyramid are expressed by such exchanges, with heads of families and nobles receiving, say, agricultural produce, or military and other services in return for protection in a violent world, or occasional gifts of valued items. Someone might give the local holy woman a sheep in return for intercession with the gods (an important 'service'). In this way goods and services act as the cement binding society together. Economic exchange is embedded within the social organization: the so-called 'embedded economy'.

Most prehistoric farming societies must have worked in this manner. More hierarchical societies, however, such as the Hallstatt D chiefdoms, may have operated a variant of the embedded economy, in which aristocrats kept much-prized goods as their own exclusive perquisites. In such a 'prestige goods' economy some items (e.g. wine) might be given sparingly to favoured dependants, perhaps ceremonially at feasts. Competition therefore arose, not only between aristocrats for control of the goods, but also among the dependants – for the mark of favour in receiving a portion. It was this competitive behaviour that may have led to the advent of the Western Hallstatt 'chiefdoms', characterized as they are by the manufacture and importing of luxury goods. The 'prestige goods' model fits the evidence for the later Iron Age even better, as we shall see.

THE HOCHDORF CHIEFTAIN

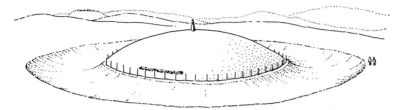

(Top) The probable appearance of the tumulus in its completed state, based on information derived from the excavations.

(Above) One of the female figures which supported the bronze couch.

In 1977, an amateur archaeologist noticed an unusual low mound or tumulus in some fields east of Hochdorf in the Baden-Württemberg region of Germany. Intrigued, she notified archaeological authorities in Stuttgart; they found the remains of a large circle of stones around the tumulus, which had been almost ploughed away. Excavations under Jörg Biel began almost at once, from 1978–79, before the site suffered further damage. The dig revealed a wooden chamber, crushed beneath a mass of overlying boulders and beams. To Biel's delight, the tomb proved (unusually) not to have been looted, and to contain a spectacular array of funerary goods. The painstaking detective work devoted to reassembling the shattered remains has borne fruit, for we now have an exceptionally complete picture of the person interred, and the society from which he came.

The tumulus

The builders had protected the burial by sinking the wooden chamber into a pit nearly 8 ft (2.4 m) deep, beneath a huge mound 200 ft (60 m) across and originally c. 20 ft (6 m) high. They had then encased the burial chamber within c. 50 tons of timber and stone blocks, further protecting the roof with four layers of wooden logs. Biel and his colleagues unearthed the remains of several lesser burials, as well as manufacturing debris indicating that many of the items in the principal grave were specially made at the site.

The Hochdorf 'prince'

The sheer wealth of the burial suggested to Jörg Biel that the deceased had been an important member of the community. A man of about 40 years of age, 6 ft 2 in (1.87 m) tall, and strongly built, this Celtic prince had been laid out on a remarkable bronze couch or bed, wearing a gold belt-plate and a decorated dagger carefully encased in gold. The mourners had placed a wide bracelet on his right arm and a large torc around his neck; both were of thin gold plate. Amber beads and gold and bronze brooches found near the body had probably once lain on the dead man's chest. Thin gold plaques, once attached to his vanished footwear, suggested that he wore ankle-length boots with slightly curled, pointed toes. This may have been a widespread, even long-lived fashion, for figures wearing similar footwear are to be seen in Etruscan murals and on an early La Tène scabbard from the Hallstatt cemetery.

A large iron razor and a wooden comb had been placed by the prince's head, together with a conical bark hat about a foot (30 cm) in diameter. It seems that the Hochdorf lord also indulged his passion for angling and the hunt. A small pouch on his chest contained several fine fish-hooks, while a quiver of iron-tipped arrows apparently hung over the back of the couch.

(Left) A fragment of embroidered textile.

(Below) One of the cast bronze lions from the cauldron.

Tomb furnishings

A unique find was the great bronze couch, c. 10 ft (3 m) long, on which the body rested. Ornamented with images of wagons and fighters or dancers in punched-dot outline, the couch is supported by eight delightful female figurines, mounted on wheels and resembling to the modern eye nothing so much as circus performers. Traces of fabrics probably came from the clothes, drapes, hangings and cushions used to upholster the couch.

The eastern half of the tomb-chamber was dominated by a four-wheeled vehicle, now brilliantly reconstructed from the iron and bronze plates that had once encased it. Whether it had a specific function, as chariot, travelling vehicle or hearse, is unclear. A wooden yoke and bronze-decorated leather horse-harness were piled on the wagon, as were a number of other items including an iron axe and a spear.

Burial attendants had placed a fine service of bronze dishes on the wagon – enough to accommodate nine people; nine large drinking horns were also hanging from hooks on the south wall of the chamber. Nine was the ideal number for the Greek *symposion*, or drinking party, so perhaps what we have here is evidence for a final ritual feast. Classical influence is certainly borne out by the presence of the large Italian bronze cauldron, found at the dead man's feet.

Fabrics hanging from the walls, and decorations of flowers and boughs, complete the magnificent burial. The deceased was clearly a man of power, although not, it would seem, particularly a man of war. For there is no warrior's panoply: rather, an emphasis on peaceful display and the pleasures of aristocratic life – feasting and the hunt.

How old is the tomb?

There is some argument about the date of the grave, but the cauldron can be dated by the style of the metalwork to about 530 BC. The other finds in the grave also seem to fit with a date of no later than 500 BC. The Celtic prince thus lay undisturbed for about 2,500 years.

(Below) Thin embossed gold plaques defined the form of a now-vanished pair of leather shoes. Note the lace holes.

(Right) Reconstruction of the grave. There may well have been other objects of which no traces have survived. For example, it seems likely that the quiver was accompanied by a bow.

(Right) The cauldron, thought on stylistic grounds to have been manufactured in the Greek cities of southern Italy.

CENTRES OF POWER: THE HEUNEBURG

The possible appearance of the Heuneburg in the early sixth century BC, seen from the north. The form of the superstructure of the towers is conjectural.

THE HEUNEBURG HILLFORT (in Baden-Württemberg, Germany) overlooked the Upper Danube, dominating this natural east-west corridor of trade and communication, and also routes to the Alpine passes. People lived here – frequently remodelling the site, which covered almost 8 acres (3.2 ha) – from the seventh century BC until its violent destruction in the later fifth century BC. The last three constructional phases were all destroyed by fire, which suggests disturbed times, unless the inhabitants were extremely careless or unfortunate. During its early existence people settled outside the defences as well.

The most famous of the Heuneburg's many phases is the early sixth century BC construction of a defensive wall with projecting towers, built in sun-dried brick on stone footings. This technique is entirely foreign to the area, but is consistent with Greek fortification methods; it is another manifestation of the powerful Classical influence also seen at the site in imported Greek goods, such as Attic black-figure pottery and wine amphorae from Massalia. In fact, the Greek method of using mud bricks was thoroughly inappropriate in the

central European climate: construction was shortly underway once more, this time using traditional Celtic techniques.

The Heuneburg was not just a centre of wealth and power, derived at least in part from the control of long-distance luxury trade: it was also a centre of manufacture. Workshops found near the entrance at the southeast corner show that local artisans worked bronze, gold, and coral from the Mediterranean, and made fine wheel-thrown pottery. One of the most important discoveries was a mould for a handle imitating that on Etruscan wine-buckets (*stamnoi* see p. 106).

Close to the site are clusters of barrows or mounds overlying the early extramural settlement. There is another cluster of tumuli more than a mile (*c.* 2 km) to the west, including the enormous mound known as the Hohmichele. Discovered just before the Second World War, this tomb's main chamber had been heavily plundered by ancient grave robbers, one of whom left a trail of small glass beads when he broke the string of a necklace. A second chamber, however, had remained undisturbed and contained the bodies of a man and a woman, together with a four-wheeled wagon. A number of later interments were inserted into the mound during the sixth century, one of which preserved the oldest traces of silk yet found in Europe.

(Below right) An aerial photograph of the Heuneburg today, with the Danube flowing past its foot. (Below left) A plan of the site based on excavations. Relatively little is known about the interior, although the foundations of some rectangular buildings have been uncovered inside the southeastern gate.

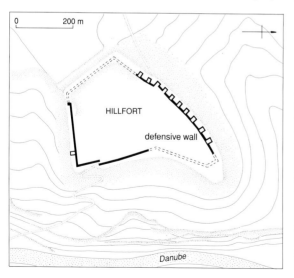

UPHEAVAL AND MIGRATION, 500–400 BC

'The Celts ... of Gaul, were under the domination of the Bituriges, and this tribe supplied the Celtic nation with a king. ... [Wishing] to relieve his kingdom of a burdensome throng, he announced that he meant to send Bellovesus and Segovesus, his sister's sons, two enterprising young men, to find such homes as the gods might assign to them by augury ... Whereupon to Segovesus were by lot assigned the Hercynian highlands [the Black Forest, Bohemia, and the Hartz]; but to Bellovesus the gods proposed a far pleasanter road, into Italy. Taking with him the surplus population of his tribes, the Bituriges, Arverni, Senones, Haedui, Ambarri, Carnutes, and Aulerci, he marched with vast numbers of infantry and cavalry ...'
Livy 5,34

THE FIFTH CENTURY BC began with the sudden extinction of the rich 'princedoms' of the Hallstatt D. Hillforts like Mont Lassois and the Heuneburg were abandoned, and the nearby rich burials ceased. At about the same time, wealthy warrior societies were evolving, mostly to the north of the princely centres: almost certainly Celtic-speakers, it was these peoples who were to develop the material culture and artistic style now called La Tène.

Shifts in trade

Broadly coinciding with these transformations came a major shift in trading patterns. Soon after 500 BC, trade with Massalia via the Rhône apparently halted. Mediterranean contacts were reorientated over the Alps, to the new part-Greek towns at Spina and Adria near the Italian Adriatic coast, and new Etruscan settlements in the Po Valley.

The items traded also changed, partly reflecting shifts in Greek fashion (red-figure pottery replacing black-figure), although they remained largely wine-drinking gear, including Etruscan bronze flagons and buckets. However, the importing zone now stretched further north, as findspots of Classical items reveal.

The cradle of La Tène

The developing La Tène societies left numerous cemeteries. Often military in aspect, some graves contain two-wheeled vehicles, probably chariots (another innovation perhaps imported from the Etruscans). The richest graves are in the middle Rhineland, in the Hunsrück and Eifel mountains and around the confluence of the Moselle and Rhine. There are parallel developments in the Champagne region of eastern France (the so-called Marne culture), where the many cemeteries are not quite so rich, but include chariot burials and many graves with weapons. Similar graves from this time are to be found as far east as Austria and Bohemia, areas which by now were also receiving imports from Italy. Some cemeteries exhibit an unbroken burial tradition from Hallstatt times: the La Tène culture evolved in these regions, it was not brought from elsewhere.

The birth of La Tène art

Alongside the Greek and Etruscan vessels, the richer graves contained items of metalwork in a new artistic style. Known as the La Tène style (pp. 15, 30), it developed rapidly in the fifth and fourth centuries BC. The earliest examples are clearly imitating and developing Classical motifs which appear on imported vessels. Local versions of bronze wine-flagons, for instance (such as those from Basse-Yutz in eastern France or Dürrnberg in Austria), copied the function, general shape and decorative elements of the Classical prototypes, but adapted and transformed them into an entirely new synthesis.

THE LURE OF FIGS AND GRAPES
'The Gauls, imprisoned as they were by the Alps ... first found a motive for overflowing into Italy from the circumstance of a Gallic citizen from Switzerland named Helico, who had lived in Rome because of his skill as a craftsman, [and] brought with him when he came back some dried figs and grapes and some samples of oil and wine: consequently we may excuse them for having sought to obtain these things even by means of war'
Pliny, *Natural History*, 12,2,5

The zone of development of the La Tène culture lay largely to the north of the old Hallstatt chiefdoms, and stretched from east of Paris to beyond Prague.

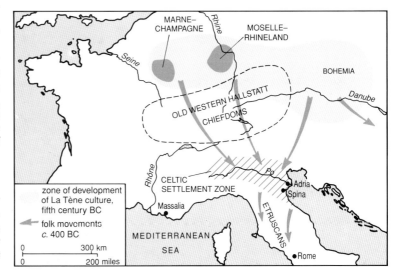

29

(Above) Detail of a flagon handle from Kleinaspergle (450–400 BC).

(Below) Reconstruction of a chariot burial from Somme-Bionne, France, as it was found. The warrior was buried with his weapons, chariot, an Etruscan bronze flagon and a fifth-century BC Greek red-figure cup.

The demise of the Hallstatt chiefdoms

What caused the collapse of the Hallstatt D chiefdoms and the birth of La Tène? The two events must surely be linked, but how? One suggestion is that the Hallstatt chiefdoms were too dependent on controlling the trade routes and on supplies of imported luxuries. This would have made them vulnerable to dislocations of trade with Massalia, or upheaval in the 'warrior fringe' to the north. The latter consisted largely of the very areas which were soon to flower into the La Tène cultures of Marne and Moselle. So the Hallstatt chiefdoms may have been destroyed by the growing power of their proto-La Tène northern neighbours. The Heuneburg was burned, but this could have resulted from internal conflict rather than external hostilities. An alternative explanation might be that the chiefdoms relied too heavily on 'prestige goods', so the interruption of supplies could have undermined the existing order. Or perhaps the scale of the Hallstatt collapse is exaggerated: in the splendid Kleinaspergle grave at Asperg, there is evidence for continuity into the La Tène period. Nevertheless, profound change is indisputable.

People on the move

Whatever the true fate of the Hallstatt chiefdoms, the process of change and upheaval continued. Several generations later, around 400 BC, massive folk-movements began north of the Alps. Vast numbers began to pour over the Alpine passes, to conquer and raid in Italy, and to settle in the Po Valley and neighbouring areas. The *Keltoi* ceased to be distant trading partners or ethnographic curiosities, and became dangerous foes. Not surprisingly, Etruscan trade with the north stopped. The invasion of Italy marks the real beginning of detailed Celtic history.

At the same time, other Celtic groups swept east into the Danube basin, marking the start of the invasion of the Balkans which, a century later, culminated in attacks on Greece and Asia Minor.

It is not entirely clear where the migrants came from. Was it the Marne-Moselle area, where La Tène culture largely developed? Certainly the tribal names Senones and Lingones are subsequently recorded in both eastern France and Italy. However, many migrants could have come from neighbouring areas which lack good cemetery evidence to tell us of their material culture. The movement may have affected most of the early La Tène world: there are signs of reductions in population in Bohemia about 400, which might indicate migration from there, too – or just changing burial rites. The Boii, who gave Bohemia its name, were among the invaders of Italy; but were they already living in Bohemia so early? Many questions remain unanswered.

(Below) Etruscan flagons like this example from the Gorge Meillet vehicle grave brought new artistic inspiration to the nascent La Tène world. Soon Celtic artisans were developing their own versions, such as the magnificent fifth-century bronze flagons from Basse-Yutz in the Moselle (left). The Celtic metalsmiths added inlays of imported coral and red glass to the basic Etruscan form. The stylized animals on the top are apparently a pack of dogs chasing a duck which 'swims' on the pouring wine, alluding amusingly to hunting – evidently a favourite pursuit of the nobility.

What triggered the migrations?

Surviving Classical accounts of the migrations contain largely anecdotal explanations, but these are often consistent with archaeology. While the more far-fetched interpretations centre on Celtic greed for luxuries and loot, Livy's tale of Bellovesus and Segovesus, if perhaps allegorical in detail, suggests that overpopulation was the main reason (as Pompeius Trogus and Plutarch specifically record). The fifth-century warrior chiefdoms were apparently unable to cope with the economic and social tensions, and avoided internal conflict by directing energies – and surplus people – outwards. We can find an interesting parallel to this in what happened several centuries earlier in Greece, when cities sent out waves of colonists to Italy and elsewhere, including Massalia, for similar reasons. La Tène societies subsequently managed to cope better with large populations, probably by developing more powerful structures of government, with proto-towns and proto-states, supported by improved agriculture (pp. 118–19).

Given that the fifth-century Celts were already in contact with the Classical lands, and some of them had visited or settled south of the Alps, it is not surprising that one of the main thrusts of the migrations was into the Po Valley. The migrations may have been triggered by internal pressures, but their direction was governed by the lure of the warm, rich lands to the south, leading the Celtic world on to its zenith.

III
THE CELTIC LANDS

*'They are wont to change their abode on slight
provocation, migrating in bands with all their battle-
array, or rather setting out with their households when
displaced by a stronger enemy.'*

Strabo

IN THE THIRD CENTURY BC, the Celtic world had reached its greatest territorial extent, and was at the height of its power. It stretched from Spain and Ireland in the west to the Danube basin and even central Turkey in the east. Here we will survey these lands, both in the north and west where Celtic-speaking peoples were already living at the dawn of documentary history, and the new conquests in Italy and the east. It reflects the great period of expansion south and eastwards, bringing the Celts to the gates of the Classical world, and the Classical world's gradual discovery of the Celtic lands north of the Alps and in Iberia. Our discussion broadly follows the chronology of these encounters: first in Italy and the Danube lands, then Spain, the interior of Gaul, and finally the British Isles.

The Celtic world was not an empire, but a mosaic of tribes, a rich and diverse pattern of chiefdoms and kingdoms. Some of these were led by robber-barons and their retinues, ruling over subject peoples of different race; others were mixed societies, as in Spain, or Italy. But most were linked by the shared traditions of La Tène material culture in its many styles and local variants – and all were linked by the common family of Celtic tongues and dialects.

*A mounted Etruscan warrior charges a naked Celt. Detail from a stone
funerary relief, Bologna, c. 400 BC.*

GAULS IN ITALY

'At the time that Dionysius was besieging Rhegium [391 BC], the Celts who had their homes in the regions beyond the Alps streamed through the passes in great strength and seized the territory that lay between the Apennine mountains and the Alps, expelling the Tyrrhenians who lived there'
Diodorus Siculus 14,113,1

SOON AFTER 400 BC, waves of Celtic-speakers came through the Alpine passes from the north and invaded northern Italy. They seized the vast Po Valley and raided deep into the peninsula. Henceforth the Po plain and adjacent areas under Celtic rule were known as Gallia Cisalpina, 'Gaul this side of the Alps'.

A bronze figurine of a naked Gaulish warrior, wearing only a belt, torc, and helmet with elaborate crests. The shield and spear or sword are lost. Said to have been found in Italy, this figure could represent one of the Gaesatae (pp. 81, 84).

The sack of Rome

The hard-pressed Etruscan city-states appealed for help from their neighbours in the face of the Celtic advance. The over-confident young Roman republic intervened in 390 or 387 BC (the chronology is uncertain) when thousands of Celtic-speaking Senones attacked the Etruscan city of Clusium. Rome broke international convention when her ambassadors took up arms against the newcomers, precipitating a Celtic march on Rome. The Roman army was routed at the Battle of the Allia, leading to one of the most notorious moments in Roman history: the sack of Rome by the Gauls. Legend has it that the Capitoline hill held out, but this is probably a patriotic fiction: the Gauls had to be bribed to go away, but not until they had ravaged the entire city. When the Romans complained at the way the ransom was weighed out, the Gallic chief Brennus is said to have thrown his sword on to the scales, saying 'vae victis!' ('woe to the conquered!'). Rome rapidly recovered from her humiliation, but it was an event with consequences lasting for centuries. Henceforth the Gauls were regarded with fear and suspicion, as a dangerous barbarian superpower in the North which posed a permanent threat to Roman security. This *terror Gallicus*, as it has been termed, continued to affect Roman attitudes to the Gauls even after the conquest of almost all the Celtic world (pp.127, 140).

In reality these invaders were not the first Celtic speakers to live south of the Alps. Some early inscriptions from the foothills of the Alps, dated to the sixth century BC, are in Celtic. They seem to belong to the archaeologically known 'Golaseccan culture', which is currently associated with the historically documented Insubres – one of the most important Celtic tribes of Gallia Cisalpina.

Division of the spoils

It was with the invasions of the early fourth century BC that the northern region of Italy became largely Celtic-speaking – and a part of the La Tène world.

The new tribal map is known in outline from Roman sources. Mediolanum, now Milan, was the capital of the Insubres, although virtually nothing is known of it at this period. The Cenomani, credited with the foundation of Brixia (Brescia), retained a distinct La Tène culture. The Carzaghetto cemetery, near Mantua, yielded fifty-six graves dating from 320 to 250 BC, including males interred with swords and belts, and females with torcs. Nevertheless they seem to have integrated closely with the non-Celtic Veneti, especially around Padua.

The Boii, whom Cato said were divided into 112 sub-tribes, had the old Etruscan town of Felsina (Bologna) as one of their centres. Some of the graves at Bologna follow Etruscan burial rites, suggesting a strong surviving native element, while others introduce the fashion for burial with La Tène weapons, drinking gear and games. The female graves indicate a range of ranks, some with La Tène brooches and Bohemian-style bracelets. Archaeological remains from the territory of the Boii are consistent with Livy's picture of villages, isolated farms and hillforts. The Boian rural site recently excavated at Monte Bibele (p. 59) reflects the mixed ethnic make-up. The tombs at this site suggest that it was in close contact with both Etruria and the wider La Tène world from 350 to 250 BC.

We know little as yet of the settlements of the Senones further south, but some cemeteries have been found – most famously that at Montefortino d'Arcevia, with 50 per cent of the male graves containing La Tène weaponry. (Interestingly, there are both La Tène-style graves with acquired local goods as offerings, and some graves made according to the native rite but including La Tène objects, suggesting a degree of 'Celticization' of local people.)

The Lingones are mentioned occasionally in the sources. Gauls are also attested in southern Italy, based in Apulia – but these are thought to have been mostly mercenaries rather than settlers. After the sack of Rome, the Gauls were quickly drawn into Italian politics: Dionysius of Syracuse (in Sicily) allied with them, and they were extensively recruited for wars in Italy.

The growing shadow of Rome

Rome signed a treaty with the Senones in 332 BC following several decades of unrest, but growing Roman power led the Senones to find common cause with the Etruscans and other Italic peoples. They were defeated, however, at Sentinum in 295 BC. In 284 the Senones destroyed two legions and killed a consul, but the Romans avenged their loss the following year, when the Boii and their Etruscan allies were also defeated. Rome then began to establish military colonies to contain the Gauls. An uneasy peace followed due to Rome's distraction by war with Carthage; this lasted for a generation, until 232 BC, when Rome seized the land of the Senones and parcelled it out to her own colonists. The most chilling débâcle took place at the Battle of Telamon in Tuscany, in 225, when a vast Celtic army was trapped between two Roman forces and completely crushed (pp. 84–85). It was now apparent to the Celtic peoples of northern Italy that it was only a question of time before they were all conquered.

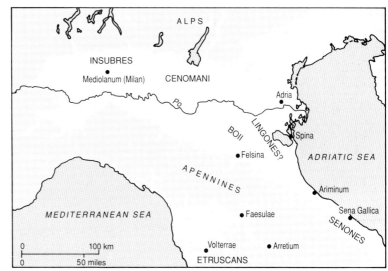

Broad outline of the Celtic settlements in the Po Valley and adjacent areas, which from the fourth century BC was known to the Romans as Gallia Cisalpina, 'Gaul this side of the Alps'.

THE ALPS, SOUTH GERMANY AND BOHEMIA

(Right) Detail from a gold torc from Erstfeld in Switzerland, late fifth or early fourth century BC. (Below) Later La Tène bronze bracelets from Valais, Switzerland.

AS WE HAVE SEEN, La Tène culture evolved not just in France and the Rhineland but in a broad strip of Europe stretching across Germany to Austria and Bohemia: all these lands probably contributed to the invasion of Italy. There is also some evidence of movements within the 'homeland'. The archaeological record attests the spread of certain La Tène-style objects in the early fourth century BC, which some scholars believe to indicate La Tène migrations into Bohemia from Switzerland and southern Germany. But equally there are signs of continuity of Hallstatt people there: probably both groups were already speaking Celtic dialects. In the late fourth century, Bohemia was producing its own variants of La Tène art and metalwork. And by the late second century BC, and perhaps much earlier, the people of this region were calling themselves Boii: hence the modern name Bohemia (*Boihaemum*, 'home of the Boii'). Whatever the sequence of events in

Bohemia, it involved great change, and probably violence: the early centre at Závist near Prague was destroyed (p. 25). A dispersed settlement pattern of small farms now prevailed.

Transalpine contacts

There is some archaeological evidence, as well as the coincidence of names, for links between the Boii of Italy and those of Bohemia. For example, there are certain very close similarities in some forms of metalwork, such as bracelet types. The two tribes may indeed have been branches of a fifth-century parent stock, and may well have maintained close contacts.

Wherever the Gauls of northern Italy actually came from, their arrival was part of a much larger series of folk-movements which, as the story of Segovesus and Bellovesus implies (p. 29), also included a push to the east. This carried Celtic settlers into the Danube basin during the fourth century, and brought Celtic armies to the gates of Greece.

The rising German threat

By the second century BC, the Celtic territories of central and southern Germany were coming under pressure from a new power to the north: the Germans. The newcomers were gradually to expand their power southwards, overrunning the Celtic territories of southern Germany, but the Boii continued to be an expansionist power: Celtic strength in the east was not yet spent.

(Right) Map of the early eastern La Tène world. The solid tint denotes areas of intense Celtic settlement; the hatched tint represents the eastward expansion and settlement of varying density.

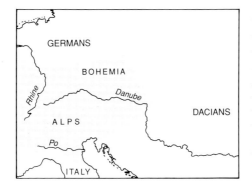

THE DANUBE LANDS AND THE ATTACK ON GREECE

'The Celti who lived about the Adriatic joined Alexander for the sake of establishing friendship and hospitality ... the king received them kindly and asked them when drinking what it was that they most feared, thinking they would say himself, but they replied they feared nothing, unless it were that Heaven might fall on them, although indeed they added that they put above everything else the friendship of such a man as he.'
Strabo, *Geography*, 7,3,8

IT IS NOT CLEAR whether the 'Adriatic' Celts who met Alexander the Great in the Balkans in 335 BC were from the Po plain or had come from the north. But whoever they were, the Danube basin was already becoming an extension of the La Tène world – although there may have been Celtic-speakers there in the Hallstatt period. In Alexander's time they were not yet a threat to the Greek-speaking world, but they would soon become one.

The conquest of the Danube lands

While early fourth-century La Tène objects have been found in the Carpathian basin, documents and archaeology suggest that actual migrations of Celtic-speakers along the Danube Valley began a few decades later. Within 100 years, substantial populations using La Tène material culture had settled in Slovakia, southern Poland around Cracow, and in many parts of the Carpathian basin, perhaps supplemented later by refugees from the Roman conquest of Gallia Cisalpina (p. 34). The middle Danube was now presumably dominated by Celtic speakers, but it was ethnically very mixed.

The threat to Greece

Quite what precipitated the massive southward migration towards Macedonia and Greece in the early third century BC is unclear: perhaps it was the lure of the fabulous riches of the Classical world as much as the search for land to settle. According to the Greek historian Arrian, the Celts sent a second delegation to Alexander at Babylon in 323 BC, following his victory over Persia. One can well imagine that the tales they brought home of the magnificent cities of Greece and the east

fostered the sense of wanderlust among succeeding generations, who took advantage of the break-up of Alexander's empire – which once stretched from the Adriatic to Afghanistan – that occurred after his death in 323 BC. The Greeks and Macedonians were very aware of the dangerous threat posed by these *Galatae* (Galatians), as they called them.

Celtic attacks on Macedonia were contained until 281 BC when Galatians under the leader Bolgios defeated and beheaded King Ptolemy Ceraunus; the way south was opened. In 279 BC Celtic forces invaded Macedonia. Eventually, internal quarrels led to a split in the invading army, with 20,000 men led by Leotarios and Leonnorios heading off on their own, ultimately to settle in Turkey and establish a Galatian state (pp. 40–41). Another part of the Galatian army – under the leaders Acichorios and Brennus (a name, or perhaps a royal title, also attested in the Celtic migrations into Italy a century earlier) – headed south towards Greece, intending to loot the great shrine at Delphi.

'It was then that Brennus, both in public meetings and also in personal talks with individual Galatian officers, strongly urged a campaign against Greece, enlarging on the weaknesses of Greece at the time, on the wealth of the Greek states, and on the even greater wealth in sanctuaries, including votive offerings and coined silver and gold. So he induced the Galatians to march against Greece ... The muster of foot amounted to one hundred and fifty-two thousand, with twenty thousand four hundred horse...'
Pausanias, *Description of Greece*, 10,19

A coin portrait of Alexander the Great, who encountered Celts in the Balkans before embarking upon a career of conquest in the Persian empire.

The great temple of Apollo at Delphi lay at the heart of a splendid complex of religious and ancillary buildings. One of the most famous holy places in the ancient world, Delphi possessed many treasury buildings containing an enormous wealth of offerings from all the Greek states.

The march on Delphi

Horror-stories of Celtic cruelty were circulating in Greece; the Galatians apparently did not even stop to bury their dead – inhuman behaviour in Greek eyes, as it left the soul to wander the earth. Would these fearsome barbarians loot and desecrate Delphi, the most holy place in Greece (the oracle of Apollo resided here) and the chief repository for many of the nation's most valued treasures? The story of the invasion and eventual destruction of the *Galatae* became famous throughout the Classical world. The sources are somewhat contradictory, as they deliberately echo the events of the famous Persian invasions of the fifth century BC, and so distort the account of the Gallic attack. There were indeed some parallels between the two assaults: on both occasions, for example, the Greeks made a

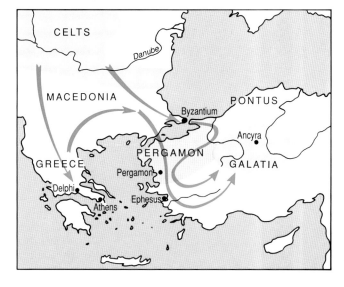

Map to show the Celts' sorties into Greece in 279 BC, and their subsequent movement by invitation into Asia Minor, the easternmost penetration of Celtic settlement.

stand at the defile at Thermopylae and repulsed the invaders, but they were out-flanked in 279 BC just as they had been 200 years earlier by the Persians. Thereafter the Celts rapidly advanced on Delphi and its sacred treasures.

The Galatians reached Delphi in mid-winter and massed close to the sanctuary. A pitched battle ensued with a Greek army, which had allegedly sought divine help. The gods responded by sending earth-quakes and thunderbolts to shake the Celtic camp, with rock-slides from Mount Parnassus on the following night. The Celts, suffering badly from the icy weather, faced a frontal attack from the Greeks at dawn, and were further surprised by a contingent that had infiltrated around their flank and poured arrows and javelins on to their unprotected rear. The Celts suf-fered serious losses but resisted strongly, especially Brennus' personal guard of par-ticularly huge warriors. But when the Gala-tian leader was injured, the invaders made a fighting retreat until dusk fell, killing their wounded as they went.

According to the Greeks the gods inter-vened once more during the hours of darkness, inducing 'panic' among the demoralized invaders ('for causeless terrors are said to come from the god Pan', wrote Pausanias). The Celts are even said to have started fighting each other, 'so that a great mutual slaughter was wrought among the Galatians by the madness sent by the god': evidently a fitting fate for the impious barbarians. They began a disorderly retreat – starving and harassed by the victorious Greeks. Celtic losses, according to Pausanias, amounted to 26,000 dead.

Aftermath

Brennus died or took his own life (allegedly by drinking undiluted wine!), and later Greek writers ascribed the salvation of the sanctuary to the courage of their ancestors and the intervention of the gods. Some ancient authorities, however, clearly believed that Delphi had in fact been plun-dered by the Celts before they were beaten off: for example, a description survives of Brennus laughing at the depiction of the Greek gods in human form in the sanctu-ary; and it was rumoured, almost certainly falsely, that some of the treasure later taken by the Romans from the shrine of the Tolosates at Toulouse was loot from Delphi. Whatever the truth, the Delphi expedition was hardly a success for the Galatians. Acichorios led the survivors back to Thrace.

The attack on Delphi, and the diversion of many of the *Galatae* to Asia (pp. 40–41), marked the high tide of Celtic expansion in Europe. In 278–277 BC, King Antigonos Gonatas of Macedonia defeated another Celtic army at Lysimachia, ending the threat to Greece. Thereafter the Celtic presence in the Danube lands gradually declined, as islands of political power like the small kingdom of Tylis in Thrace were extinguished, and others merged with the native populations, losing their identity.

THE GALATIANS AT THERMOPYLAE
'The Galatians were worse armed than the Greeks, having no other defensive armour than their national shields ... On they marched against their enemies with the unreasoning fury and passion of brutes. Slashed with axe or sword they kept their desperation while they still breathed; pierced by arrow or javelin, they did not abate of their passion so long as life remained. Some drew out from their wounds the spears, by which they had been hit, and threw them at the Greeks or used them in close fighting.'
Pausanias, *Description of Greece*, 10,22

ATROCITY STORIES: TRUTH OR PROPAGANDA?
'The fate of the Callians at the hands of [the Galatians] is the most wicked ever heard of, and is without a parallel in the crimes of men. Every male they put to the sword, and there were butchered old men equally with children at their mother's breasts. The more plump of these sucking babes the Gauls killed, drinking their blood and eating their flesh.'
Pausanias, *Description of Greece*, 10, 22

WRATH OF THE GODS
'Brennus and his army were now faced by the Greeks who had mustered at Delphi, and soon portents boding no good to the barbarians were sent by the god ... the whole ground occupied by the Galatian army was shaken violently ... with continuous thunder and lightning. The thunder ... terrified the Galatians and prevented them from hearing their orders, while the bolts from heaven set on fire not only those whom they struck but also their neighbours'
Pausanias, *Description of Greece*, 10,23

THE GALATIANS IN ASIA

'To the Trocmii the coast of the Hellespont was assigned [as raiding land]; the Tolistobogii received by the lot Aeolis and Ionia; the Tectosages the interior parts of Asia. And they exacted tribute from all Asia on this side of the Taurus, but established their own dwellings along the river Halys. And so great was the terror of their name, their numbers being also enlarged by great natural increase, that in the end even the King of Syria did not refuse to pay them tribute.'
Livy 38,16,12–13

ALTHOUGH THE TERM *Galatae* was used by Greeks to denote Celts in general, the Galatians *par excellence* came to be the people who settled in central Turkey in the third century BC, carving out a state in northern Phrygia.

The Asian adventure of these wandering tribes from the Danube is one of the most fascinating, yet neglected chapters of Celtic history. The archaeology of the Galatians has yet to be discovered: to date the only pieces of La Tène metalwork known from Turkey are three brooches! Literary sources, however, refer to hillforts and strongholds which should be identifiable

(Ancyra, now modern Ankara, was one of these), and there may well be cemeteries with recognizably La Tène burial rites and artifacts. But for the present, to build a picture of the Galatians we must rely solely on Greek and Roman writings, and a few sculptures.

The coming of the Galatians

In 278 BC, Nicomedes of Bithynia invited three Celtic tribes (the Tectosages, Trocmii and Tolistobogii) across the Hellespont to help fight a war. They came across with their families, under the leadership of Leonorius and Lutarius. Although the Celtic forces were defeated by Antiochus I of Seleucia in 275, they managed to establish themselves as a major force in Asia Minor. They appear to have forged an alliance with Mithridates of Pontus (302–266 BC), who settled them in lands belonging to Seleucia. King Antiochus II was unable to dislodge them, and indeed was killed by a Celt in 261. Their depredations were gradually curbed by their neighbours, notably by Attalus of Pergamon, who defeated them around 240 BC.

The Galatians, while numerous, ruled a substantial pre-existing population, although they seem to have kept themselves aloof, preserving their culture and identity for generations. However, Greek names later appear among them, and there are other indications of a trend towards assimilation with their Hellenized neighbours by the last century BC.

Tribes and government

The proximity of Galatia to the literate

The famous statue of the Dying Gaul, actually a Galatian. A marble copy of a bronze originally dedicated in the second century BC to Athena by Attalus of Pergamon. Note the spiky hairstyle, also attested among the Gauls of France. Like other Celts, the Galatians are recorded as going naked into battle.

Greek world has resulted in the survival of considerable detail regarding Galatian political structure. Each tribe was divided into four 'septs' or clans, probably with distinct territories. Each sept was ruled by a chief called a *tetrarch* (from Greek, *tetra-*, 'four'; *arkhos*, 'chief'). He was assisted by a general, two deputy generals and a judge. It is not clear whether these were elected magistracies such as the Greeks would have understood (and like those which developed among some of the states of Gaul); later, when the system was collapsing, the tetrarchs appear to have become petty kings.

The twelve tetrarchies sent a total of 300 'senators' (perhaps the five officials plus twenty others from each sept) to a national assembly, probably held annually at a central shrine called *Drunemeton*. There was no central government or any real mechanism for establishing a national policy; the tribes were too jealous of their independence, and often seem to have fought amongst themselves. At least one man, Ortiagon, tried to unite them under his sole rule, but failed.

The robber kingdom

The role of Galatia in third- and second-century BC Asia Minor was frankly destructive. Like other Celts, Galatians were particularly keen to accumulate wealth in the form of loot and cattle. They periodically burst out of their territories on plundering raids, bringing back prisoners as well as goods; and in the third century Galatia became a centre for trading slaves and holding prisoners for ransom. Surrounding states raised special taxes to free those taken. The Galatians inspired widespread terror, especially since they had a reputation for sacrificing prisoners: people committed suicide rather than fall into their hands.

Galatian religion

The best recorded instance of Galatian human sacrifice occurred in 165 BC, when prisoners not about to be ransomed were offered to the gods. Virtually nothing is otherwise known of Galatian religion, beyond the existence of the central shrine, *Drunemeton* ('oak-sanctuary'). Despite this indication of veneration for the oak, there is no evidence that Druids existed among the Galatians.

Swords for hire

Because of their fearsome image, Hellenistic rulers found these easternmost Celts a useful source of mercenary power. The Galatians' first clashed with Rome as allies of Antiochus III of Seleucia – at the decisive battle of Magnesia in 190 BC; in a punitive campaign the Romans defeated the Celtic forces, and took 40,000 prisoners. Later, however, Rome too found a use for the Galatians – as a tool in the labyrinthine politics of the Hellenistic East. So Galatian power continued under Roman hegemony, until the first century BC (pp. 122–23).

(Above) Part of a frieze from Pergamon depicting arms captured from the Galatians and others. Note the upside-down chariot-yoke (almost identical to an actual example from La Tène). Helmets like the one with large curving crests have been found in Italy. Compare the oval shield with that from Chertsey (p. 113).

(Below) The political structure of the Galatians, based on Greek evidence.

PROBABLE POLITICAL ORGANIZATION OF THE GALATIANS IN ASIA

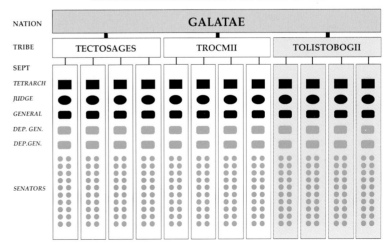

SPAIN AND PORTUGAL: THE CELTIBERIANS

The Flannery brooch depicts a Celtic warrior with accurately observed weapons, including a La Tène sword (the blade is lost, as are the helmet crests). It is of Classical workmanship, but reflects Spanish brooch types. Perhaps it was commissioned by a Celtiberian patron. Probably third century BC.

'In ancient times these two peoples, namely the Iberians and the Celts, kept warring among themselves over the land, but when later they arranged their differences and settled upon the land altogether, and when they went further and agreed to intermarriage with each other, because of such intermixture the two peoples received the appellation [Celtiberians] ... And since it was two powerful nations that united and the land of theirs was fertile, it came to pass that the Celtiberians advanced far in fame ...'
Diodorus Siculus 5,33–34

SPAIN and Portugal are relatively neglected parts of the Celtic-speaking world. They are also the only places other than Gaul where the use of the term 'Celt' is clearly attested in antiquity. The name Celtius, and tribal names such as Celti Praestamarici, are recorded. The Celts were just one group of peoples among many in the Iberian peninsula, and the extent of their settlement is almost as obscure as their origins. In the second century BC, Celtiberia proper was quite a limited area of north-central Spain, but the distribution of place-names and other documentary evidence suggest that Celtic dialects were widely spoken in western and northern Iberia as well.

According to Herodotus, Celts were living in Spain by the fifth century BC. Linguistic evidence and inscriptions corroborate this account, indicating that Celtic was spoken alongside Iberian and other tongues: many place-names incorporate Celtic elements, e.g. *-briga* and *nemet-*. On the other hand, the *-dunum* suffix, generally associated with linguistic developments in the northern Celtic lands, is relatively rare in Spain.

Seeking the Spanish Celts

Iberia is particularly curious in that it did not become part of the La Tène world: there were some contacts, and stylistic influence is detectable on Spanish metalwork (e.g. on some brooches and weapon types), but there was no general adoption of La Tène art or other aspects of material culture.

Iberia is important in showing that not all Celts used La Tène material culture: equally important, it proves that the Celtic-speaking world was not entirely the result of migrations from the supposed central European homeland in the fifth century BC and after. If the Spanish Celts had only just arrived from central Europe in the fifth century, they should have been the bearers of final Hallstatt or early La Tène culture: but they were not. Indeed their material culture is not readily distinguishable from their Iberian neighbours, with whom they were so closely connected (a major reason for the difficulty in identifying them archaeologically). So when did the Spanish

Celts arrive? Various theories have been proposed, including migration during the late Bronze Age. Alternatively, however, it is possible that the Celtic speakers of Spain never immigrated at all, that their language and culture instead developed locally, with contacts across the Pyrenees (p. 21).

The words of Diodorus suggest that Celts were closely integrated with their Iberian neighbours. Indeed other than the name and the evidence for language there is little distinctively 'Celtic' about them: the Celtiberians were warlike and warrior-dominated, but so were other Iberians. They were adapted to the heat of the uplands in summer, and the cold of the mountains in winter, living in high, fortified settlements. Much of their warfare may have arisen from competition for land.

Celtiberian life

Diodorus records that the Celtiberians were very hospitable to strangers; they also made formal hospitality pacts among themselves, which were virtual alliances in war. There was little formal political organization beyond the tribal units, although some groups – notably the Arevaci, based at Numantia (pp. 122–23) – managed to gain hegemony over their neighbours. Their cemeteries (they practised cremation) reveal a wide range of wealth, and include burials with weapons. Gold torcs of distinctive Iberian type are also known. The Celtiberians won a fine reputation as mercenaries (notably in Carthaginian service), providing particularly good cavalry. Violence was as prevalent here as it was in the rest of the Celtic world, with touchy pride leading to frequent duels: warfare and cattle-raiding were endemic. Chieftains had retinues of sworn followers. These aspects echo life in Gaul, but are also paralleled among the non-Celtic peoples of Iberia.

The Celtiberians posed a particular challenge to the growing power of the new Roman provinces in eastern and southern Spain from the second century BC, and subsequently provided the best auxiliary cavalry for Roman armies. One curious Spanish practice the Romans did not care for: 'Careful and cleanly as they are in their ways of living, they nevertheless observe one practice which is low and partakes of great uncleanness; for they consistently use urine to bathe the body and wash their

(Left) A gold torc from northwest Iberia, second or first century BC.

teeth with it, thinking that in this practice is constituted the care and healing of the body' (Diodorus Siculus 5,33). It may be observed that today urea, the main constituent of urine, is used as the active ingredient in some dental health chewing gum! The Romans regarded this habit with disgust, as Catullus makes clear in his scorn for that 'paragon of long-haired dandies, Egnatius, son of rabbity Celtiberia, made a gentleman by a bushy beard and teeth brushed with Spanish piss' (*Poems* 37).

(Below) Stone relief of a warrior, from Osuna in southern Spain. Note the large La Tène-type body-shield.

GAUL, 400–100 BC

'Gaul is inhabited by many tribes of different size; for the largest number some 200,000 men, and the smallest 50,000, one of the latter [the Aedui] standing on terms of kinship and friendship with the Romans, a relationship which has endured from ancient times down to our own day'
Diodorus Siculus 5,25,1

BY THE TIME THE ROMANS arrived in the Rhône Valley late in the second century BC, it was clear to them that all of what is now France, the Rhineland and the Alpine region was occupied by similar, largely Celtic-speaking peoples. Evidence from slightly later times suggests that the same was also true of the British Isles.

Eastern France has long been seen as part of the traditional Celtic homeland in Hallstatt times and especially in the early La Tène period. It formed the western part of the development zone of La Tène material culture, which from the fifth century BC spread west and north, to Britain and then to Ireland. This gradual expansion of La Tène culture has been used to support arguments for either a westward wave of migration from the Celtic 'homeland', or a process of peaceful Celtization (through trade and exchange, contact and competition). But – as we have seen for northern Italy and Spain – it is more likely that Celtic tongues were already widely spoken during Hallstatt times, and that the observed change in material culture during the fifth century BC was simply the movement of a stylistic fashion between kindred Celtic-speaking peoples on the Atlantic seaboard of Europe.

(Left) The zone of renewed contact between the Gallic and Classical worlds in the second century BC. Rome was drawn into the politics of Gaul by the military problems her ally Massalia encountered with local Celtic and other peoples, and by her own need for communications with Spain.

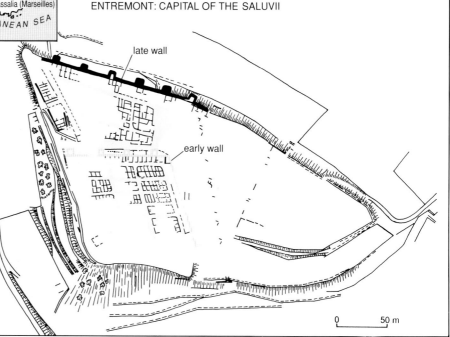

ENTREMONT: CAPITAL OF THE SALUVII

(Right) A plan of the capital of the Saluvii at Entremont. The Saluvii were probably of mixed Celto-Ligurian stock.

The western half of this stone-built hilltown has been extensively explored, revealing a Greek-inspired street grid, and two successive sets of defences with projecting towers which closely follow Hellenistic models. There were also apparently public buildings for decidely un-Greek activities, such as the display of severed heads.

The site was abandoned after the establishment of the Roman military station at nearby Aquae Sextiae (Aix).

Turning from the Mediterranean

One of the major characteristics of the period, contrasting strongly with what had come before and what would happen later, is the virtual absence of evidence for trade with the Mediterranean world after about 400 BC: apart from an Italian bucket in the Waldalgesheim grave in Germany, there is almost nothing in central or eastern Gaul until the second century BC. Trade along the Alpine routes to Italy was probably disrupted because the Celtic incursions into the Po Valley c. 400 BC destroyed the north Etruscan trading centres. After this date, northern Italy and the Balkans became zones of direct Celtic-Classical contact, through which some Classical ideas – such as coinage, which was adopted in some of the Celtic lands during this period – may have entered Gaul. However, the failure of Greek Massalia (Marseilles) to trade up the Rhône on any significant scale is harder to explain. It may have been a failure of supply, in that the city – her commercial activities hemmed in by Carthage – turned her back on trade and became a small-scale territorial power in southern Gaul. She certainly engaged in conflicts with local tribes, which may not have been as defensive as has been made out by Roman writers;

(Left) Archaeology has revealed important economic contacts between Massalia and Entremont. Many amphorae were found at the site, and the presence of grape and olive presses shows the enterprise of the Saluvii in beginning to supply themselves with these commodities. The Saluvii also imitated aspects of Greek art, and developed considerable skill in stone sculpture as may be seen from this head of a woman wearing a headcloth. They also produced full-length statues of seated gods, chiefs and warriors (p. 82)

(Below) A detail of Entremont's impressive masonry defences.

A coral-inlaid bronze disk from a vehicle grave at St-Jean-sur-Tourbe, Marne. Late fifth to early fourth century BC; c. 10 in (245 mm) in diameter.

it was one such conflict that brought Rome into direct contact with the Transalpine Gauls (see below).

The other, more interesting possibility is that the Gauls did not want or need such trade at this period, for social or even ideological reasons. If the southward and eastward migrations around 400 BC were some kind of release of population pressure and political stresses, Gaul may well have been left with a less densely-settled landscape, with generally smaller-scale politics, and less competition needed to achieve local power. There may even have been a reaction against foreign fashions. Whatever the cause, the evidence suggests a period of relative isolationism from the fourth to the second centuries BC, with the Transalpine Celtic world developing in its own way.

The coming of Rome

Rome was drawn into Gaul in the second century BC by two factors: first, Rome's need for secure land communications with her new Spanish provinces (p. 122); secondly, appeals for help from her old ally, Greek Massalia.

Rome was already operating in the zone between the Rhône mouth and the Pyrenees when she received requests for aid from the Massiliotes against the Saluvii, a powerful part-Gallic tribe whose main stronghold was at Entremont, on a hill above modern Aix-en-Provence. Roman intervention in this conflict triggered a chain reaction with enormous consequences.

The siege and destruction of Entremont in 124–123 BC was followed by the establishment of a Roman military stronghold at Aquae Sextiae (Aix). Roman demands for the surrender of the fugitive Saluvian leader led directly to war with the Gallic Allobroges in 122 BC. This in turn drew in the Arverni west of the Rhône – already a major Gallic power, and probably nominal overlords of the Allobroges and other tribes. In 121, the Arvernian King Bituitus sent ambassadors to negotiate with the Romans. Rebuffed, he led his large army into battle and was defeated. Roman power now reached far up the Rhône corridor, incorporating the Allobroges (who were not finally subdued until the 60s BC). With the establishment of a strategic colony at Narbo (Narbonne) in 118, and the construction of a road from Italy to Spain, the foundations were laid for the province of Gallia Transalpina, later known simply as The Province (hence the modern name, Provence). The unoccupied remainder of Gaul came to be referred to as Gallia Comata, 'hairy Gaul'.

Rome was now in direct political contact with the Gallic interior; one important tribe, the Aedui, found they had common cause with Rome against the power of the Arverni, and from 122 BC were established as the 'friends and brothers' of the Roman people. This sequence of political and military moves suggests that, as Caesar reported seventy years later, Gaul was already divided into tribal power-blocs. The friendship between Rome and the Aedui dates from this period: the Aeduan appeal may have been made purely on the basis that 'my enemy's enemy is my friend', but it was to be a vital factor in Caesar's conquest of Gaul.

The second century BC was a time of profound change for Gaul. Extensive interchange was slowly revived with the Classical Mediterranean, both via the Rhône and via Toulouse and the western coasts. These contacts quickly expanded with the establishment of the Roman province in Gaul. Parallel with these, and inextricably linked to them, were other fundamental changes, which were carrying at least parts of Gaul towards urban civilization (p. 118).

The second century BC ended with an ominous foreshadowing of the future. Gaul was invaded by the Cimbri and Teutones, the first recorded incursion of a growing power in the north: the Germans.

IRON AGE BRITAIN

'The inhabitants of Britain who dwell about the promontory of Belerion [Cornwall] are especially hospitable to strangers and have adopted a civilized manner of life because of their intercourse with merchants and other peoples ... they work tin into pieces the size of knucklebones and convey it to an island which lies off Britain and is called Ictis ... On the island the merchants purchase the tin of the natives and carry it from there across the Strait to Gaul; and finally, making their way on foot through Gaul for some thirty days, they bring their wares on horseback to the mouth of the river Rhône.'

Diodorus Siculus 5,22,1–4

BRITAIN WAS A LAND of mystery to the Classical world, and it is only with Caesar's raids of 55 and 54 BC (p. 128) that we get our first reliable eyewitness account of the land.

British contacts with the Mediterranean world were tenuous but continuous throughout the Iron Age, with for example coral reaching the island. They increased later, especially after the establishment of the Roman province of Gallia Transalpina, with goods travelling via Brittany and Biscay to and from the Garonne and Tolosa (Toulouse), and so to Narbo and Massalia. Imports included glassware and wine in amphorae, which have been found across England south of the Thames. The documentary sources reveal that the continental traders wanted British tin, which was assembled at Ictis, possibly St Michael's Mount off the coast of Cornwall. Hengistbury Head, near Christchurch on the Dorset coast, was an important commercial centre. Excavations here revealed imported amphorae, while exports included iron, copper and tin from Cornwall and Wales, and black shale from Kimmeridge in Dorset. Other commodities were probably traded too, like hides or slaves (both are attested in later times). The traders perhaps included Massiliotes and occasionally Romans, but most will have been Gauls: Caesar records that the Veneti of Armorica (Brittany) regularly crossed in their sturdy sailing ships to an unnamed *emporium* in Britain – perhaps Hengistbury.

It is easy to exaggerate the importance of these early Classical contacts. Britain, like Gaul, was largely self-sufficient and developed in its own way.

LAST RESTING PLACE OF A WARRIOR, CHIEF OR PRIEST?

The grave of an adult male, buried c. 200–100 BC, was recently found at Deal in Kent (below). Accompanied by a sword and shield, he was wearing a bronze 'crown', (right, restored replica).

Who was he? Warrior burials are rare, especially in

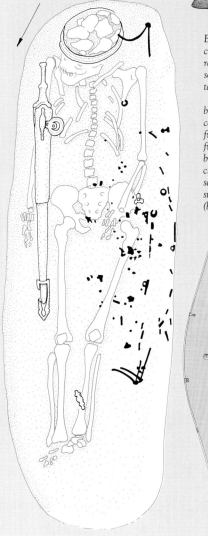

Britain. The 'crown' is without close parallel, but could represent priestly authority or some other status as much as temporal power.

The fragmentary shield can be largely reconstructed (below centre). Bronze decorations from the shield board were too fragmentary to restore. The bronze bindings reveal a characteristically British shape, seen on votive model shields such as this from a recent find (below right).

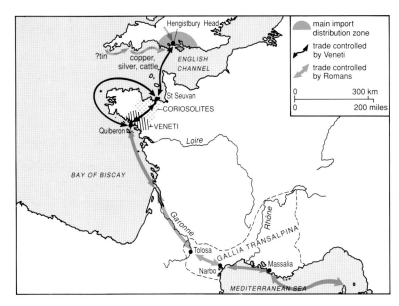

Key:
- main import distribution zone
- trade controlled by Veneti
- trade controlled by Romans

0 ——— 300 km
0 ——— 200 miles

By the first century BC, Britain was connected to the trading networks which stretched to the Roman province in southern Gaul, via Brittany and the Garonne. The distribution of early imports of Italian wine jars in central southern England, for example, fits well with the archaeological evidence for an important (indeed, perhaps the only) point of entry at Hengistbury Head.

While trade from the Mediterranean to Biscay was probably operated by the Romans, evidence from Caesar suggests that the northern trade routes, around Brittany and across the English Channel, were controlled by the powerful Veneti, who dominated their neighbours as well as the seas.

Changing views of the British Iron Age

This picture of (literally) insular development with limited overseas contacts contrasts strongly with older views of Iron Age Britain. Until the 1960s, developments during the Iron Age were explained as the result of invasions from the continent by Celtic speakers, who brought to Britain aspects of Hallstatt and La Tène material culture. This now seems simplistic (p. 21). We can now see that there was continuity from the Bronze Age in many fundamental aspects of life: for example, in pottery styles, or house design – the British roundhouse was not replaced by the rectangular house more typical of Gaul. Hillforts can also often be traced back to Bronze Age beginnings.

On the other hand, Caesar records that the north Gallic Belgae had recently raided Britain, and stayed to settle. For many years scholars believed these Belgae were represented in the archaeological record by the appearance of continental-style pots and cremation burials in Kent and parts of the Thames Valley (p. 103), but this is now thought to be a post-Caesarian phenomenon. In fact, the Belgae in Britain are invisible archaeologically: perhaps, as has recently been suggested, they crossed from the Seine to the Solent region, and their name was then preserved in the Romano-British tribal canton, whose capital was at Venta Belgarum (Winchester). But the debate continues.

Tradition, change and exchange

The reality was probably a rich mixture of continuity with a (perhaps already Celtic-speaking) Bronze Age past, with some immigration from the continent (e.g. of aristocrats such as Commius, who arrived about 50 BC), and some small-scale raiding. The absorption of continental ideas and practices – of which the adoption of the La Tène art style is just the most archaeologically visible – could have come about through political or kinship links with Brittany and, increasingly importantly, Belgica. (Caesar records that 'within living memory' Diviciacus of the Belgic Suessiones held some kind of sway over parts of Britain.)

Britain also developed her own trends, for example the fashion for painting the body blue, or the characteristically British shield-shapes and mirror designs. More importantly, she was not a passive recipient of ideas and goods from the continent: British La Tène metalwork is today considered as fine as any. Moreover, Britain actively participated in the wider Celtic world. For example, a British-developed style of hillfort defence appears on the continent. But the most famous British 'export', it would seem, was Druidism, which apparently originated there (pp. 90–91). Mercenary service in Gaul may also have been an important route for exchange: British warriors fought Caesar in Gaul, and the practice may have been long established.

A land much like Gaul

The Britain that Caesar found when he raided the island in 55 and 54 BC (p. 128) was in many respects like Gaul, with tribal units and a dominant warrior aristocracy. The archaeology likewise indicates a similar pattern of an increasingly densely settled agrarian landscape, dotted in some areas with hillforts, and a material culture which emphasized aristocratic display and war (p. 57–62). But Caesar's description of the Britons of the interior as blue-painted savages was probably hearsay, and may show that the traditional north–south antagonism in Britain is of great antiquity! In reality people were as sophisticated, rich (and well dressed) as those in adjacent areas of Gaul, and the Britons were to share in the great changes that affected the Gauls as the shadow of Rome loomed.

EARLY IRELAND, 600–1 BC

> 'Concerning this island I have nothing certain to
> tell, except that its inhabitants are more savage
> than the Britons, since they are man-eaters as well
> as heavy eaters, and since, further, they count it an
> honourable thing, when their fathers die, to
> devour them, and openly to have intercourse, not
> only with the other women, but also with their
> mothers and sisters; but I am saying this only with
> the understanding that I have no trustworthy
> witnesses for it …'
> Strabo 4,5,4

(Right) At Navan in Co.
Armagh a huge circular timber
structure, perhaps roofed, was
erected in about 94 BC. Navan
was already a centre of
communal display by this time.

To STRABO, Ireland was a land of even greater mystery than Britain. Strabo himself doubted what he had been told: we cannot untangle truth from tall travellers' tales among the few early references to the island. The archaeological evidence is likewise sparse and enigmatic. Hillforts are known, but dating evidence for them is uncertain, as it is for other settlements – Ireland seems to have imported few datable Classical goods, and minted no coins. The wet climate has, however, preserved an abundance of ancient wood, which can now be dated by the method of counting tree rings. On this basis we know that the royal site of Navan, County Armagh (the ancient Emhain Mhacha, capital of Ulster) was already occupied in the middle Iron Age, suggesting continuity of centres of political power for centuries before they appear in early medieval sources.

The Irish Celts: invaders or natives?

The medieval *Book of Invasions* purports to give an account of waves of invaders, but it is very garbled, and probably largely invented. It talks of the Gaels and the *Fír Bolg* coming to Ireland, groups which might seem to equate with continental Gauls and Belgae. But the idea of large-scale immigrations of Celts in the Iron Age fits the archaeological evidence no better in Ireland than it does in Britain; the pattern is rather one of strong continuity with the preceding Bronze Age, followed quite late by the adoption of the La Tène artistic tradition – which was adapted to the needs of Irish society. Hallstatt C swords reached Ireland, but late Hallstatt and early La Tène material is almost non-existent. La Tène metalwork does appear by 250 BC: for example spear butts and seven scabbards

(of distinctive Irish styles, but derived from British and continental prototypes) have been found. These may have been inspired by imports such as the Clonmacnois torc (c. 300 BC), which, if not actually made in the Rhineland, shows strong stylistic influence from this region. The Irish La Tène is still very fragmentary and little understood.

Ireland may well have shared in the developing sense of Celtic identity, through trade, diplomatic contact, and perhaps some limited immigration, especially later. By the early centuries AD Ireland was fully a part of the Celtic world, even if, like Spain, peripheral, idiosyncratic and distinctive.

(Below) An aerial photograph of Navan today. Note the ditch within the (now tree-grown) bank: this was not a defensive site. The great timber building reconstructed above was shortlived. After perhaps only a decade it was levelled, and a massive stone mound was built over it, clearly visible in the photograph within the far side of the enclosure.

IV
THE
PATTERNS OF
LIFE

'They lived in unwalled villages, without any
superfluous furniture; for ... they slept on beds of leaves
and fed on meat and were exclusively occupied with war
and agriculture'
Polybius 2,17,8, on the Gauls of northern Italy

THE ROUTINES of daily life in early Celtic societies
must have varied greatly from region to region.
Our attention will most naturally focus, however, on the heartlands of the Celtic world – on Gaul
and neighbouring areas – for it is here that we have the
best documentary evidence. Coincidentally, these same
areas have yielded perhaps the richest archaeological
evidence for the La Tène period.

We see a range of societies across the Celtic world,
from loose tribal structures to centralized kingdoms.
Each was far from static: there was continual change,
sometimes slow, sometimes very fast. Archaeology and
history suggest that, at least among the Celts of central
Gaul, the Alpine region and as far as Bohemia, great
changes were taking place during the last two centuries
BC in the ways people lived and dealt with each other,
and especially in how they ordered their government.
Tribes were evolving into states.

The huge Longbridge-Deverill Cowdown house under reconstruction at
Butser experimental farm. Most Iron Age Britons lived in more modest
dwellings such as the Moel-y-Gaer house reconstructed in the
foreground.

THE SHAPE OF SOCIETY

'Throughout Gaul there are two classes of persons of definite account and dignity. ... one consists of Druids, the other of knights ... These [knights], when there is occasion, upon the incidence of a war ... are all engaged therein; and according to the importance of each of them in birth and resources, so is the number of liegemen and clients that he has about him. This is the one form of influence and power known to them.'
Caesar, *Gallic War*, 6,13–15

EARLY CELTIC SOCIETY is often characterized as 'heroic', dominated by the warrior ethic. Greek and Roman observers tended to see the Celts at best as noble savages, at worst as ignoble and dangerous foes. Either way, their apparently bizarre customs and great energy were eternal sources of fear and fascination. But Classical writers also found much to admire about the Celts, especially the mental agility and eloquence of the Gauls. Caesar remarked on their wit and adaptability, and their quickness to learn: their speed in copying aspects of Roman military tactics caused him serious difficulties during the 50s BC.

New archaeological discoveries, new ideas about what they mean, and in particular a reassessment of the documentary record from an anthropological viewpoint, are helping us to understand how complex and sophisticated the Celtic societies of Iron Age Europe actually were.

The character of Gauls and Gallic society

The Gauls, about whom we know most historically, were renowned for their excitability, love of boasting, and dangerous demeanour especially when drunk – which apparently they often were. Gallic men and women were fiercely proud of themselves, their deeds, and their ancestry, and were swift to respond to insults. On the other hand they revelled in their highly elaborated verbal style, which involved much allusion and circumlocution. Celtic societies were largely non-literate (see box), so it is not surprising to find that the Gauls excelled at oratory and verse speaking – especially as they were very fond of conferences and councils. It is believed that they possessed a large and sophisticated oral

literature, similar to that of Homeric Greece or Celtic Ireland (p. 158–61). This would mostly have been in the charge of the bards and priests, but sadly not a single Gallic epic or praise-song survives.

The make-up of Celtic societies

The most fundamental division – as in probably every society – was between men and women. Celtic women, particularly noblewomen, had a more prominent role than their Roman or Greek sisters (pp. 66–69), but all the Celtic realms seem to have remained thoroughly male-dominated.

We have a few tantalizing hints of interesting patterns in family life. What, for example, are we to make of Caesar's observation that it was thought shameful in Gaul for a son to appear in his father's presence in public before he came of age? Does this imply the fostering-out of noble sons attested later in Ireland? According to Livy, the legendary Celtic leaders Bellovesus and Segovesus were the sons of the sister of King Ambigatus. Did the king choose these two young men to command the quest for new lands because he had no sons of his own, or was it the tradition among the Gauls for sons to move to their uncle's home? Similar practices have been observed in more recent societies.

Both the Gauls of the first century BC and the Irish of the early centuries AD had privileged classes of nobles, warriors, and individuals with special skills (known in Ireland as 'men of art'), including priests, seers, bards and artisans. Similar classes were probably to be found across most of the Celtic world, but there was no complete uniformity: Druidism, for example, was probably limited to Gaul and the British Isles (pp. 90–91).

The priests played a vital part in maintaining the identity and well-being of the people, and in their relations with the gods, the dead, and other communities (pp. 90–91). Bards probably shared with priests the role of living repository of oral tribal history and tradition, besides their peculiar role of praise-singing, extolling the virtues of the nobility – another form of aristocratic status display (pp. 70–71). The impor-

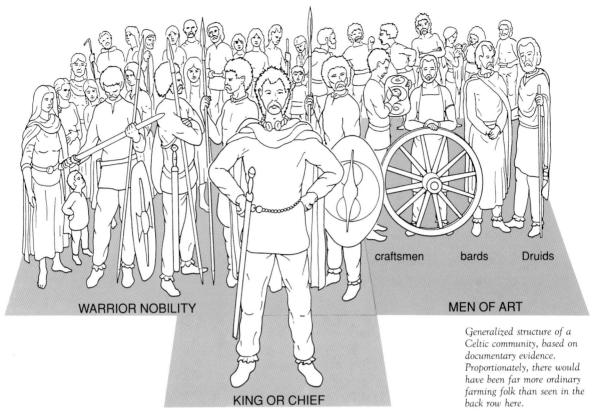

craftsmen   bards   Druids

WARRIOR NOBILITY   MEN OF ART

KING OR CHIEF

Generalized structure of a Celtic community, based on documentary evidence. Proportionately, there would have been far more ordinary farming folk than seen in the back row here.

tance of artisans lay in their ability to make not only the tools and equipment necessary for everyday life, but also much of the finery which the Celtic lords wore to express their wealth and high rank (p. 115).

Of the mass of the ordinary *free* people we hear almost nothing in the texts. Slavery existed, although on a smaller scale than in the Classical world: slaves may have been most important as export commodities.

Besides distinct classes and ranks, Celtic societies may also have had various other social subdivisions, such as age-sets, which boys entered when they reached manhood. Young males of the same age, especially budding warriors, probably spent much of their time together, perhaps before starting families or political careers of their own. The continental *Gaesatae* – a large group of warriors outside the tribal structure, seen by the Romans as mercenaries (pp. 81, 84–85) – may have provided a safety valve for such young men to seek their fortunes beyond the tribe for a limited time. Classical writers mention the widespread practice of homosexuality among the Celts – particularly perhaps among groups like the *Gaesatae*.

Tribes and states

Recent research, particularly regarding central and northern Gaul, suggests that the Celtic societies of the middle and later Iron Age generally consisted of small, territorially-based sub-tribes known to the Romans as *pagi*. These were essentially kin-groups – extended families and clans – with attached followers and dependants such as slaves and clients. The *pagi* came together into the large tribal units recorded by Caesar. Multi-tribal confederations proved distinctly unstable, constantly splitting and coalescing according to political fortune. Tribes were typically governed by kings or chiefs (often in pairs) with limited powers, weighty decisions being taken by the popular assembly of all the free men of the tribe. There was also a council of several hundred leading nobles (referred to by Caesar as a 'senate'), from which the rulers were chosen and wherein much real power lay.

It is noteworthy that social or political identity was much more a matter of kinship and community than particular territory: chiefdoms and kingdoms were potentially 'portable', and could migrate to new lands – as the Helvetii tried to do in 58 BC (p. 124).

FATHERS AND SONS
'... *they do not allow their sons to approach them openly until they have grown to an age when they can bear the burden of military service, and they count it a disgrace for a son who is still in his boyhood to take his place publicly in the presence of his father.*'
Caesar, *Gallic War*, 6,18

THE CELTS AND HOMOSEXUALITY
'*And among barbarians the Celts also, though they have very beautiful women, enjoy boys more: so that some of them often have two lovers to sleep with on their beds of animal skins.*'
Athenaeus, *Deipnosophistae*, 603a

CELTIC HUSBANDRY

'All the rest of the country produces grain in large quantities, and millet, and nuts, and all kinds of livestock. And none of the country is untilled except parts where tilling is precluded by swamps and woods. Yet these parts too are thickly peopled – more because of the largeness of the population than because of the industry of the people; for the women are not only prolific, but good nurses as well, while the men are fighters rather than farmers.'
Strabo 4,1,2 on Gaul

(Below left) Gaulish and British Iron Age domestic animals – shown here in light colour – were generally smaller than modern breeds. The bones of Iron Age sheep suggest that these animals were small and goat-like, virtually identical to the modern Soay breed from the St Kilda Islands, Scotland (below right) – perhaps direct survivals of Iron Age varieties. Their wool is short and coarse, and usually dark. Since the Soay sheep had returned to a wild state, it is hard to know whether Iron Age domesticated sheep behaved exactly like these agile, quite intelligent and 'unsheeplike' animals, which may even attack sheep-dogs!

IRON AGE CELTIC SOCIETY was essentially rural: most people spent their lives on the land, engaged in raising crops, tending herds, managing woodlands and all the other tasks of the farmer's year. What we know of pre-Roman agriculture comes almost entirely from archaeology.

Most of our evidence relates to the broadly similar environments of northern Gaul and Britain. We know about the range of crops, animals and other resources exploited, and also something of farming methods. Research has shown that changes were taking place in the later Iron Age: for instance, cultivation of the vine had begun in Gaul (wine was hitherto imported from the Mediterranean); the Saluvii of southern Gaul started to grow olives (p. 45); and heavier soils were drained and cultivated in both Gaul and Britain. Moreover, we can begin to challenge old preconceptions, such as the idea – gleaned partly from Caesar – that upland Britain was almost entirely pastoral in its economy: archaeology shows that arable farming was also important in northern and western areas of the country.

Farm animals

For livestock, Celtic farmers relied primarily on sheep, cattle and pigs, although the varieties kept were different from today's. Pigs were much closer in appearance to their wild ancestors, and the sheep looked more like goats. Sheep seem to have been exploited for their wool (which was very coarse on most of these early breeds) and perhaps milk rather than meat, on the evidence of the (old) age at which they were usually butchered.

The cattle, a now-extinct variety known as the Celtic Shorthorn, were quite small. They had been carefully bred over many generations to produce compact, powerful oxen for pulling ploughs and heavy wagons. Horses, mostly ponies of about 12 to 14 hands (c. 1.2–1.4 m at the withers), were raised for light draught work and for war rather than for heavy tasks. The horse collar was unknown in antiquity and the harness used did not allow the animal to make full use of its strength. Caesar records the Gauls' delight in horse-dealing, and the enormous prices they paid for fine animals.

Many breeds of dog existed, from varieties so small they can only have been pets, to large animals which were perhaps the hunting dogs mentioned by Strabo. The Celts butchered dog carcasses, not so much for the meat as for the skins – the Gauls sat at their ease on such pelts. Today no farmyard would be complete without chickens and cats, and both can be traced back to Celtic times – the former a recent introduction from the Orient, the latter present at the southern British hillfort of Danebury (although perhaps a trapped wild, rather than a domesticated, animal). Donkeys, and therefore mules, on the other

(Left) Newly-felled coppice poles lie stacked at the experimental Iron Age farm at Butser in Hampshire, ready for use in building, fencing or as fuel.

(Below) Cattle were vital for draught work, especially ploughing. Here modern Dexter cattle – the closest modern equivalent to the extinct Iron Age breed, the Celtic Shorthorn – pull an ard (simple plough) at Butser.

hand, were not introduced until the Roman period.

Animal carcasses provided a range of important raw materials in addition to meat: bone and horn (which were the plastics of the ancient world), skins for leather, and tough sinews.

Crops and woodlands

The Celts grew a number of cereals, notably several varieties of wheat (emmer, spelt and breadwheat) and barley. Millet was a major crop in Gaul. Beans were also cultivated, as were peas and lentils. Bitter Vetch, Fat Hen, Gold of Pleasure and other plants now regarded as wild may have been cultivated, or at least collected. From these plants, and from fruits and berries, people had access to good sources of protein, carbohydrates and vitamins. Flax was also grown for linen, as an alternative to wool, and probably for its oil.

Pieces of wood surviving in waterlogged conditions serve to remind us that timber was as important to the farmer as arable land and livestock. Woodlands must have been carefully managed to ensure that stands of mature trees could provide timber for buildings. Other trees were cut close to

HUNTING

Celtic lords and lesser folk undoubtedly indulged in hunting, to keep down pests and for sport. Dogs were bred for the purpose, while bows and slings, although used in war, were primarily weapons of the chase. Caesar mentions a special wooden projectile used by the Gauls for bird-hunting. The boar, an important Celtic symbol of ferocious power, was surely pursued, but archaeology indicates that red and roe deer and hare were also popular quarry (the rabbit was unknown in Britain or Gaul). Wolves, foxes and badgers were likewise hunted, not least for their pelts. However, hunting made a limited contribution to the table: only a small proportion of the animal bones recovered from settlement sites come from wild species.

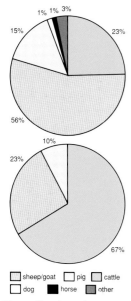

Diet at Danebury, from animal bones: (top) numbers of individual animals; (bottom) relative quantities of meat.

sheep/goat ☐ pig ☐ cattle ☐
dog ☐ horse ■ other ▨

PROVIDING FOR HUNGRY TIMES: THE ENIGMA OF THE PITS

It was essential to be able to store the summer's crops, to ensure that supplies lasted through the winter months until the next harvest. In a world without refrigeration, food was preserved in a variety of ways, not least by salting: Gallic salt pork was exported to Italy. Salt was an essential commodity. The dry storage of vegetable foods and seeds, in pots or sacks in granaries were other possible options, as was smoking.

One of the enigmas of Iron Age archaeology, particularly in Britain, has been the function of the large number of pits found on excavated sites. Charred grain has been discovered in some of the deeper pits. Could they have served as underground silos? It may seem a nonsensical idea to try to store grain in damp holes in the ground, but experiments carried out at Butser ancient farm suggest that the technique is surprisingly effective. Provided there is an airtight seal to the pit, the grain in

the ground (coppicing) in order to produce an abundant supply of long straight poles that were essential when it came to making wattle walls, fences and for fuel.

By the Iron Age, much of the British and Gallic landscape had been under the plough for over 3,000 years. Beginning about 100 BC, however, a major change took place, at least in Britain, with the increasingly intensive use of land. The remaining wildwood – the natural cover of the landscape – was cleared at an unprecedented rate, and what had once been marginal land in wet valleys with heavy clay soils was drained and brought under the plough. This development ran parallel with changes in farming methods, and an increasing emphasis on cattle (suited to wet pastures and required to plough the new fields). The plough itself was improved, with iron share and coulter. Perhaps crop rotation and manuring were practised, although to what extent is unknown.

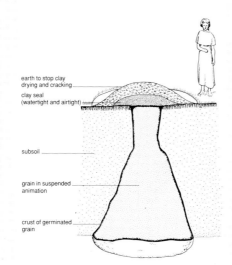

earth to stop clay drying and cracking
clay seal (watertight and airtight)
subsoil
grain in suspended animation
crust of germinated grain

contact with the damp walls germinates, using the available oxygen and releasing carbon dioxide. This puts the bulk of the grain into suspended animation. It usually keeps perfectly for months, until the seal is broken. Many of the pits found on Iron Age sites could, therefore, have been used to store grain.

A substantial increase in population accompanied these changes: quite possibly both were aspects of a wider process, in part triggered by an improving climate – which by about AD 1 was similar to today's. In its broad outline, the British countryside before the Roman conquest was already much as we see it today: a patchwork of woodlands, pastures, and ditched, fenced, walled or hedged fields (even if modern fields are generally much larger).

The farming regime

Many Iron Age crop varieties such as emmer wheat still survive, and some existing breeds of domestic animal are likewise similar to their pre-Roman forerunners – Soay sheep from the Hebrides, for example, appear to be direct descendants of the typical British Iron Age breeds. What better way, therefore, to gain an insight into Celtic farming methods than to recreate a typical Iron Age farm using, as far as possible, Iron Age crops and livestock? Peter Reynolds established just such a long-term experimental programme in 1972 at Butser, Hampshire.

The project has yielded some surprises. The grain varieties, for instance, have consistently given far higher yields than expected. This has far-reaching implications for our basic understanding of the Iron Age. Many archaeologists used to assume that pre-Roman agriculture was primitive, subsistence farming which produced enough for survival but little more. Now there are grounds for thinking that farmers could count on substantial, and fairly reliable surpluses each year. Such surpluses would indeed have been needed in a society that supported classes who presumably did not produce their own food: the aristocrats, craftsmen and other 'men of art'. It may be that the Celts exported grain and cattle to the Roman Empire in far greater quantities than we had guessed. The agricultural richness of Gaul and Britain could in fact have proved a major attraction to the Romans. Yet, for all their apparent competence, Celtic farmers will have been as much at the mercy of the elements and disease as any others. From Britain comes evidence of soil depletion and erosion, while Caesar refers to serious crop failures in Gaul causing unrest. The lot of people on the land has never been easy.

FARMS AND VILLAGES

'The building [was] surrounded by forest as the dwellings of the Gauls usually are – for to avoid the heat they generally seek the neighbourhood of woods and rivers ...'
Caesar, *Gallic War*, 6,31

AIR PHOTOGRAPHY and excavation in northern Gaul and southern Britain show a typical rural pattern of dispersed farmsteads or small hamlets, consisting of one to several houses. Modern ploughs have frequently scoured away all but the post-sockets of the ancient buildings, and the pits and ditches. Nevertheless, archaeologists believe that these scant remains were once home to one or more extended families and their dependants within a farmyard area often delimited by a bank and ditch. It is the ditches, more to keep animals in or out than for defence, that are often seen from the air. Deep pits are usually found within the farmyard, and post-sockets for smaller structures which were probably raised granaries or stores. Farmers would originally have used the pits as silos (p. 56), but filled them with rubbish – and perhaps offerings (p. 92) – once they were redundant. These deposits are of vital importance to archaeologists, since they hold many clues about the activities that took place on the site.

It is clear that there were other types of settlement besides farmsteads: there were larger, unwalled villages in some areas; several sorts of gathering places, such as religious centres (pp. 92–94); and defended sites such as hillforts. In late Iron Age Britain settlements began to expand on to marginal land – in some areas for industrial purposes, such as coastal salt workings around the Wash. Trading centres also sprang up, as at Hengistbury Head.

Houses

Houses tended to be circular in Britain and Ireland, and roughly rectangular in Gaul

(Below right) Plan of an early Iron Age house excavated at Pimperne, Dorset; all that remained of the building were post-sockets. This plan was combined with information about the properties of the likely building materials to reconstruct the house (below centre and, below left, reconstruction at Butser). The walls might have been a little higher, the roof a little steeper, but not much flatter or the thatch would leak. Once the roof was assembled the earthfast principal rafters seen in the drawing could be cut away. Many details are unknown: there could have been other elements such as internal partitions.

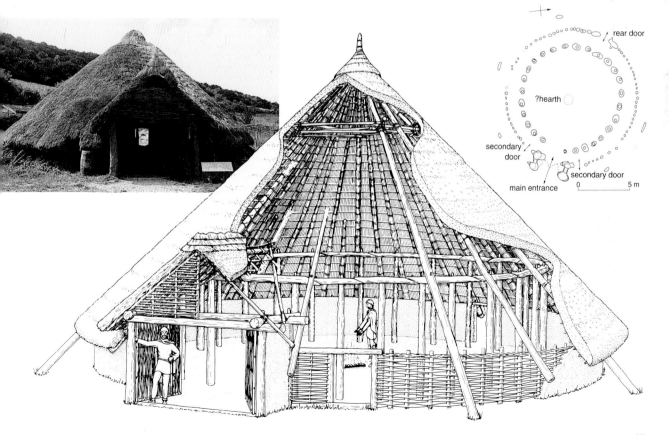

rear door

?hearth

secondary door

secondary door

main entrance

0   5 m

(Right) A reconstruction at Chassemy of a late Iron Age Gallic house from the oppidum at Villeneuve-St-Germain near Soissons, France. Constructed – like many British houses – of timber, wattle, daub and thatch, but of rectangular plan, Gaulish houses leave fewer traces than many British roundhouses and are consequently harder to reconstruct with confidence. The thatch on the original would have been thicker than shown here.

and elsewhere – there being no apparent reason for the difference. Britain is unusual in yielding a reasonably representative sample of house-types: these have been reconstructed almost solely from their foundations, for very few fragments of the timber superstructures have been discovered (other than the material from the lake villages of the Somerset Levels). The predominantly circular houses vary greatly in size, from about 15 ft to over 50 ft (5–15 m) in diameter. The smaller buildings, often unthinkingly dismissed as huts, may in reality have been components of larger dwellings. These could have consisted of more than one roundhouse, with other ancillary buildings such as cooking-shacks or work-sheds, plus storage facilities.

Even the smaller roundhouses offered considerable floor-space under a conical roof, without the need for freestanding roofposts: the weight of the roof could be transmitted directly to wattle walls. Weatherproofed with clay daub, these

(Left) The lofty interior of the completed Pimperne house at Butser (p. 57). Most British roundhouses were much smaller than this building, which could have housed considerable gatherings for feasting and meetings. There was no need for a smoke-hole in the conical roof: the smoke seeped through the thatch. With a constantly burning central fire, the roofspace could store large quantities of dried and preserved foodstuffs in the oxygen-poor atmosphere above head-height. (Far left) The even larger Longbridge-Deverill-Cowdown house during reconstruction at Butser, 1992.

circular walls – the ring completed by the wooden door-lintel – were remarkably strong. Heavy, unmortared stone walls were used where local geology permitted or required.

Larger houses usually had an inner post ring to provide additional support for the long rafters, but the unencumbered central floor area could be enormous. Some of these bigger dwellings may have been the residences of the nobility. For example, the massive houses from Pimperne and Longbridge Deveril Cowdown in Dorset (recently reconstructed at Butser), may well have been nobles' 'manors' or feasting-halls. Were the houses of the rich elaborately carved and decorated? Given the

Celtic love for *portable* wealth and finery, perhaps aristocrats invested in movable furnishings such as embroidered hangings, leaving the structures themselves plain and simple. This would not be so surprising given that kings and major nobles probably moved between multiple residences, taking feasting-gear and favourite furnishings with them. In the sources we hear of the Gauls sitting on pelts and using low dining-tables. Excavations have unearthed all sorts of domestic equipment, such as drinking gear, gaming counters, cooking utensils like cauldrons, and iron fire dogs. It seems likely that all these articles were packed into wagons which the Gauls in particular appeared to need when on the move.

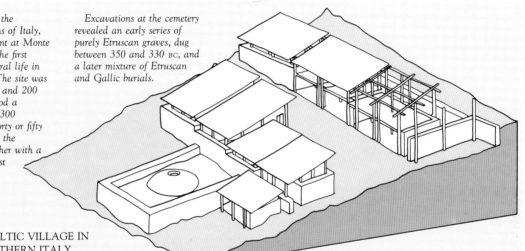

Perched high up in the Apennine mountains of Italy, the ancient settlement at Monte Bibele has yielded the first clear evidence of rural life in Celtic-ruled Italy. The site was settled between 400 and 200 BC; during this period a population of 200–300 constructed about forty or fifty houses terraced into the mountainside, together with a cemetery and at least two shrines.

Excavations at the cemetery revealed an early series of purely Etruscan graves, dug between 350 and 330 BC, and a later mixture of Etruscan and Gallic burials.

A CELTIC VILLAGE IN NORTHERN ITALY

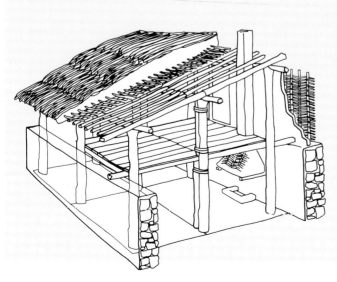

Archaeologists have attributed the gradual and apparently smooth addition of these Celtic elements in the graves to the arrival and assimilation of Celtic settlers. Monte Bibele was evidently home to a mixed community of local Etruscans and Gallic Celts, with the latter presumably forming a martial élite.

The houses were built of stone and timber, probably thatched, and may have had an upper floor. They were arranged according to a systematic pattern in small groups – perhaps suggesting that the settlement was planned. Inside the houses, their occupants would have sat upon an earthen floor, in front

of clay hearths. Excavators found the ground strewn with pottery (used for storing or preparing food), loom-weights and animal bones. Water was supplied to the community by a nearby spring, which fed into a well-constructed cistern.

The settlement was destroyed by fire in about 200 BC, which aided the preservation of wood and foodstuffs by carbonization. Investigations of a storehouse revealed several hundred pounds of wheat, oats, broad beans, lentils, peas, flax, acorns, olives, garlic, hazelnuts, apples and grape-seed: a mix of local and imported produce. The inhabitants clearly had a varied diet.

HILLFORTS, BROCHS AND MAJOR SETTLEMENTS

CELTIC PEOPLES built defended sites across many parts of Europe, as indeed did some of their neighbours, and peoples before them. Within the Celtic lands there are regional variations, such as the extraordinary brochs and crannogs (artificial islands) of northern Britain. Spain also represents a very different picture, with its own traditions of village settlement later giving rise to fortified towns such as Numantia (pp. 122–23). But it is the often spectacular hillforts which, naturally enough, most attract our attention.

Hillforts

Many hillforts remain breathtaking feats of construction, even after millennia of

(Left) Model showing the organized roadway at Danebury lined with rows of rectangular post-built structures, thought to be raised granaries for the storage of very large quantities of grain. These types of granary provided good ventilation and kept vermin out.

erosion. The sheer effort of moving thousands of tons of earth and stone by unaided musclepower, and the creation of systems of banks and ditches and gateways of bewildering complexity, can still inspire awe.

Many hundreds of hillforts are known: they are almost the only trace of later prehistoric times still visible in many European landscapes. Scholars used to believe that they were the main form of Iron Age settlement in Britain and Gaul, which may indeed have been true in some areas and at particular times – for example in the Rhône corridor in the second century BC, where it appears that most of the population lived in fortified hilltop villages. Nevertheless we can be certain that several regions, such as east Yorkshire, had few or no hillforts, while in others hillforts were progressively abandoned.

What were hillforts for?

Hillforts probably had many functions. Some were refuges in times of trouble, where the community would move their cattle and property during war. Some may have been lived in permanently, others only seasonally. Danebury (see below)

(Right) Excavations at Danebury hillfort in 1986, seen from the northern rampart. The topsoil has been removed to reveal the chalk bedrock and archaeological features. The dark circles are the mouths of refilled pits awaiting excavation. In the foreground is the quarry hollow from which material used to strengthen the rampart had been dug. Here, the foundations and floors of many houses were well preserved by soil washing down from higher ground.

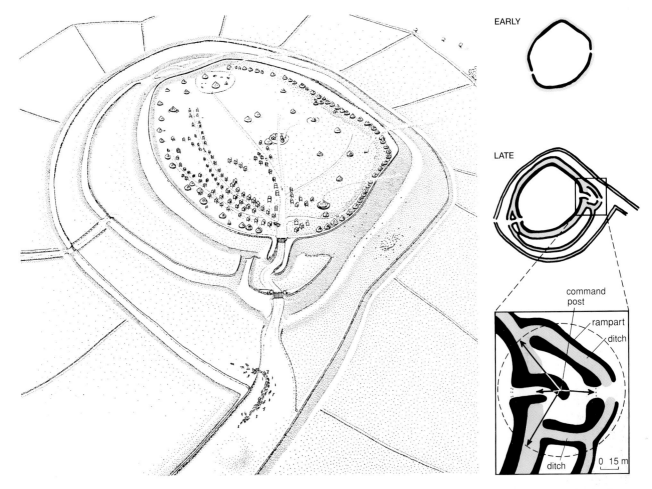

EARLY

LATE

command
post

rampart

ditch

ditch

0   15 m

apparently served both as village and secure communal food-store for the surrounding district, in case of war or famine. Hillforts might also have provided the facilities for trade and manufacture, or housed a religious centre; still others might have had more to do with display of power of the community and its rulers than with the exigencies of war.

In the later Iron Age, as larger and more complex societies and states arose, new settlement types were founded, most notably the sprawling *oppida* or proto-towns. These represent a fundamental change in the landscape and contemporary ways of life: for much of Celtic Europe was beginning to move towards urbanization (p. 118).

The British hillfort at Danebury

Danebury is one of the most prominent of many Iron Age hillforts that once defended the chalk hills of Hampshire. Over half of the 5-hectare (12-acre) interior

has been excavated during two decades of work by Barry Cunliffe and his colleagues, making it the best-explored hillfort in Britain. Literally hundreds of thousands of artifacts and bones have been unearthed. In addition, Cunliffe's team has conducted a detailed survey of the surrounding landscape, giving us some idea of how the hillfort fitted into the local pattern of settlement.

Occupied from about 650 to 100 BC, the hillfort went through many changes: its interior layout was reorganized several times, with its ramparts and gate becoming increasingly elaborate. A visitor, having passed the defended gateway, would have seen small round houses of traditional British type, mostly in the lee of the rampart on this windswept prominence. The short-lived wood and wattle dwellings had frequently to be rebuilt. Fortunately for the excavators their remains (floors as well as foundations) were prone to coverage by silt

Danebury was originally built with two entrances and a single rampart (top right). In about 400 BC the defences were increased, and over the next couple of centuries the site acquired outer earthworks and more complex gates (centre right).

The reconstruction (above left) shows the appearance of Danebury in the second century BC. The west gate was blocked, while the remaining double gate had a central 'command post' giving an all-round view of the gate area (above right). To reach the inner gate attackers had to expose their unshielded side to missiles hurled from here.

washing down from the crown of the hill and the back of the rampart, and so were quite well preserved. (Elsewhere floors rarely survive erosion by later ploughing.)

Much of the interior seems to have been devoted to storage, on a massive scale. The occupants had cut thousands of pits from the chalk, of which perhaps a few score were in use at any one time. They were probably used for storing foodstuffs, especially grain (p. 56). After use, the pits were filled with rubbish, including fragments of pottery, animal bones, seeds and imported goods (shale bracelets, querns, glass). The four-post structures found in some numbers at the site are thought to have been raised granaries. Later dwellers at the fort built these granaries in lines along well-defined internal roadways.

Curiously, the storage capacity of the pits and granaries appears to have greatly exceeded the requirements of the small population of the hillfort (no more than a couple of hundred, perhaps less at some seasons). Weed seeds found in samples of carbonized grain from the site confirm that crops from a variety of soils, in the valley bottoms as well as on the chalk, were stored in the hillfort. The careful layout of the granaries along the internal roads of the fort further suggests the organizing hand of a central authority, most likely a chieftain or petty king, who need not have resided in the fort in peacetime. All this hints at Danebury's role as a place of secure food storage, and probably of political control, for the people of its hinterland.

That the danger of war was real, and the defences around the fort were not solely for prestige, is evident from the ultimate fate of Danebury, whose gate was burned in about 100 BC. The site was then abandoned, the victim, it would seem, of tribal warfare.

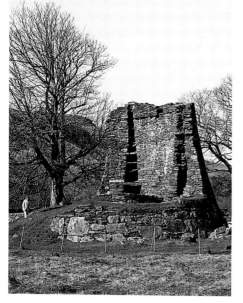

SCOTTISH BROCHS
(Left) Dun Telve in Gleann Beag in the western Highlands is one of the best preserved brochs in mainland Scotland. Such circular defensive towers, which appear by about 100 BC, are a peculiarity of northern Scotland and the Isles. Constructed entirely of unmortared stone, their elegant, tapering shape possessed great strength. The surviving portion of Dun Telve reveals the 'casemate' construction of the inner and outer facings, with slabs linking the two and forming the floors of rooms and stairs within the thickness of the wall.

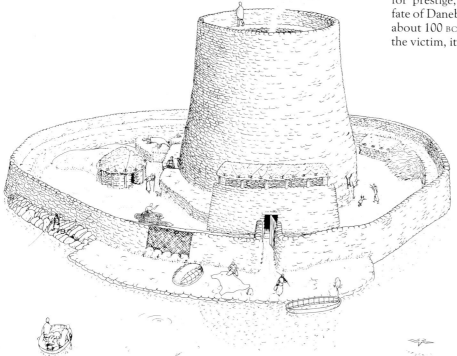

(Left) A reconstruction of the broch of Clickhimin, Shetland, which was in use from the first century BC to the second century AD. The tower was supplemented by an outer wall and a blockhouse guarding the entrance. Although nearly 500 brochs have been found, none have survived intact, so we do not know how – or if – such towers were roofed, or exactly how tall they were. It has been conjectured that these were strongholds belonging to the nobility of small maritime tribal powers.

PEOPLE, POPULATION AND DISEASE

'I have already told the number of the Helvetii, and of the Arveni, and of their allies – from all of which the largeness of the population is manifest, as is also the thing of which I spoke above – the excellence of the women in regard to the bearing and nursing of children.'
Strabo 4,3,3

IT IS CLEAR from the Classical sources, and from the number of Iron Age settlements found, that Gaul and Britain were densely settled. Modern surveys, using aerial photography and field-walking (searching fields for pottery and other traces of buried settlements churned up by ploughing), have located farms, hamlets and larger agglomerations in their thousands. Not all of these were occupied at once, of course, but even so, recent estimates put the population of late Iron Age Britain as high as 2–3 million, and that of Gaul at 6–8 million. There had evidently been rapid growth in the last two centuries BC, because during the early Iron Age in Britain at any rate the population was much smaller.

What did they look like?

The Gauls had a reputation for enormous physical stature by comparison with Greeks and Romans, although the archaeological evidence from Britain at least does not suggest that the Celts were especially tall on average (p. 100). On the other hand, there is a wealth of diverse archaeological data, anecdotal evidence in the Classical texts, and some (frequently stylized) depictions, which give us a broad picture of what the early Celts looked like, and how they dressed (pp. 64–69).

Illness and medicine

Disease was common among early communities. Poor hygiene and ignorance resulted in a host of ailments, from intestinal worms and eye complaints to dental disease and poorly-healed injuries. But there was not a total lack of medicine. Herbal remedies were doubtless widely used, and people certainly appealed to supernatural powers: wooden models of afflicted organs have been found at water-shrines in Gaul. Several healing springs exploited in Roman times were probably already in use in the Iron Age, for example at Nemausus (Nîmes, France) and at Bath (England, p. 89). Surgery was also carried out: several graves containing medical instruments have been unearthed. For instance, the grave of a 'warrior-surgeon' equipped with weapons and surgical instruments was discovered at München-Obermenzing in Germany (third or early second century BC). The instruments include retractors, probes and a trephining saw. Trephining (making holes in the skull) may have been a fairly common treatment for head injuries and perhaps psychological disorders; trephined skulls have been found in Austria. Whether medicine was a speciality of, say, priests or local wise women is unknown. In medicine, as in so many other areas, the Celts stand favourable comparison with the Classical world; here there was a similar mix of herbal remedies, magic, religion and limited surgery for those who could afford it – and were prepared to risk its hazards and agonies.

(Above) This aerial photograph reveals the enclosing ditch of an Iron Age farmstead at Little Woodbury, Wiltshire. Thousands of similar sites are now known in Britain.

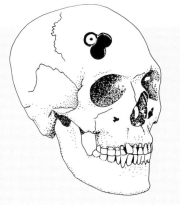

PREHISTORIC NEUROSURGERY: THE HAZARDS OF KNIFE AND SAW
People have made holes in the skulls of the living for thousands of years, especially to relieve neurological symptoms caused by injuries. Specialized saws for the purpose have been found in La Tène tombs in Celtic central Europe, including one with the 'warrior-surgeon' from München-Obermenzing (see text).
Cylindrical skull-drills (trepans) were also developed and widely used by the Greek surgeons, as was a more complex version (the trephine) with a central guiding pin to stop the bit from slipping. The trephine was imported and adopted by central European Celts, as gruesomely revealed by this skull from a third-century BC cemetery at Katzelsdorf, Austria. Note the characteristic central hole in the third, incomplete cut. The patient probably died at the surgeon's hands: there is no sign of any healing. Surprisingly, archaeology has shown that some patients survived the shock and risk of infection from such ordeals.

CELTIC MEN

*'The Gauls are tall of body, with rippling muscles,
and white of skin, and their hair is blond, and not
only naturally so, but they also make it their
practice by artificial means to increase the
distinguishing colour which nature has given it.
For they are always washing their hair in lime-
water, and they pull it back from the forehead to
the top of the head and back to the nape of the
neck, with the result that their appearance is like
that of Satyrs and Pans, since the treatment of their
hair makes it so heavy and coarse that it differs in
no respect from the mane of horses. Some of them
shave the beard, but others let it grow a little; and
the nobles shave their cheeks, but they let the
moustache grow until it covers the mouth.
Consequently, when they are eating, their
moustaches become entangled in the food, and
when they are drinking, the beverage passes, as it
were, through a kind of strainer.'
Diodorus Siculus 5,28*

TO THE GREEKS AND ROMANS, the continental
Celts were striking in appearance, because
of their great height, blond or reddish hair
and pale complexions. This has sometimes
puzzled modern people, as many Celts
today, such as the Welsh and Bretons, are
stereotyped as relatively short and dark.
These differing perceptions merely under-
line the fact that the ancient and modern
Celts are a cultural and linguistic grouping,
and not a biologically distinct race.

Hairstyles

The Gauls had a shaggy appearance, due to
the fashion for long hair, beards and,
among the aristocracy, large moustaches.
Spiking the hair by washing it in chalky
water was perhaps to enhance fearsomeness
on the battlefield. It was probably not a
universal practice: it would be hard, for

instance, to wear a helmet over spiked hair.
There were regional fashions too; statuary
suggests that in the last century BC southern
Gauls were clean-shaven and short-haired,
perhaps under Graeco-Roman influence.

Gauls are also said to have shaved their
body hair. Razors and tweezers have been
found, and the site at La Tène produced
'toilet sets' consisting of an iron razor and
a pair of sprung iron shears. The Britons
were unusual in that they painted or tat-
tooed their bodies blue (p. 96).

Dress

Some items of clothing have been recovered from Iron Age bog-bodies in the
north, beyond Celtica. Together with fragments of textiles from graves and the
Hallstatt mines, these have given some
substance to the sartorial accounts of Gauls
in France and Italy. Descriptions show that
Celtic dress was colourful and fine, and
that people took a great interest in their
appearance, to impress each other and to
alarm their foes.

During the later Iron Age, the Gauls
generally wore long-sleeved shirts or tunics,
and long trousers (*bracae*, 'breeches'),
which the Romans regarded as both effeminate and particularly barbaric. It is often
said that breeches were probably invented
by horse-riding peoples of Asia, for reasons
of practicality when in the saddle; but the
cold climate of northern Europe rather
than horse-riding probably had more to do
with the adoption of trousers by the Celts
(and Germans), since relatively few Celts
rode. Certain Celtic groups, such as the

*(Left) A stone head from
Mšecké Žehrovice in Bohemia,
perhaps depicting a god. Note
the torc, swept-back hair,
shaven chin and fine
moustache, also seen on a
small bronze head from
Welwyn (right), and on a
depiction of a Gaul on a
Roman silver denarius (far
right). The last figure has a
goatee beard, and perhaps
lime-washed hair.*

Irish, appear not to have worn trousers at all. Clothes were made of wool or linen, with some silk used by the rich. Celtic nobles wore brightly coloured cloths, with gold thread and elaborate embroidery: traces of embroidery have recently been found in a grave at Bruton Fleming in Yorkshire. Much of the colour would have become fairly subdued, owing to the use of vegetable dyes which tend to fade.

Cloaks were also worn, especially in winter. The coarse wool of Gallic sheep made a very superior cloak called the *sagus* (wool retains its insulating properties even when wet), which was exported to Italy. Cloaks are specifically mentioned as being patterned in checks, and fabrics with tartan- or tweed-like designs have been found in Iron Age contexts. Brooches (*fibulae*), of iron or bronze and sometimes decorated with coral, were used to fasten the cloak at the right shoulder. The fibula worked like a modern safety pin, with a spring and a catch-plate to hold the point. It appears that they were normally worn with the catch-plate upwards.

A belt was also often worn, especially the sword-belt by the nobility. According to Strabo, the Celts would 'endeavour not to grow fat or pot-bellied'; he further mentions that a fine was imposed on those who became too obese to do up their belts, but this was probably more connected with vanity than an interest in physical fitness!

Jewellery

Brooches, essentially dress fasteners, could be elaborate. Armlets are also frequently mentioned, but the most famous item of jewellery is the metal neckring or torc. Although especially associated with the Celts, it was also worn by other peoples, and was later adopted by the Romans as a military decoration: torcs are often mentioned as spoils of war. Did they have a specific symbolic meaning, beyond a simple expression of wealth? Quite possibly so, since many are not made of precious metal, but of iron or copper alloy. They may have served as a particular indication of rank or status, nobility or power. And they may have had religious associations as well: they are known to have been dedicated to the gods, and appear on figures of deities (pp. 88–89). No doubt the specific meaning varied across the Celtic world, and through time.

A BRITISH NOBLE COUPLE OF ABOUT 200 BC

Portrait of a wealthy northern British couple, based on archaeological and documentary evidence from Britain and neighbouring lands. The woman's hairstyle and peplos-type dress are based on Danish bog-finds, as are the patterns on the cloaks. Her jewellery and the man's sword and armour derive from east Yorkshire cemetery evidence. Although the blue body-colour is known to have been worn by Iron Age Britons, we can only guess that it was applied in sinuous La Tène patterns as seen here. Similarly, descriptions of lime-washed hair refer to the Gauls, but it is reasonable to suggest that Britons may also have treated their hair in this way. Painting by Peter Connolly.

CELTIC WOMEN

BOUDICA: QUEEN OF THE ICENI

'In stature she was very tall, in appearance most terrifying, in the glance of her eye most fierce, and her voice was harsh; a great mass of the tawniest hair fell to her hips; around her neck was a large golden necklace; and she wore a tunic of diverse colours over which a thick mantle was fastened with a brooch. This was her invariable attire. She now grasped a spear to aid her in terrifying all beholders and spoke...'
Cassius Dio 62,2

A fur cape, and wrap-around skirt, from a fifth-century BC bog body found at Huldremose in Denmark. Although from beyond the Celtic world, it shows that the tartan-like fabrics mentioned in documents were widely available from early times.

'The women of the Gauls are not only like men in their great stature but they are a match for them in courage as well.'
Diodorus Siculus 5,32

CELTIC WOMEN were remarked upon by Greeks and Romans for their beauty, fecundity, and their courage. Women were not, however, treated as equals in Celtic societies, although compared especially with their Greek equivalents, noblewomen enjoyed considerable freedom of action and even power.

The lives of women are underrepresented in the very male-orientated Classical sources, although archaeology sheds considerable light on the female world, for example through offerings found in women's graves. It is risky to make simple assumptions about gender roles. It would be unwise to imagine, say, that men were necessarily responsible for agriculture and women for the home and activities such as the weaving of textiles. While the limited evidence does suggest that crafts like metalworking were male preserves, food production and other essential craft activities (from pottery to basketry and leatherworking) may well have been in the hands of women.

Marriage seems to have been far more of a partnership than in the Roman world, where a woman passed from the power of her father into that of her husband. According to Caesar, the practice among the Gauls was for the husband and wife to pool equal amounts of money, and to share any gains – at death, the surviving partner inherited everything. Despite this apparent equality of the sexes, Caesar says men had power of life or death over their wives – although this may have been as theoretical as it had become among the Romans. Some noblemen apparently practised polygamy. As in Rome, the privileged lot of noblewomen was counterbalanced by the burden of being pawns in the dynastic marriages with which Gallic aristocrats sealed alliances. For example, Dumnorix, an ambitious noble among the Aedui, secured a private alliance with the Helvetian prince Orgetorix by marrying the latter's daughter, and also married his own female relatives into the nobility of other tribes, to further his personal scheming for power.

Caesar records that some women in Britain shared several husbands. This passage is often dismissed as fabulous, but such polyandry is paralleled in later societies elsewhere in the world. The possibility that some early Celtic groups recognized the primacy of matrilinear descent, in which an individual's status depended on the identity of the mother rather than the father, has been raised by scholars. The evidence is thin, but it is reasonable to think that the female line was of considerably greater importance than it was in the Classical world.

Pride, courage and morality

Celtic noblewomen scandalized Roman opinion by their alleged promiscuity, and Queen Cartimandua's elopement is a case in point (see box). It seems clear that in sexual relations Celtic women were much more open and independent than Roman women. They also shared the pride and eloquence for which their people were renowned, witness the words attributed to the wife of the Caledonian chieftain Argentocoxus when she was challenged by the empress Julia Augusta about her morals: 'We fulfil the demands of nature in a much better way than do you Roman women: for we consort openly with the best men, whereas you let yourselves be debauched in secret by the vilest' (Dio 77,16,5).

The fierce pride of Celtic noblewomen, and the sense of personal honour which demanded vengeance for any insult or injury, is graphically shown by the story of Chiomara, wife of the Galatian noble Ortiagon (p. 41). She was captured by the Romans in 189 BC, and fell into the hands of a centurion, who, failing to seduce her, raped her. Subsequently, she was able to persuade him that her people would ransom her. A deal was duly struck, and her kinsmen brought the ransom to a secret meeting, where the centurion, pleased at the prospect of wealth, made his farewells – whereupon at a word from Chiomara her kinsmen killed him. She returned to her husband, and presented him with the head of her enemy. Ortiagon, commenting on the betrayal of the ransom bargain, said: 'Woman, a fine thing is good faith'. 'A better thing only one man should be alive who had intercourse with me', she replied (Plutarch, *On the Courage of Women*, 22).

Women and power

Women could, and at least sometimes did, play an overt role in politics: for example, Plutarch reports that they intervened to prevent war among the Italian Gauls in the early fourth century BC. There were also priestesses, but their role and status are obscure (p. 90). The modern notion of sword-wielding Celtic Amazons is more difficult to substantiate: although women were often present on the battlefield, there seems to be no evidence of them bearing arms – except in Dio's description of Boudica (p. 66).

Women among the nobility sometimes achieved considerable direct political power. Boudica, queen of the Iceni, is surely the most famous of all ancient Britons, eclipsing her northern British contemporary Cartimandua of the Brigantes. And Irish tales provide the legendary Medb (Maeve) of Connaught, who wielded more power than her husband. It is beyond doubt that Celtic noblewomen possessed considerable personal status and prestige from the earliest times, as the Vix grave of the sixth century BC (p. 22–23), the Waldalgesheim grave of the fourth century

BRITISH QUEENS AND THE ROMAN CONQUEST

A Victorian view of Boudica and her daughters.

The careers of the British queens Boudica and Cartimandua show the courage, ambition and political skill which Celtic noblewomen could exhibit when the opportunity arose. They were central players in the drama of the Roman annexation of Britain, but can we assume from this that the idea of female rulers was widely accepted among the British peoples? Detailed scrutiny of the historical context raises doubts. It may be no coincidence that the figures of Boudica and Cartimandua both appear in the context of gradual Roman conquest, when the imperial presence was a new and distorting factor in native politics.

Boudica, queen of the Iceni of East Anglia, undoubtedly led the rebellion against the Romans (p. 139), but her leadership may have been symbolic. It may simply have resulted from the extraordinary circumstances prevailing at the time, for she was the consort of the late King Prasutagus, and the personal humiliation and abuse she and her daughters received at Roman hands were an affront to tribal honour. She thus became the focus for the outrage felt by the tribe at large at the perceived injustice of the Roman takeover. Whether she would have been accepted as her husband's successor in the absence of the Romans and their brutality is an interesting question.

Cartimandua was queen of the powerful Brigantes of northern England, married to one Venutius. They may have shared power, or one may have been the executive ruler and the other simply a consort. What is clear is that Cartimandua was ambitious for personal power, to the point of a break with Venutius. To achieve her ends she became politically closely associated with the Roman invaders, upon whom she relied more and more – and to whom she eventually fled. It is impossible to tell now whether the increasing hostility many of the Brigantes displayed towards her was the cause or effect of this growing rapprochement. Did they attack her because she was seen as an overweening female, whose rule was unacceptable? The fact that she had an affair with Venutius' armour-bearer hardly helped! Or did they attack her because she was collaborating with the invaders? Both answers may be true.

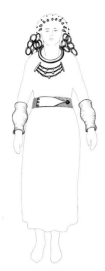

BC, and the woman in the third-century cart burial recently found at Wetwang Slack in Yorkshire (p. 101) all testify, to give but a few examples. However, how common it really was for women to hold supreme political power in their own right is more open to question. It is hard to know what to make of semidivine figures like Medb, while Boudica and Cartimandua may not in fact be the clear examples they seem (p. 67). Otherwise there is no known mention of female rulers among the various native British and Gallic chieftains, monarchs and magistrates of the late Iron Age.

Female dress

Most clues to the types of dress worn by Celtic women come from the combinations of brooches and other jewellery found in graves; the textiles themselves have perished. There are also a few remarkably well-preserved female garments from Iron Age bog-bodies found in Denmark. Although strictly outside the recognized areas of

(Above) A woman's finery, based on a body from the Magdalenenberg tumulus, sixth century BC. (Below) Some of the jewellery from the cemetery at Hallstatt.

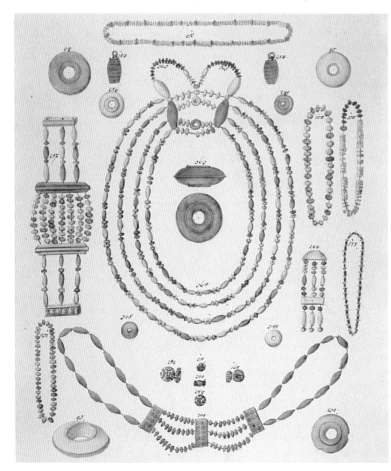

Celtic culture, they nevertheless show the same features inferred from cemetery evidence.

A common form of dress was probably the *peplos*, apparently worn by many peoples from the Baltic to the Mediterranean, including Greek women. It consisted essentially of two rectangles of fabric, fastened up the sides, and typically held together at the shoulders by a pair of *fibulae*, sometimes linked by swags of decorative chain. The *peplos* was a simple and practical garment, the shoulder fastenings being particularly convenient for breast-feeding mothers. There were other types of garment too. The Danish finds have produced a checked wrap-around skirt. This, and other pieces from Denmark and Hallstatt in Austria, preserve bold check patterns; the original colours of these have faded, but they nonetheless attest the tweedy/tartan patterns characteristic of much Celtic clothing, according to Classical sources. Skirts are likely to have been calf- or ankle-length, to avoid the mud. The widespread fashion for wearing anklets also suggests that skirts were worn short enough for these ornaments to be seen. Cloaks are mentioned too. The fabrics available were wool, linen and, very occasionally, some imported silk. There is, as yet, no evidence for the nature of women's footwear.

Hairstyles and cosmetics

Hair was apparently worn long. Female burials, especially from the Hallstatt period, sometimes have hairpins in situ around the skull, suggesting elaborate hairstyles. There are no references to headdresses or hats, although stone carvings from Entremont (p. 45), and a wooden statue from Chamalières (Puy-de-Dôme, first century AD) show headcloths or scarves.

Even less is known about cosmetics, although small bronze objects identified as cosmetic grinders have been found in late Iron Age British contexts. And during the 20s BC, Propertius criticized Roman women for 'aping the painted Briton' by wearing a fashionable cosmetic called *belgicus color*, perhaps an imported Celtic eye-shadow or blusher!

Jewellery: status and fashion

Celtic women, like their Greek and Roman sisters – and indeed their own menfolk – loved jewellery. Bracelets and anklets of

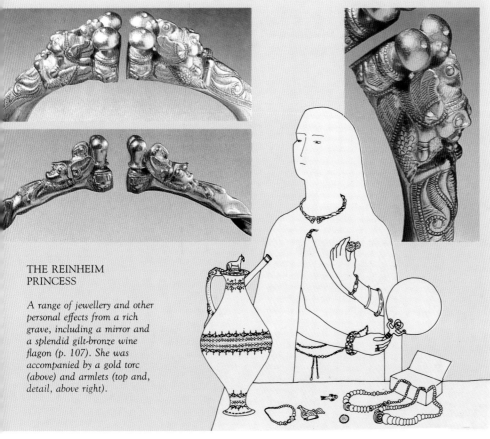

THE REINHEIM PRINCESS

A range of jewellery and other personal effects from a rich grave, including a mirror and a splendid gilt-bronze wine flagon (p. 107). She was accompanied by a gold torc (above) and armlets (top and, detail, above right).

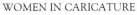

WOMEN IN CARICATURE

'a whole band of foreigners will be unable to cope with one of the [Gauls] in a fight, if he calls in his wife, stronger than he by far and with flashing eyes; least of all when she swells her neck and gnashes her teeth, and poising her huge white arms, begins to rain blows mingled with kicks, like shots discharged by the twisted cords of a catapult. The voices of most of them are formidable and threatening, alike when they are good-natured and angry. But all of them with equal care keep clean and neat, and in those districts, particularly in Aquitania, no man or woman can be seen, be she never so poor, in soiled or ragged clothing, as elsewhere.'
Ammianus Marcellinus 15,12,1 (fourth century AD)

HUSBANDS AND WIVES

'The men, after due reckoning, take from their own goods a sum of money equal to the dowry they have received from their wives and place it with the dowry. Of each sum account is kept between them and the profits saved; whichever of the two survives receives the portion of both together with the profits of past years. Men have the power of life and death over their wives, as over their children; and when the father of a house, who is of distinguished birth, has died, his relatives assemble, and if there is anything suspicious about his death they make inquisition of his wives [sic] as they would of slaves, and if discovery is made they put them to death with fire and all manner of excruciating tortures.'
Caesar, Gallic War, 6,19

bronze (sometimes enamelled) and other materials, are particularly common, as are the *fibulae* mentioned above. Neck jewellery was also widely worn, not least torcs, but also necklaces of coral, amber or glass beads. Finger-rings and earrings, beloved of the Classical world, were apparently little worn north of the Alps before the Roman conquest.

There were many regional fashions, such as the black shale bracelets of Britain, and fashions also evolved over time. In the Münsingen-Rain cemetery in Switzerland, women during the fifth century BC were typically buried wearing a pair of anklets, two bracelets and a necklace. In the following century the necklace went out of fashion, while the number of anklets increased to four. After 250 BC anklets disappeared, and elaborate bronze chain waist-belts were introduced; the bronze bracelets were replaced by glass bangles of excellent quality and colour, notably cobalt blue. Similar but varying patterns are seen in many parts of Celtic Europe.

Another interesting possibility is that, as in many more recent societies, the way women dressed depended not only on their wealth and rank, but on their age, marital or maternal status. For example, it has been observed that in the female graves of the Hallstatt period around Asperg, mature women often have three fibulae at the shoulder, while girls and some older women only have one or two. Could this be because the latter were unmarried? Further patterns will doubtless become apparent as more cemeteries are studied in detail.

Mirrors

In late Iron Age Britain, mirrors became increasingly elaborately decorated. Iron and bronze examples are known, the latter being both better preserved and more finely worked, showing complex inscribed decoration on the back of the mirror plate, and sometimes red enamelling. These beautiful and ostentatious objects seem to have been status-markers, and are sometimes found in female graves in Britain.

FEASTING AND FIGHTING: HOW SOCIETY FUNCTIONED

Coin showing the Gallic leader Dumnorix (p. 118), armoured, and with a boar and severed head – symbols of power and war.

'When a large number dine together they sit around in a circle with the most influential man in the centre, like the leader of the chorus, whether he surpass the others in warlike skill, or nobility of family, or wealth. Beside him sits the host and next on either side the others in order of distinction. Their shieldsmen stand behind them while their spearmen are seated in a circle on the opposite side and feast in common like their lords. The servers bear around the drink in terracotta or silver jars like spouted cups.'
Poseidonius, quoted in Athenaeus 4,36

ANCIENT CELTIC SOCIETIES were held together by a complex web of kinship ties and other obligations, such as guest-friendship, a bond arising from providing hospitality to an outsider. Within this network, individuals strove to attain rank and prestige, a famous name and wide renown.

Celtic lords were famous for ostentatious public displays of generosity, which seem to have been essential for the maintenance of their place in the social pecking-order. Intellectual qualities such as eloquence were also valued. Personal courage was an essential commodity, and success in war was a vital source of prestige, power, dependants, and the material wealth (notably gold and cattle) to retain them. This system of competition for wealth, power and followers led to the development of an unstable hierarchy, in which nobles constantly sought new means of enhancing their prestige to boost their standing. Not surprisingly, 'prestige goods' assumed a great importance, whether finery (rich clothes, elaborate weaponry, ?gold torcs), the exclusive use of which expressed privilege; or valued commodities (e.g. gold coins or Italian wine), which were selectively bestowed to reward supporters. This would explain Diodorus' famous statement that Gauls would exchange a slave for an amphora of wine. To an Italian merchant it was a bargain, but the purchaser was not stupid: within his own world the wine was of most use if it appeared to be fabulously valuable, so that the offer of a drink was a great honour and mark of favour. It made sense ostentatiously to inflate the price paid. This precious liquid could then be dispensed publicly, for maximum effect, at the feasts which Gauls loved so much.

WHO OWNED THE LAND?
The traditional basis of noble wealth in Europe has been the ownership of the land, and the consequent direct control of agricultural produce – the lifeblood of the economy in pre-industrial societies. In some areas, however (perhaps in all until late in the Iron Age), land may have been held communally by the tribe, with grazing rights for personally owned stock or plots for arable farming allotted to individuals or families. There is no mention of estates belonging to the nobility, although their houses are referred to. The ownership of land may not have mattered: it was the control of surplus produce and the possession of herds which were important.

We currently believe that the Celts operated a so-called embedded economy (p. 25), meaning that no matter who owned or farmed the land, the aristocracy probably came to control its produce – through their ties of mutual obligation (whether kinship or clientage) with those who did the farming. In return for protecting their dependants, the lords could expect to receive plenty of livestock and produce.

Feasting

Feasts could be wild, drunken, even deadly affairs, but above all they were important social gatherings, at least sometimes with ceremonial or religious overtones. Nobles would sit in formal order of status, attended by their retinues. At such events the relative ranks of the various warriors present could be tested in public, in mock combat, or (if Poseidonius is to be believed) in duels to the death over the right to the champion's portion – the choicest cut of meat.

The religious element of such feasts is evident from Poseidonius' account of the (sacred?) feasting enclosures built by Lovernius, and of people making death-pacts at feasts. The provision of plentiful food and drink, the entertainment even of strangers, the praise-singer, and story-telling were other vital ingredients. An interesting role at the feast was played by the satirist, whose barbs at the expense of warrior pride were much feared in a society where 'face' was all-important.

(Left) A cauldron and its suspension chain, from La Tène.

Patrons and clients

Wealth came from war, or (later in the Iron Age) from the control of foreign trade (pp. 118–21), and especially from agriculture. Another increasingly important source of power was the acquisition of clients.

Clients were people under obligation to nobles to support and serve them, in return for protection and perhaps a living (e.g. artisans making splendid 'prestige goods' such as weapons and gold torcs). As the authority of the nobility grew, they were able to control more and more of the agricultural and other wealth of the community. They could even acquire clients in other tribes, and to form personal alliances with noble families among neighbouring peoples. In the later part of the Iron Age (at least in Gaul), it seems that these ties of clientage became more important than kinship or other relations. The rising power of the élites meant that increasing numbers of the free poor became dependent on them, pledging themselves as clients in return, presumably, for help through crop-failure or other difficulties. This may well explain Caesar's description of the ordinary people as little better than slaves, to whom no attention was paid (*if* Caesar correctly understood, and honestly reported, what he saw!).

The idea of clientage also applied to entire peoples, with weaker groups coming under the protection of the stronger, as demonstrated by the power of the Aedui, for example. In the growing importance of clientship, Gallic aristocracies in particular were strikingly similar to that of Rome, where the great senatorial clans built their powerbases and competed in much the same way. Some Roman politicians like Caesar mounted social events such as gladiatorial games, entertainments and feasts to enhance their own personal prestige. In many respects, the Celts and Romans were far more similar than many realize.

'Their possessions consisted of cattle and gold, because these were the only things they could carry about with them everywhere according to circumstances and shift when they chose. They treated comradeship as of the greatest importance, those among them being the most feared and most powerful who were thought to have the largest number of attendants and associates'
Polybius 2,17,9–12, on the Gauls of northern Italy

'Lovernius, father of Bituitus who was dethroned by the Romans ... in an attempt to win popular favour rode in a chariot over the plains distributing gold and silver to the tens of thousands of Celts who followed him; moreover, he made a square enclosure one and a half miles each way, within which he filled vats with expensive liquor and prepared so great a quantity of food that for many days all who wished could enter and enjoy the feast prepared, being served without a break by the attendants. And when at length he fixed a day for the ending of the feast, a Celtic poet who arrived too late met Lovernius and composed a song magnifying his greatness and lamenting his own late arrival. Lovernius was very pleased and asked for a bag of gold and threw it to the poet who ran beside his chariot. The poet picked it up and sang another song saying that the very tracks made by his chariot gave gold and largesse to mankind.'
Poseidonius, quoted in Athenaeus 4,37

'... according to the custom of Gaul, it is a crime in dependants to desert their patrons, even in desperate case.'
Caesar 7,40

GALLIC EATING HABITS THROUGH GREEK EYES

'The Celts sit on dried grass and have their meals served up on wooden tables raised slightly above the earth. Their food consists of a small number of loaves of bread together with a large quantity of meat, either boiled or roasted on charcoal or on spits. They partake of this in a cleanly but leonine fashion, raising up whole limbs in both hands and biting off the meat, while any part which is hard to tear off they cut through with a small dagger which hangs attached to their sword-sheath in its own scabbard. Those who live beside the rivers or near the Mediterranean or Atlantic eat fish in addition, baked fish, that is, with the addition of salt, vinegar and cummin. They also use cummin in their drinks.'
Poseidonius on southern Gaul, early first century BC; quoted in Athenaeus 4,36

'The drink of the wealthy classes is wine imported from Italy or from the territory of Marseilles. This is unadulterated, but sometimes a little water is added. The lower classes drink wheaten beer prepared with honey, but most people drink it plain. It is called corma. They use a common cup, drinking a little at a time, taking no more than a mouthful, but they do it rather frequently.'
Poseidonius, quoted in Athenaeus 4,36

'When they dine they all sit upon the ground, using for cushions the skins of wolves or of dogs. The service at the meals is performed by the youngest children, both male and female, who are of a suitable age; and near at hand are their fireplaces ... and on them are cauldrons and spits holding whole pieces of meat ...
'They invite strangers to their feasts, and do not inquire until after the meal who they are and of what things they stand in need.'
Diodorus Siculus 5,28

'The Celts sometimes engage in single combat at dinner. Assembling in arms they engage in a mock battle-drill, and mutual thrust-and-parry, but sometimes wounds are inflicted, and the irritation caused by this may lead even to the slaying of the opponent unless the bystanders hold them back ... And in former times ... when the hindquarters were served up the bravest hero took the thigh piece, and if another man claimed it they stood up and fought in single combat to the death. Others in the presence of the assembly received silver or gold or a certain number of jars of wine, and having taken pledges of the gift and distributed it among their friends and kin, lay stretched out face upwards on their shields, and another standing by cut their throat with his sword.'
Poseidonius, quoted in Athenaeus 4,40

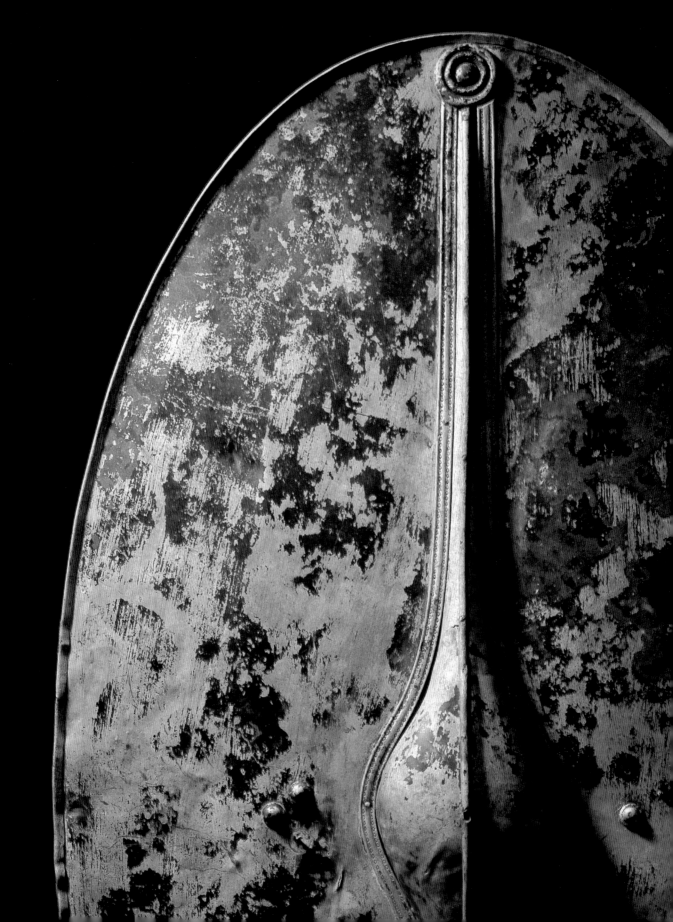

V
THE
CELTS AT WAR

'The enemy ... even when their hope of safety was at an end, displayed a prodigious courage. When their front rank had fallen, the next stood on the prostrate forms and fought from them; when these were cast down, and the corpses were piled up in heaps, the survivors, standing as it were upon a mound, hurled darts at our troops, or caught and returned our javelins. ... This engagement brought the name and nation of the Nervii almost to utter destruction. ... From six hundred tribal councillors they had been reduced to three, and from sixty thousand to barely five hundred that could bear arms.'

Caesar on the Battle of the Sambre, *Gallic War*, II, 29

THE ANCIENT CELTS had a fearsome reputation for aggressiveness, even among the militaristic Romans, and there can be no doubt that war played a key role in Celtic politics and society. Personal courage was very important to Celtic nobles and the bearing of weapons may have been regarded as a primary mark of free manhood. The aristocracy distinguished themselves from the rank and file by carrying particularly splendid arms. For, as with other aspects of Celtic life, display is a key idea. The impression given by archaeology and Classical descriptions of Celtic armies is one of ostentation: of brilliantly made weapons and of gorgeous decoration – the Celts loved to dazzle the enemy with their pride, and their wealthy dress and arms. Many Celtic weapons are boasts in bronze and iron: swords chased with delicate patterns, or helmets surmounted with fantastic crests.

Detail of the bronze shield recently found in the gravels of the river Thames at Chertsey.

THE SPECTRUM OF VIOLENCE

A late Iron Age bronze
statuette of a Gaulish warrior
from St-Maur-en-Chausée,
France.

*'The whole race ... is war-mad, and both high-
spirited and quick for battle, although otherwise
simple and not ill-mannered ...'*
Strabo 4,4,2

THE COMPLEX WEB of clientage and alliance
which Caesar reveals in Gaul was largely
based on the outcome of frequent wars.
The theatre of combat was where many
personal and tribal relations were tested,
broken and forged. We may suppose conflicts ranged from great wars associated
with migrations of whole peoples to mere
brigandage, inter-family feuds, and cattle
raids by individual warriors seeking quick
wealth and prestige. Probably most Celtic
warfare was on a small scale, involving no
more than a few score men on each side.

The population was growing and states
were developing in late Iron Age Gaul, and
this may have led to an increase in the scale
of warfare. But it is clear that the vast
armies commanded by Vercingetorix and
others were assembled only as a response
to the great threat from Rome (p. 127). In
fact, Rome changed the very rules of Celtic
warfare, bringing large armies into an area
where, internally at least, they may have
been much rarer before. Certainly, the
Gaul described and conquered by Caesar
showed no signs of exhaustion by internal
wars – it was a rich and prosperous land –
so means were evidently found for limiting
the damage war could cause. Caesar says
that the Druids were involved in disputes
and in the decision to wage or end war,
providing some evidence for the existence
of limiting social mechanisms. War did not
threaten the fabric of society as a whole,
even if the fortunes of individual clans and
tribes did wax and wane. It would probably
also be wrong to think that love of war was
confined to the nobility, at the expense
of the suffering of a pacifist peasantry:
admiration for the warrior ethic appears to
have been general, and was not restricted
to men either (see box). Violence was
endemic, but sufficiently intermittent for
most people to get on with their lives
successfully most of the time: warlike display was at least as important as actual
fighting.

WOMEN AND WAR
*Despite the popular idea that
there were Celtic amazons,
there is no hard evidence that
women took an active role in
fighting. But there were some
famed female leaders such as
Boudica (pp. 67, 139), and
women are documented as
spectators on the battlefield. In
Italy, at least, they are also
recorded taking a role in
deciding on war or peace.*

THE TECHNOLOGY OF WAR: WEAPONS AND ARMOUR

*'Their arms correspond in size with their physique;
a long sword fastened on the right side and a long
shield, and spears of like dimension ...'*
Strabo IV,4,3; first century BC

THE BASIC ARMS OF IRON AGE Celts were normally an iron-tipped spear and a shield, to which the wealthy might add a sword, a helmet, and in later times a shirt of iron mail. There were considerable changes over the last four centuries BC, reflecting tactical developments and growing wealth and sophistication, but it is likely that most warriors throughout the La Tène period were armed with spear and shield alone. These arms may have served more often as symbols of free status and hunting gear than for war.

Spears and projectile weapons

A wide range of spearhead forms are known, some enormous, others viciously serrated. Some were weirdly shaped or elaborately decorated, more for show than for function. Complete spears, 8 feet (2.5 m) long, have been found at La Tène.

Caesar records numerous archers in Gaul, but these seem to have made little impact on warfare. Slings may have been of greater importance, and dumps of what are thought to have been slingstones have often been found in Britain, where the great elaboration of some hillforts has been seen as a response to this highly effective weapon. However, many modern authorities believe the multiplication of British hillfort ramparts was as much a display of power as the result of military necessity (p. 130).

Swords

Swords exhibited various general and local fashions during the La Tène period. Blades were short from the fifth to the third centuries. Improvements in iron technology and changes in fighting style resulted in slashing swords of often enormous length in the second and first centuries BC. Perhaps surprisingly they were worn on the right, hanging from a waist-belt of metal chain and/or leather, which passed through a loop on the back of the scabbard. It is in fact quite easy to draw even a long blade from this position (Roman legionaries also wore their swords on the right). Polybius describes how some Celtic swords were of poor metal which bent on impact, requiring the owner to retire and stamp the blade back into shape with his foot before re-entering the fray! This is contradicted by modern observations of Celtic blades, which suggest the weapons were very well made, with a good edge and great flexibility.

Shields

Normally flat boards of wood, it is probable that shields were usually faced with leather to protect them against the weather, and splitting caused by blows. Examples found at La Tène stood about 3 ft 9 in (1.1 m) tall, but later depictions of Gauls leaning on shields suggest that in the late Iron Age some were larger than this, perhaps 4 ft 6 in to 4 ft 10 in (1.3–1.4 m) tall, like the contemporary Roman legionary shield. In shape they were often tall ovals, or long rectangles with rounded ends. Circles, long hexagons and (in Britain) ovals with concave ends were known. Given the Celts' apparent love of colour, we may assume that the shields were brightly painted, while depictions and surviving metal facings from ceremonial shields (too flimsy for combat) show that they were embellished with symbols such as torcs and animal figures (p. 115).

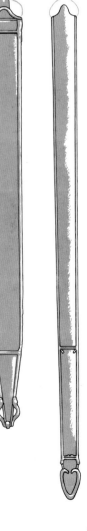

(Below) Swords and scabbards of the La Tène period. Left: an example from the Marne region, dating probably to the fourth century BC. Right: a sword from the Thames near London, probably first century BC.

(Left) A Gallic sword and belt; the latter consists of two chains linked by a leather band which passes through the suspension loop on the back of the scabbard. The belt was closed by engaging a hook on the long chain in a ring on the short one.

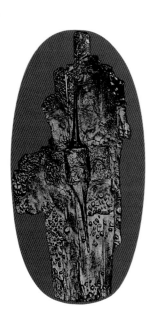

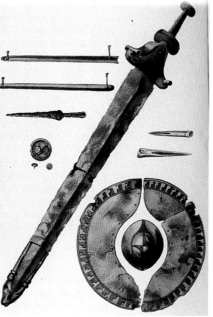

Shields were wielded by a single central handle, set into a hole in the board; this grip was horizontal, and the shield was carried like a suitcase. The fist was protected by a projecting wooden boss on the front, frequently extended into a spine running up and down the face of the board. There was no forearm strap. Like Roman shields, but unlike those of a Greek hoplite or medieval knight, Celtic shields were also weapons of offence; besides warding off blows, they served as mailed fists to strike the opponent in a two-handed fencing style, with spear or sword in the right hand. Shields were often provided with an iron or bronze boss-plate for strength and decoration, and sometimes metal edging.

Helmets

In Gaul, iron helmets were made from the fourth century BC and had gradually ousted weaker bronze versions by the time of the Roman conquest, perhaps in response to the development of large slashing swords. Typically, helmets possessed an elaborated top button and an integral neckguard. They also usually had hinged cheekpieces, a feature thought to have been adopted from Italy. They were often decorated, and some were embellished with extraordinary crests.

Horned helmets are mentioned in the Classical texts, and the best archaeological example is the Waterloo helmet from London; this was probably more for ceremonial use than war. The same is true of fabulous pieces such as the Agris helmet (pp. 104–5), which is decorated with gold and coral inlay. The eve of Caesar's conquest was a period of innovation in Gallic helmet design, with new iron forms appearing such as the 'battle-bowler' type with a smooth

(Above left) A wooden shield, one of several almost complete examples from the deposit at La Tène. Note the axial spine which flares to cover the central handgrip, a vulnerable area reinforced by a simple iron shield boss. Contemporary depictions suggest that shields were brightly painted.

(Above) Sword, metal shield fittings and other items from a grave at Grimethorpe Wold, east Yorkshire.

(Left) A Gallic noble of about the time of the Caesarean conquest, leaning on his shield. Note his shirt of iron mail, the sophisticated iron helmet, and the enormously long slashing sword suspended at his right hip.

(Right) The mid-fourth century BC helmet from Amfreville, France, plated with repoussé gold and inlaid with red glass.

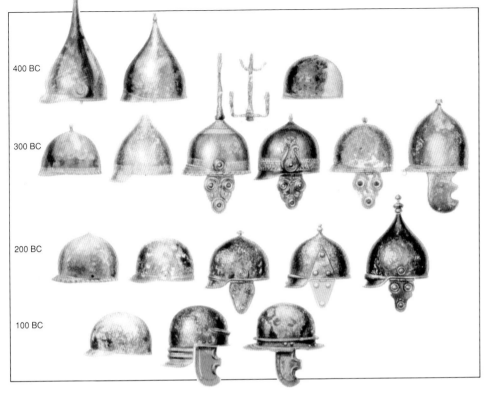

400 BC

300 BC

200 BC

100 BC

A range of bronze and iron helmets from France, Austria, Italy, Switzerland and other Celtic lands.

'Their armour includes man-sized shields decorated in individual fashion. Some of them have projecting bronze animals of fine workmanship ... On their heads they wear bronze helmets which possess large projecting figures lending the appearance of enormous stature to the wearer. In some cases horns form one part with the helmet, while in other cases it is relief figures of the foreparts of birds or quadrupeds. Their trumpets are again of a peculiar barbaric kind ... and produce a harsh sound which suits the tumult of war. Some have iron breastplates of chain mail, while others fight naked ...'
Diodorus Siculus V,30,2–3; first century BC

top and a brim. Some of these late Gallic helmets were the ancestors of a family of Roman legionary helmet types.

Armour and heroic nudity

Although the Classical world used a variety of body defences such as metal plate, scale, and padded linen, the Celts apparently used no armour before the invention of mail (so-called chain-mail), soon after 300 BC. This matrix of individually-forged, interlocking iron rings required the highest standards of blacksmithing to produce, and seems to have been a Celtic invention, appearing in graves in the third century. It was very labour-intensive (and therefore expensive) to make, and so was never very common, probably being confined to the senior warriors only. Weighing up to 35 pounds (15 kg), these body defences were highly prized and were soon adopted by the Romans. It is possible that the number of such shirts available grew over time, for in addition to the newly made shirts, old ones may have outlasted their owners and thus been handed on. However, the majority of Celtic warriors continued to fight with no armour at all.

Indeed there are descriptions of Gauls fighting naked at least until the third century BC, a practice followed in earlier times by the Greeks. Paradoxically, this might actually have been sensible for an unarmoured man, in that wounds contaminated with dirty cloth are highly prone to infection. But it is more likely that there was some religious reason, now lost to us. Whatever the case, fighting naked appears to have gone out of fashion on the continent by the time of Caesar.

(Right) Spearmen from a fifth-century BC scabbard found in the cemetery at Hallstatt. Note the apparently decorated oval shields, and the pointed shoes (p. 27).

CHARIOTS AND CAVALRY

MASTERS AND SLAVES IN BATTLE

'to each horseman were attached two servants, who were themselves skilled riders and, like their masters, had a horse. When the Galatian horsemen were engaged, the servants remained behind the ranks and proved useful in the following way. Should a horseman or his horse fall, the slave brought him a horse to mount; if the rider was killed, the slave mounted the horse in his master's place; if both rider and horse were killed, there was a mounted man ready. When a rider was wounded, one slave brought back to camp the wounded man, while the other took his vacant place in the ranks ... This organization is called in their native speech trimarcisia, for I would have you know that marca is the Celtic name for a horse.'
Pausanias 10,19,5 on the Galatae who attacked Greece

Armed with lances but no shields, these horsemen are from an early La Tène period scabbard found in the cemetery at Hallstatt, Austria.

'In chariot fighting the Britons begin by driving all over the field hurling javelins, and generally the terror inspired by the horses and the noise of the wheels are sufficient to throw their opponents' ranks into disorder. Then, after making their way between the squadrons of their own cavalry, they jump down from the chariots and engage on foot. In the meantime their charioteers retire a short distance from the battle and place the chariots in such a position that their masters, if hard pressed by numbers, have an easy means of retreat to their own lines. Thus they combine the mobility of cavalry with the staying power of infantry; and by daily training and practice they attain such proficiency that even on a steep incline they are able to control the horses at full gallop, and to check and turn them in a moment. They can run along the chariot pole, stand on the yoke, and get back into the chariot as quick as lightning.'
Caesar, *Gallic War*, V,1; first century BC

CHARIOTS were important in early Celtic warfare: vehicles identified as such have been found in early La Tène graves, and depictions of them are known from Italy, and on Roman and Gallic coins. Except in Britain and Ireland however, they appear to have fallen out of favour by the second century BC, although they were probably built and used in Gaul for some time after their obsolescence in war, primarily as transport for the nobility. Even in their heyday, it may well be that they were mostly used as 'battle taxis' for the rapid movement of warriors who actually dismounted to fight – the chariot was a convenient means of withdrawal. Caesar also reported the use of British chariots for hurling javelins at high speed.

Descriptions and depictions of chariots suggest that they were single-axled vehicles, drawn by two ponies and carrying a driver and a warrior. Remains of wheeled vehicles have been recovered from La Tène graves in Gaul (p. 15), and a few from east Yorkshire in Britain (p. 100–2), but it is not certain that these were chariots rather than hearses or buggies (and in any case they are too badly decayed to say much about their construction except that they were small and light). Surviving wheels from water-logged deposits, and more complete remains from earlier Hallstatt burials, show that the standard of carpentry was very high, and equal to anything the Classical world could produce (p. 114). The quality of metal fittings indicates the wealth lavished on such vehicles.

In continental Europe, the last recorded use of chariots in war was at Telamon in 225 BC (p. 84); Caesar only encountered them on the battlefield in Britain, where they remained in use for generations after. Tacitus mentions chariots in the Caledonian army defeated by his father-in-law, Agricola, at Mons Graupius, Scotland in AD 84. According to later tales, chariots survived for several centuries on the battle-grounds of Ireland.

Cavalry

Chariotry was increasingly supplanted by cavalry in the later Iron Age. Among the Gauls and the Celtiberians in particular, military horsemanship attained high levels of skill. The apparent growth in the importance of cavalry, which broadly coincides with the abandonment of chariotry on the continent, seems to mark a real change in

THE FOUR-POMMEL SADDLE, A KEY TECHNICAL INNOVATION

(Right) Front view of a reconstructed saddle of Roman imperial times, a type now thought to have been in use by the Celts during the later Iron Age. The rider can maintain a thoroughly secure seat by pressing his thigh against the front pommel (left).

the technology and tactics of Celtic warfare. Depictions show that the horse was ridden to war throughout the La Tène period, and even in Britain riders fought alongside the chariots. Yet it has traditionally been thought that until the introduction of the stirrup in the post-Roman period, cavalry can only have been of limited effectiveness – due to the supposed precariousness of the rider's place in the saddle. However, scholars have recently demonstrated that the saddle used in northwest Europe during the late Iron Age and early Roman period was actually remarkably effective, giving riders a seat as firm as that provided by stirrups. This was achieved by means of four tall pommels, two behind the rump

and one angled out over each thigh: the rider sat in, rather than on the saddle. Since it is now clear that the same basic form was used by the Parthians in the Middle East as well, it seems likely that this saddle developed among the rider-peoples of central Asia in the last centuries BC and spread west and south. It is tempting to link the change from chariots to really effective cavalry with the introduction to Gaul of the four-pommel saddle (and perhaps the appearance of improved breeds of riding horses?), around the third or second century BC. Whatever the case, cavalry became one of the most powerful arms of Celtic warfare, and Gaul and Spain provided much of the best horse in the Roman armies of the late republic and early empire.

(Below) Reconstruction of a Celtic chariot, based on archaeological finds, written descriptions, and pictures – e.g. on a stone from Padua (below left, c. 300 BC) and republican Roman coins (above). Recent finds in Yorkshire (p. 101) suggest that British chariots were very light, and easily dismantled.

THE CELTS ON CAMPAIGN

'It is also their custom, when they are formed for battle, to step out in front of the line and to challenge the most valiant men from among their opponents into single combat, brandishing their weapons in front of them to terrify their adversaries. And when any man accepts the challenge to battle, they then break forth into a song in praise of the valiant deeds of their ancestors and in boast of their own high achievements, reviling all the while and belittling their opponent, and trying, in a word, by such talk to strip him of his bold spirit before the combat.'
Diodorus Siculus 5,29

DURING THE CAMPAIGNING SEASON – which started when springtime dried out the roads and cleared the passes, and finished when the winter rains began – forces were levied as necessary from the men of the state, apparently on clan and tribal lines: there were no standing Celtic armies. According to Caesar, confederate armies, or those of powerful states and their clients, were organized by tribe, with each contingent having a designated area in the camp and its own place in the battle line. Allies and subject peoples, as well as mercenaries, might be called up.

On campaign

On the move, Gallic armies had great numbers of carts, and it was not only on migration that women, children and vast swarms of hangers-on moved with the column (a feature of many other armies in history, from the Roman legions themselves on occasion, to Wellington's Peninsular army). Progress could thus be very slow, and the lack of discipline made organization ramshackle. Under such circumstances, hygiene in the camp would probably have been non-existent, causing Celtic armies to be more vulnerable to disease than Roman ones. (Even as recently as the American Civil War armies routinely lost more men to sickness than to battle.)

The touchy pride of the individual chieftains and even contingents made it very difficult for leaders to control large armies: it required exceptional force of personality, such as that possessed by Vercingetorix or Ambiorix, to get their men to face arduous tasks.

Mercenaries

It was common for Celtic warriors to go freelance, literally, seeking their fortune as mercenaries outside their own tribe. Perhaps a mechanism for peacefully removing surplus young men from within a group, this seems to have become a highly organized practice. In the third century BC there

The Belgic Nervii attack Caesar's legions at the Battle of the Sambre in 57 BC (p. 73). The limited use of armour by Gallic armies, and the need to swing long slashing swords or wield thrusting spears, rendered the Gauls vulnerable to the short stabbing swords of the legionaries, who were well protected by their huge shields. Painting by Peter Connolly.

were thousands of warriors in Transalpine Gaul called *Gaesatae*, meaning 'spearmen'. Polybius wrongly (but significantly) translates the word as 'mercenaries', because they were available for hire. The *Gaesatae* mounted expeditions of their own volition, and it was their appearance uninvited in Italy that precipitated the campaign culminating in the battle of Telamon in 225 BC (pp. 84–85). The *Gaesatae* had a powerful *ésprit de corps*, and contemporary observers noted that they in particular fought naked at Telamon: their Cisalpine Gallic allies fought in breeches and cloaks.

Celtic mercenaries were quite willing to serve foreign masters, especially in the Greek states of the eastern Mediterranean. The Galatians provided a reservoir of mercenary power in Anatolia, Celts served in the armies of Macedon and Egypt, Celtiberians were much employed by the Carthaginians, and Gauls from the Po Valley were recruited by Hannibal during the bloody Second Punic War (p. 122). Gallic and Spanish cavalry also served the Romans as auxiliaries during the later Republic.

The face of battle

Once a Gallic army came into contact with its foe, it deployed into line of battle, by tribal contingents. There were battle-standards, which often appear to have been animal figures on staves. These probably symbolized the individual clan and tribal contingents, and formed rallying points. The standards also had a religious function, as indeed did Roman ones (most notably the eagle of a legion), and Caesar describes the Gauls taking solemn oaths before them.

We hear of the warriors sitting in the battle-line, on bundles of straw or twigs, waiting for fighting to commence. As the armies faced each other, complex rituals were enacted, notably the issue of challenges to single combat between champions. Prominent warriors would approach the enemy, reciting their ancestry, boasting of their own prowess, and intimidating their opponent. There are recorded cases of Roman generals engaging in duels with Celtic leaders, including Manlius Torquatus in 367 BC, and M. Valerius Corvinus in 348 BC. (The historicity of these cases may be questioned, but such combats between Roman and other generals are attested in later times as well.)

Overtures to carnage

As the moment for battle approached, the warriors created a huge din – of war-cries, battle-songs, boasts and taunts, to which was added the fearsome sound of the *carnyx* or animal-headed battle-horn. Thus opposing forces worked themselves into battle frenzy, often helped with quantities of alcohol (one band of Celtic mercenaries in Sicily in 250 BC was reportedly so drunk that it was easily overwhelmed by the Romans). The other object was to overawe and terrify the enemy with the size, splendour of appearance, arms, din and rapid manoeuvres of warriors, chariots and horse. Finally the Celts would burst forward in their dreaded charge, and hurl themselves on the enemy. It was at this moment that unnerved opponents broke ranks and ran for their lives.

Gallic infantry at least sometimes fought in close masses according to Caesar, who describes their overlapping shields pinned together by Roman javelins. However, their big thrusting spears and long slashing swords required a lot of room to swing, which suggests a fairly open order, suited to their individualistic fighting style and national temperament.

Death or glory

Few battles in ancient times lasted more than a day, and were often decided in no more than a few hours, with one side breaking and running. This was the moment for cavalry to give chase, and the slaughter could continue until darkness, unless the attraction of looting the dead (and perhaps the enemy's camp) proved stronger. Cattle, gold, women and severed heads were especially highly prized as booty. Defeated peoples might become clients and dependants of the victors, and

Duelling continental Celtic warriors of about the third century BC. On the left is a noble in a newly-fashionable mail shirt, with the typical early Celtic cape-like double-thickness shoulder reinforcement. Most warriors of the period would have been armed only with a spear and shield, unless they were lucky enough (as was perhaps the man on the right) to win a sword or other items as battle trophies.

THE HEADHUNTERS

'*When their enemies fall they cut off their heads and fasten them about the necks of their horses; and turning over to their attendants the arms of their opponents, all covered in blood, they carry them off as booty, singing a paean over them and striking up a song of victory, and these first-fruits of battle they fasten by nails upon their houses, just as men do, in certain kinds of hunting, with the heads of wild beasts they have mastered. The heads of their most distinguished enemies they embalm in cedar-oil and carefully preserve in a chest, and these they exhibit to strangers, gravely maintaining that in exchange for this head some one of their ancestors, or their father, or the man himself, refused the offer of a great sum of money.*'
Diodorus Sirculus 5,29

The taking of heads was one of the Celtic habits which most outraged the Classical writers: they thought it appalling to desecrate the bodies of the dead in this way, on both religious and moral grounds. The gruesome habit appears to have served a number of functions, most obviously providing concrete proof of the courage of a warrior in defeating an opponent; such bloody trophies can thus be seen as important prestige possessions.

Headhunting may also have had a religious purpose: the Celts apparently believed that the head was the dwelling place of the immortal soul. By keeping control of the head of an enemy, they may have thought that the spirit was also controlled.

Fragment and reconstructed statue from Entremont (p. 45).

would give hostages against their good behaviour. (Hostages might also be exchanged between allies as a means of securing good faith.)

Storm and siege

The many defended sites across the Celtic world imply the possibility of attack, and sometimes archaeological traces such as burnt gates are found which suggest assaults on strongholds: Danebury, for instance, may have ended its days in fire and sack (p. 62). While some of the hugely elaborate defences constructed around British hillforts such as Maiden Castle or continental *oppida* like Manching are now thought to have been at least in part designed to display power, the construction of the timber-and-stone *murus gallicus* (p. 121) was particularly sophisticated, and implies much practical experience of defence construction and basic siege warfare. However, there is no sign that the Gauls or other Celts possessed the complex machines and catapults used by Graeco-Roman armies.

Death, defeat and the gods

Defeated Celtic generals often sought death in combat or committed suicide. Caesar records such cases during the Gallic War, including one which suggests that this was for religious reasons as much as the anguish of defeat: King Catuvolcus of the Eburones hanged himself from a yew-tree, which smacks of literal self-sacrifice, as does the later suicide of Sacrovir (see pp. 85, 136). Livy describes an interesting example of a Republican Roman general behaving in much the same way. At the Battle of Sentinum in 295 BC, the Consul Decius – facing impending defeat by Gauls and Samnites – dedicated himself and the souls of the enemy to the *manes* (Roman ancestral spirits): 'and having added the usual prayers that he was driving before him fear and panic, blood and carnage, and the wrath of the gods celestial and infernal, and should blight with a curse the standards, weapons and armour of the enemy, and that one and the same place should witness his own destruction and that of the Gauls and Samnites ... he spurred his charger against the Gallic lines ... and hurling himself against the weapons of the enemy met his death' (Livy 10,28). This vividly illustrates that Roman armies and generals were much closer to the Celts in their thinking and behaviour than is generally assumed.

WAR WITH THE GREEKS AND ROMANS

WHEN THEY FIRST APPEARED, Celtic armies were the terror of the ancient world. The fanaticism of their charge became legendary. If the first wild onslaught did not break the enemy, some Celts – such as the Nervii at the Battle of the Sambre in 57 BC – fought to the death (p. 73). Determined leaders such as Vercingetorix showed a quality of strategic insight and generalship which demanded even Caesar's respect, while the Celts' speed at learning gave him several frights. The Gauls quickly copied Roman siege tactics, and some used sophisticated mining techniques to disrupt Roman assaults on strongholds. In Britain, unable to beat the Romans in the field, the leader Cassivellaunus used a 'scorched earth' policy to hinder Caesar, hemming in his reconnaissance patrols with lightning attacks by guerrilla forces of chariots, while trying to force a Roman retreat by ordering an attack on the bridgehead far to Caesar's rear. This bold move was beaten off: had it succeeded, Caesar would have been in grave difficulties. Cassivellaunus was only defeated by treachery.

Exploiting Celtic weaknesses

Many Celtic generals lacked the skills of a Cassivellaunus, however, and their armies were far less tenacious than the Nervii: if not quickly victorious, they rapidly lost heart and fled. Greeks and Romans learned this lesson well. The largely unarmoured Celts proved vulnerable to javelins and arrows delivered from a safe distance. Legions used heavy javelins to break the deadly impetus of the Celtic charge, then employed their great shields to bundle the enemy together while stabbing at their unprotected abdomens and armpits with short swords. The Celts faced the choice of death or flight.

Celtic armies were fragile, virtually clouds of individuals almost as much in competition with each other for glory as in conflict with the foe. They consequently lacked cohesion: if part of the line wavered, panic could spread with great speed. In contrast, Roman legionaries were trained to fight as teams, to trust each other and remain steady under pressure. This difference gave the legions a decisive tactical advantage, while the Celtic lack of discipline and tenacity gave Rome a clear strategic edge. Celtic armies were bad at supplying themselves: Caesar dealt with one large Gallic army by the simple expedient of waiting for it to get hungry and go home. In weapons, and in courage, individual Gauls were equal to the Romans, and against Caesar they frequently had great numerical advantage. Yet this was more than offset by the Romans' *quantitative* advantage in arms: by the second century BC, legionaries were all mail-clad, helmeted and armed with swords. Only the Celtic chieftains were consistently equipped as well as this; their armies mostly remained of unarmoured spearmen.

(Above) A trumpeter with the carnyx or animal-headed war-horn. From the Gundestrup cauldron.

CONTRASTING CONCEPTIONS OF WAR

Perhaps the root of the Roman conquest of the majority of the Celtic peoples lay in the contrasting natures of the two societies, which led them to think about and wage war in very different ways. For the Celts, war – and one's role in it – was a very personal affair, in which one could display valour and win prestige and booty. (Paradoxically, the Roman nobility had much the same attitude: Caesar's conquest of Gaul was an exercise in personal glory-seeking and plunder.) But for the Romans generally, war was a very serious business, on which learned treatises were written. Method and planning were important, and it was conceived on a scale which, ultimately, overwhelmed the Celtic armies. For example, no Celtic army could have matched Caesar's legions in their ability to throw a bridge across the Rhine in ten days or to organize a fleet of 800 ships to attack Britain.

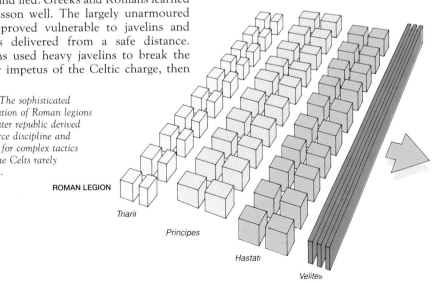

(Right) The sophisticated organization of Roman legions of the later republic derived from fierce discipline and allowed for complex tactics which the Celts rarely matched.

ROMAN LEGION

Triarii

Principes

Hastati

Velites

THE BATTLE OF TELAMON, 225 BC

A chieftain of the Insubres as he might have appeared on the field of Telamon.

ONE OF THE GREATEST of all the many battles between the Romans and the Cisalpine Gauls occurred in 225 BC at Telamon, on the coast midway between Rome and Pisa. A large force of *Gaesatae* (p. 81) crossed the Alps into Gallia Cisalpina, and the Insubres, Boii and others joined them for an attack on the Romans. They invaded Etruria with about 50,000 infantry and 20,000 horse and chariots. Threatening Rome itself, they shattered a Roman force in a stiff fight near Faesulae, but then discovered another army, under the Consul Lucius Aemilius, hot on their heels. Laden with booty the Gauls commenced a fighting retreat, withdrawing up the Etrurian coast, cautiously followed by Aemelius. Neither army was aware that the other Consul, Gaius Atilius, transferring his army from Sardinia, had landed at Pisa and was advancing south to cut off the Gauls. The scouts of the converging forces met at Telamon, and Atilius rapidly discovered from prisoners that the Gauls were now trapped between two Roman armies. Deploying his troops, he led his cavalry to seize control of a tactically important hill overlooking the road along which the enemy were approaching. The Gauls, discovering another army to their front, disputed the hill with their own horse and light infantry. A general engagement developed in a piecemeal fashion around it. Realizing that they were caught between two armies, the Gauls drew up their main battle-line, facing both ways: there was no escape. Polybius's vivid description of the ensuing struggle is a classic account of a Celtic army at war:

'Aemilius, sending on his cavalry to help those who were fighting on the hill ... advanced to attack. The Celts had drawn up facing their rear, from which they expected Aemilius to attack, the Gaesatae from the Alps and behind them the Insubres, and facing in the opposite direction, ready to meet the attack of Gaius' legions, they placed the Taurisci and the Boii. ... Their wagons and chariots they stationed at the extremity of either wing and collected their booty on one of the neighbouring hills with a protecting force round it ... The

Insubres and Boii wore their breeches and light cloaks, but the Gaesatae had discarded these garments owing to their proud confidence in themselves, and stood naked, with nothing but their arms, in front of the whole army ... At first the battle was confined to the hill, all the armies gazing on it, so great were the numbers of cavalry from each host combating their pell-mell. In this action Gaius the Consul fell in the mêlée, fighting with desperate courage, and his head was brought to the Celtic kings; but the Roman cavalry, after a stubborn struggle, at length overmastered the enemy and gained possession of the hill. The infantry were now close upon each other ... [The Romans] were on the one hand encouraged by having caught the enemy between their two armies, but on the other hand they were terrified by the fine order of the Celtic host and the dreadful din, for

THE BLOODY FIELD OF TELAMON

It is hard to be certain of the exact location of the battle or the disposition of troops in relation to the known site of Telamon itself. It is likely that the Gauls, who clashed with the cavalry of Atilius on the hill overlooking the town, probably avoided the narrow defile and deployed in the valley to the east, where they were trapped.

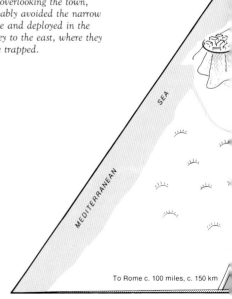

SEA

MEDITERRANEAN

To Rome c. 100 miles, c. 150 km

there were innumerable trumpeters and horn-blowers, and ... the whole army were shouting their war-cries at the same time ... Very terrifying too were the appearance and the gestures of the naked warriors in front, all in the prime of life, and finely built men, and all in the leading companies richly adorned with gold torcs and armlets. The sight of them indeed dismayed the Romans, but at the same time the prospect of winning such spoils made them twice as keen for the fight. But when the javelineers advanced ... from the ranks of the Roman legions and began to hurl their javelins in well-aimed volleys, the Celts in the rear ranks were indeed well protected by their breeches and cloaks, but ... the naked men in front ... found themselves in a very difficult and helpless predicament ... At length, unable to drive off the javelineers owing to the distance and the hail of javelins, and reduced to the utmost distress and perplexity, some of them, in their impotent rage, rushed wildly on the enemy and sacrificed their lives, while others, retreating step by step on the ranks of their comrades, threw them into disorder by their display of faint-heartedness ... but the main body of the Insubres, Boii, and Taurisci, once ... the Roman maniples attacked them, met the enemy and kept up a stubborn hand-to-hand combat. For, though being almost cut to pieces, they held their ground, equal to their foes in courage, and inferior only, as a force and individually, in their arms. The Roman shields, it should be added, were far more serviceable for defence and their swords for attack, the Gaulish sword being only good for a cut and not for a thrust. But finally, attacked from higher ground and on their flank by the Roman cavalry, which rode down the hill and charged them vigorously, the Celtic infantry were cut to pieces where they stood, their cavalry taking to flight.

'About 40,000 Celts were slain and at least 10,000 taken prisoner, among them the King Concolitanus. The other king, Aneroestes ... put an end to his life and to those of his friends ...'

Polybius 2,28–31

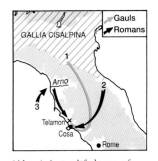

(Above) A simplified map of the campaign which ended at Telamon. 1 = Gaulish army; 2 = legions of L. Aemilius; 3 = legions of C. Atilius.

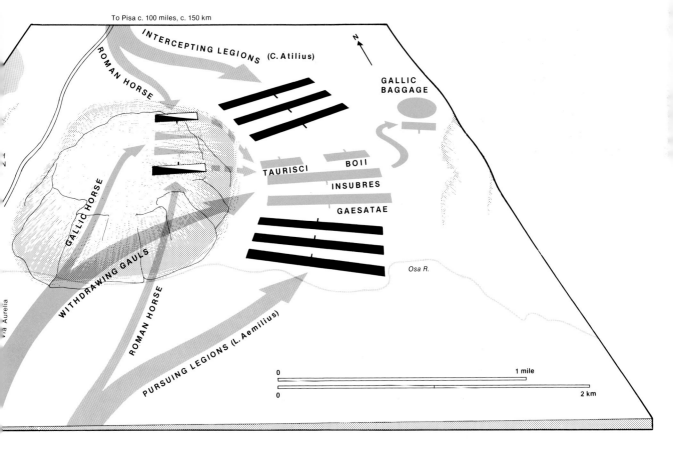

VI
GODS AND
THE AFTERLIFE

'The whole nation of the Gauls is greatly devoted to ritual observances, and for that reason those who are smitten with the more grievous maladies and who are engaged in the perils of battle either sacrifice human victims or vow to do so, employing the Druids as ministers for such sacrifices. They believe, in effect, that unless for a man's life a life be paid, the majesty of the immortal gods may not be appeased'

Caesar, *Gallic War*, 6,16

To MODERN OBSERVERS, Celtic religion seems deeply exotic and alien, its mystery compounded by blood-curdling tales of human sacrifice and the shadowy figures of the Druids. The Celts were an extremely superstitious people, beholden to their gods, the spirits, and the priests. Their lives were regimented by rituals and taboos. Even the landscape was suffused with the supernatural, and dotted with ritual enclosures or shrines.

In many ways, the realm of the sacred remains an enigma to us. Belief itself leaves no direct archaeological traces, and the Druids, for instance, eschewed the use of writing to record religious matters (according to Caesar). But the Classical writers offer fascinating, sometimes wildly exaggerated, glimpses of Celtic beliefs and burial rites, symbolism and sacrifice, as well as descriptions of the gods and the Druids. And the recent explosion in the number of shrines, cemeteries, offerings and sacrifices discovered has also greatly enriched our understanding of Celtic religious practice.

Stone 'Janus' heads from the sanctuary of the southern Gaulish Saluvii at Roquepertuse.

THE CELTIC GODS

(Below) A small stone carving from Euffigneix, Haute-Marne, probably late Iron Age. In addition to the torc and the boar figure, there are eye symbols on the sides. Perhaps the figure represents a deity capable of shifting between human and boar form. (Right) A sandstone stela with horned 'Janus' heads, from Holzgerlingen, Germany, c. 500 BC. (Opposite) A bronze statuette from Bouray, Seine-et-Oise. It retains one of its inlaid glass eyes. Seated in typical Gaulish cross-legged pose, this figure probably represents a deity, again perhaps one with animal aspects: his feet may be hooves.

THE CELTS, like their Greek and Roman counterparts, were polytheistic – they believed in a multiplicity of deities. If later Irish myths are anything to go by, their gods were as unpredictable, fallible and dangerous by turns as the Olympian gods. Dealing with the deities, and perhaps a host of other spirits and supernatural forces, was a serious but everyday business. They could be appeased by the correct propitiatory rites and sacrifices at the appropriate time and place, in rituals often conducted by priests such as the Druids. How far did Celtic religious rites parallel those of their Classical neighbours? For instance, did the Celts too worship family gods and a host of godlets covering all aspects of life (from childbirth to the drains)? We are not truly sure, but it does seem likely that religious practices took place in the home as well as at shrines. The fixing of severed heads to houses (p. 82) was probably a religious rite in part. There were also sacred aspects to hospitality, feast-giving, and the taking of oaths.

Myriad gods

Many gods are known to us by name from texts and inscriptions dating to the Roman period, or from recorded place-names (e.g. Lugdunum, 'stronghold of Lug' – modern Lyon). Others have come down to us through Irish traditions. Some were only acknowledged locally, and many such regional deities have undoubtedly vanished without trace. Others were very widely worshipped across the Celtic world. Lugh, for example (from the Irish for 'shining light'), is known from Ireland to Gaul and Spain; he may have been a sun-god, and was also associated with the raven (*lugos*). However, there was no universal pantheon which compares with that of the major Graeco-Roman gods, such as Zeus/Jupiter, Aphrodite/Venus or Ares/Mars. In fact, there may not have been any distinct, universally worshipped Celtic deities at all, perhaps because of the diverse histories and origins of the Celtic peoples.

Some widespread deities may really have been multiple cults. Teutates, for example, means 'god of the tribe', and was perhaps

a common title for many different gods rather than the name of one.

Certain deities were associated with particular locations, remote places like mountains and forest glades, and most notably springs and stretches of water, obvious sources of life. Examples from Gaul include Nemausus (at Nîmes) and Glan (at Glanum, near St-Rémy), and from Britain, Sul – the goddess of the hot spring at Bath. Water cults were not solely Celtic: they can be traced back at least to the Bronze Age. The early Germans, as well as the Classical world, shared them.

The nature of the gods and the Other World

Many deities were venerated in triads, or were three aspects of one god, sometimes depicted as three-faced. Some gods were shape-shifters, able to adopt various animal guises at will, at least in the Irish myths. For example, ravens feeding on the dead on the battlefield were thought to be manifestations of the war-goddess in Ireland: the bird on the Ciumeşti helmet from Romania may be a much earlier representation of the same idea, at the other end of the Celtic world.

The Celts apparently had no conception of heaven or hell as a reward or punishment for their conduct during life: rebirth into the afterlife was, it seems, thought to be automatic. The belief in some kind of 'Valhalla' helps to explain why Celtic warriors characteristically seemed to have no fear of death. The barriers between the world of the living and that of the gods and the dead were ill-defined, and apparently disappeared altogether at the great festival of Samhain. (This was celebrated on 1 November to mark the passing of summer and the beginning of winter; the normal laws of the world were temporarily thrown into chaos during the festival.) Irish tales tell of living heroes visiting the realm of the dead (p. 155).

In contrast to the Classical world, the Celts did not envision their deities in human shape until late in the Iron Age – or at least few idols or statues have been found prior to this period. Indeed, the Celtic leader, Brennus, is said to have mocked statues of the gods at Delphi: 'when he came only upon images of stone and wood he laughed at them, to think that men, believing that gods had human form,

should set up their images in wood and stone' (Diodorus Siculus 22,9,4). Significantly, anthropoid depictions of deities later became common in those areas close to Greek and Roman settlements and temples: Classical influences were probably at work once more. By Caesar's time images of the gods had become general in Gaul; Caesar refers to frequent wooden statues of 'Mercury'.

In war the Celts were not afraid to loot sanctuaries, making war on their enemies' gods as well as their goods. On the other hand, the Celts – like the Romans – were prepared to worship foreign gods: Gauls apparently made offerings at Massalia; and Britons conducted sacrifices on the Capitol at Rome. It is likely that other aspects of belief and rite were also partly Romanized in places – even though religion is often an area of particular conservatism and resistance to foreign ideas.

SOME EARLY CELTIC
GODS AND GODDESSES

Andastra
Victory goddess of the Iceni?

Belenus
'Bright' or 'brilliant': a Gaulish sun-god and healer

Artio
'Bear', a forest goddess

Camulos
A war god (Britain and Gaul)

Cernunnos
'The horned one', lord of animals (pictured above)

Epona
Gallic horse goddess, with fertility aspects

Esus
'Lord'

Lenus
Healer-god of the Treveri

Sequana
Goddess of the Seine

Sucellus
The 'good striker', hammer god related to the Irish deity, the Dagda

Taranis
'The thunderer': an enigmatic sky god

Teutates
'God of the tribe', perhaps the title of many different gods

Vasio
God of the Gallic Vocontii, at Vasio (Vaison-la-Romaine)

DRUIDS, PRIESTS AND SEERS

SOOTHSAYERS AND PHILOSOPHERS

'Philosophers, as we may call them, and men learned in religious affairs are unusually honoured among them and are called by them Druids. The Gauls likewise make use of diviners, accounting them worthy of high approbation, and these men foretell the future by means of the flight or cries of birds and of the slaughter of sacred animals, and they have all the multitude subservient to them ... And it is a custom of theirs that no-one should perform a sacrifice without a "philosopher"; for thank offerings should be rendered to the gods, they say, by the hands of men who are experienced in the nature of the divine, and who speak, as it were, the language of the gods, and it is also through the mediation of such men, they think, that blessings likewise should be sought.'
Diodorus Siculus 5,31

(Right) A detail of the fragmentary bronze calendar from Coligny, France. Probably dating to the earliest Roman period in Gaul, the letters are Latin but the language is Celtic. Reckoning by nights rather than days, it lists well-omened and ill-omened days for important activities. Such calculations were probably the preserve of the priesthoods.

'[The Druids] are concerned with divine worship, the due performance of sacrifices, public and private, and the interpretation of ritual questions: a great number of young men gather about them for the sake of instruction and hold them in great honour. In fact it is they who decide in almost all disputes, public and private; and if any crime has been committed, or murder done, or if there is any dispute about succession or boundaries, they also decide it, determining rewards and penalties ...'
Caesar, *Gallic War*, 6,13

THE DRUIDS were greatly esteemed in Celtic society – as intellectuals, judges, diviners, astronomers and mediators with the gods. They were not in fact the only priestly orders: other, less prominent holy men and seers existed, such as the Vates whom Strabo describes as 'diviners and natural philosophers'. The Celts also appointed priestesses (although not apparently Druidesses), at least in Gaul, Galatia and Britain. Priestesses reportedly stood alongside the Druids to call down the wrath of the gods when the Romans stormed Mona (Anglesey).

The Druids are shrouded by a veil of mystery. They passed their wisdom from one generation to the next in the form not of written texts but of memorized verse, so their secrets have ultimately died with

them. They left no clearly identifiable archaeological traces. Immortalized in the (frequently overimaginative) Classical sources and later Irish folklore, their true ways have been further obscured by the romantic myths and misconceptions that have accrued in recent centuries.

The Druidical orders

According to Caesar, the Druids were a highly organized intertribal brotherhood, which met annually in the territory of the Carnutes in Gaul to confer and elect a Chief Druid. They reportedly assembled in a sacred place – perhaps a forest clearing. The word 'Druid' is connected with the Celtic term for oak, and trees and sacred groves undoubtedly loomed large in Celtic religious life (the gathering place of the Galatians was known as *Drunemeton* or 'oak sanctuary').

Contrary to popular belief, the Druids were not unworldly ascetics: disputed elections were sometimes known to end in fighting! There is no reason to think that, except at sacrifice, Druids differed in appearance from other prominent Gauls or Britons. Like most Roman priests, they were probably integrated closely into society and daily life. We are not sure whether each tribe had its own specific group of Druids, although later Irish tales record that kings were served by a personal Druid.

The role of Druidism

The Druids, other priests and perhaps the bards would have been responsible for sustaining the sense of identity and continuity of each community. They were the guardians of the tribe's traditions, and administered tribal law. Furthermore, like Roman priests, they probably maintained the calendar – fixing festivals and naming lucky days for conducting business or sacrifice, and unlucky days when nothing important should be transacted.

As privileged members of a learned class, the Druids were exempt from military service and taxation. They were nevertheless closely involved in politics and diplomacy, in the declaration of war and the negotiation – even enforcement – of peace.

Strabo describes them as 'the most just of men', and they were frequently called upon to mediate in disagreements or mete out justice to criminals. The Druids wielded considerable power over the community, including the authority to 'excommunicate' or ban offenders from attending sacrifices and other public ceremonies, thus withdrawing their religious or legal status.

The aspect of a Druid's responsibilities to attract most attention in the texts was his role in conducting sacrifices. The Celts practised both animal and human sacrifices (pp. 92–95), and the Classical writers describe the latter in particular with a lurid mixture of fascination and horror, although the Romans themselves were no strangers to torture and slaughter.

Other duties included teaching and preparing novices for initiation into the Druidical orders, divining, astronomical studies, healing, as well as interceding with the gods on behalf of the community. Some Classical writers reported that the Druids preached a belief in the immortality of the soul, which passed to another body after death.

The origins and extent of Druidism

The Classical texts refer to Druids in Britain and Gaul, but not in Italy, Spain, the Danube or Galatia. According to Caesar, novices were often sent from Gaul to Britain where they reputedly received the best training; indeed, Druidism may have evolved in Britain and subsequently spread from there. Its distribution may suggest that it was introduced to continental Europe after the migrations over the Alps in the early fourth century BC.

Becoming a Druid

Caesar was evidently struck by the exacting nature of Druidical training. Novices were apparently expected to memorize a great number of verses, laws, histories, magic formulae and other traditions. It could sometimes take as long as twenty years for a Druid to complete his studies, so training often began early, in boyhood. Not all Druids, consequently, were old men with long white beards: some would have been in their thirties. Most were probably recruited from the aristocracy. Their high birth, combined with the secrecy surrounding the priestly orders, would have lent them great authority.

William Stukeley's fanciful 1740 conception of a Druid, complete with Bronze Age axehead on his belt. Except for Pliny's famous (but suspect) description of a mistletoe-collecting ceremony (p. 95), we do not know how Druids really dressed.

HOLY PLACES AND SACRIFICE

'After a victory they sacrifice such living things as they may have taken, and all the other effects they gather in one place. In many states heaps of such objects are to be seen piled up in hallowed spots, and it has not often happened that a man, in defiance of religious scruple, has dared to conceal such spoils in his house or to remove them from their place, and the most grievous punishment, with torture, is ordained for such an offence.'

Caesar, *Gallic War*, 6,17

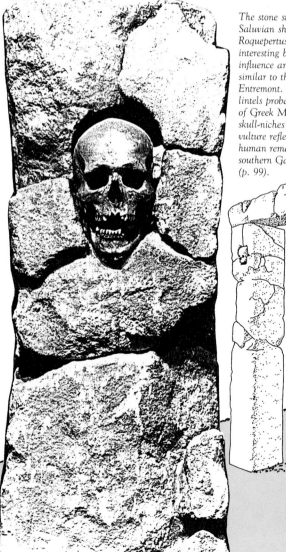

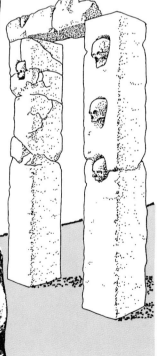

The stone structures at the Saluvian shrine of Roquepertuse display an interesting blend of Greek influence and native symbolism similar to that at their capital, Entremont. The uprights and lintels probably echo the shrines of Greek Massalia, while the skull-niches and a carved vulture reflect the treatment of human remains among southern Gauls and in Iberia (p. 99).

IN CELTIC LANDS, as in Greece and Rome, religion permeated all aspects of life to a degree which modern Westerners would find strange: yet the distinction between secular and religious is a quite recent Western conceit. The Celts probably worshipped in the home and other domestic settings as well as in specific holy places: at Danebury hillfort (pp. 61–62), for example, thank-offerings seem to have been made to earth-deities whenever a storage pit went out of use and was filled in.

Shrines were often situated close to powers of nature, remote from habitation, on hilltops or in grottoes. Classical writers mention sacred groves, holy lakes, pools and springs, as well as formal religious enclosures or temples. The Celtic word for shrine or sanctuary was *nemeton*, which appears to be related to the Greek *temenos*, an area defined as a sanctuary.

Sacred groves

The romantic image of white-clad Druids performing their rituals deep within a forest glade is not entirely unfounded, for trees were of great importance in Celtic worship. As we have seen, the word Druid is related to 'oak', and Pliny describes the collection of mistletoe from oak trees. The wooden statues or votive offerings (dating from the late Iron Age and early Roman times) found at Gallic river sources are usually of oak.

Classical writers made much of ritual and gruesome Celtic sacrifice in dark forest groves, perhaps because worship in such fearsome places was so alien to the outwardly ordered, urban life of the Mediterranean.

Permanent sanctuaries

Greeks and Romans would have felt little more at ease in the temples and holy enclosures built by the Celts. Scholars have long been aware of certain impressive religious sites in southern France, but recent excavations in northern France and elsewhere have started to add rich detail to our picture of Celtic temples.

Roquepertuse, 10 miles (15 km) west of Aix-en-Provence, is thought to be a sanctuary of the Saluvii, the people of probably

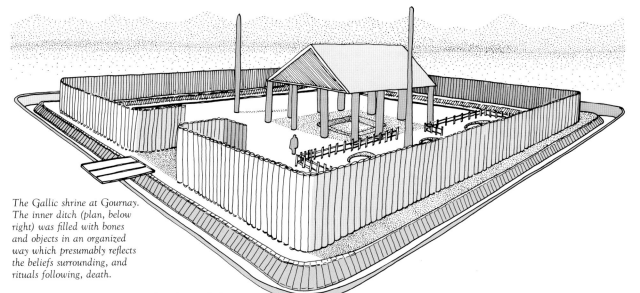

The Gallic shrine at Gournay. The inner ditch (plan, below right) was filled with bones and objects in an organized way which presumably reflects the beliefs surrounding, and rituals following, death.

mixed Celto-Ligurian stock whose defeat led to the establishment of Roman power in southern Gaul (p. 46). The painted limestone sculptures – including a vulture, perhaps the local equivalent of a raven deity, which sat on top of a construction of stone pillars and lintels – owe much to the influence of the Greeks of nearby Massalia (Marseilles). But many of the other details are emphatically un-Greek, not least the niches for human skulls cut into the stone pillars. Architectural evidence for the cult of the severed head also comes from the Saluvian capital at Entremont, which yielded dramatic sculptures of stacked heads and the skulls of fifteen adult males (p. 82).

Semi-Classical shrines like Roquepertuse and Glanum (St-Rémy-de-Provence, which has produced similar sculpture) were confined to Mediterranean Gaul. The North developed its own traditions, initially little influenced by Classical practices. The shrine at Gournay (Oise) lay near the border of three Belgic tribes, the Bellovaci, Ambiani and Viromandui. Its location may have had political importance as much as religious. Perhaps it was asserting the rights of a community to certain disputed border lands. Alternatively it may have been a politically neutral place where the gods could oversee intertribal relations. Gournay had a long history, thriving from the third century BC to the first, a period in

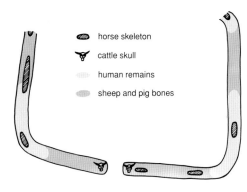

horse skeleton
cattle skull
human remains
sheep and pig bones

which it underwent various remodellings. It consisted of a ditched enclosure, roughly 130 ft (40 m) on a side, with its entrance to the east. Within the enclosure a group of ritual pits was eventually covered by a wooden building. Cattle, pigs and sheep were sacrificed here: thousands of animal bones have been recovered. The excavators also found many human bones, and some 2,000 iron weapons which had been 'ritually killed' by hacking, bending and breaking – a widespread procedure in the Celtic world. The objects and the bones were laid in the ditches in a careful system of zones, reflecting the unknown ceremonies that were performed there.

OFFERINGS TO THE GODS
'And a peculiar and striking practice is found among the upper Celts, in connection with the sacred precincts of the gods; for in the temples and precincts made consecrate in their land, a great amount of gold has been deposited as a dedication to the gods, and not a native of the country ever touches it because of religious scruple, although the Celts are an exceedingly covetous people.'
Diodorus Siculus 5,27,4

'DIONYSIAC' RITES
'there is a small island ... off the mouth of the Loire ... inhabited by the women of the Samnitae, and they are possessed by Dionysus ... it is a custom of theirs once a year to unroof the temple and roof it again on the same day before sunset, each woman bringing her load to add to the roof; but the woman whose load falls out of her arms is rent to pieces by the rest, and they carry the pieces around the temple with the cry "Ev-ah", and do not cease until their frenzy ceases ...'
Strabo 4,4,6

RITUAL SHAFTS

One of the strangest aspects of Celtic religious practice was the digging of shafts deep into the ground, often at Viereckschanzen. Archaeologists have suggested that it represented a Celtic expression of a Mediterranean belief that shafts were a means of communicating with the underworld. There is no reason to suppose, however, that the tradition was imported from the Classical world, for shafts dating to the Bronze Age (well before the Roman expansion northwards) have been found across Europe, and especially in Britain.

Many of the deep pits were filled with votive offerings. At

Holzhausen in Bavaria, for instance, one of several shafts contained a timber post in the bottom, surrounded by chemical traces of flesh and blood. Other examples from France – which continued in use into Roman times – contain animal and human bones, wooden figures, and sometimes logs or tree-trunks, perhaps sexual symbols. A scene on the Gundestrup cauldron may show a man being thrust head-first into a sacred shaft, rather than a ritual drowning or immersion as once suggested. The rites performed at the shafts perhaps parallel the offerings made in domestic storage pits.

THE DIVERSE METHODS OF HUMAN SACRIFICE

'They used to strike a human being, whom they had devoted to death, in the back with a sword, and then divine from his death-struggle. But they would not sacrifice without the Druids. We are told of still other kinds of human sacrifices; for example, they would shoot victims to death with arrows, or impale them in the temples, or, having devised a colossus of straw and wood, throw into the colossus cattle and wild animals of all sorts and human beings, and then make a burnt-offering of the whole thing.'
Strabo 4,4,5

'[They] use figures of immense size, whose limbs, woven out of twigs, they fill with living men and set on fire ... They believe that the execution of those who have been caught in the act of theft or robbery or some crime is more pleasing to the immortal gods; but when the supply of such fails they resort to the execution even of the innocent.'
Caesar, *Gallic War*, 6,16

A similar sanctuary has been excavated at Ribemont-sur-Ancre (Somme), yielding weapons, the remains of animal sacrifices, and the bodies of at least 1,000 men and women aged from 15 to 40. These bear gruesome evidence of decapitation and dismemberment, their defleshed bones carefully stacked on top of each other.

How widespread such sanctuaries may have been is unclear, but a pre-Roman shrine with some weapon offerings underlies the Roman temple on Hayling Island in England (p. 145), and a site similar to Gournay is said to have been found at the Monte Bibele settlement in Italy.

Holy waters

Worship and sacrifice at pools, springs and rivers had a long tradition, stretching back into the Bronze Age. This was no uniquely Celtic phenomenon: the peoples of the Classical world practised many cults connected with springs and lakes, and the Germans sacrificed goods and people in bogs and pools until the early centuries AD.

The importance and scale of Celtic water-sacrifice is exemplified at Tolosa (Toulouse), where in 107 BC the Roman general Caepio is said to have looted as much as 50 tons of gold and a similar amount of silver from the temple and the sacred lakes, figures which defy belief – although Caesar was later able to clear his vast debts and finance his career with the loot from Gaul and her shrines. Another famous example

of Celtic water offerings comes from Llyn Cerrig Bach on Anglesey, where a great quantity of metalwork and other objects was recovered during the Second World War from what had once been a pool. La Tène itself is now generally thought to have been such a place of offering (below).

The substantial amount of very fine metalwork recovered from riverbeds, especially in Britain, may have been deposited during funerary rites as well as propitiatory sacrifices to the gods. The ancient Britons, for instance, may have defleshed the bodies of the deceased, placing at least the skulls in rivers with offerings of weapons.

Viereckschanzen

The German term *Viereckschanze* ('quadrangular earthwork') is used to refer to mysterious rectangular banked enclosures of obscure function. Sites identified as *Viereckschanzen* have been found from Britain to Bohemia. There is rarely much trace of activity within them, ritual or otherwise – but many rites need leave no trace. Were they meeting places for ceremonies and festivals, perhaps accompanied by feasting, games and competitions – as in Greece, Rome and later in Ireland? The religious connection of some is affirmed by the presence of so-called ritual shafts (see box).

(Right) Detail from the first-century BC Rynkeby bronze cauldron, found in a bog in Denmark. Although it is from outside the Celtic world, like the Gundestrup cauldron it bears Celtic motifs, such as the torc-wearing figure and the cattle heads. (Cauldrons with heads, especially of animals, ultimately betray Classical influence, but such representations had long become a part of Celtic artistic and religious expression.)

Rites and sacrifices

What did people want of their gods, other than to appease them? Later evidence from Roman times reflects the expected range of human concerns, including private and public appeals for good harvest, fortune, relief from disease, and the redress of wrongs suffered (p. 144).

How did the Celts try to procure these favours? They seem to have conducted a wide variety of ceremonies, including the deposition of votive offerings, as well as sacrifice. From late Bronze Age times cauldrons were used both as sacred vessels and prestige items (as they were in Greece). Strabo describes how prisoners of war were sacrificed by having their throats cut over a cauldron, and cauldrons have also been found as water offerings, both inside and outside the Celtic world. The most famous example is the extraordinary silver Gundestrup cauldron, and the less well-known bronze vessel from Rynkeby is also spectacular; both are from Denmark, and, if not actually Celtic, are heavily influenced by La Tène art and life.

Some objects with no obvious function (e.g. tiny model shields found mostly in Britain) may be votive offerings. Others, such as deliberately destroyed weapons, could be elements of funerary ritual rather than direct offerings to the gods. In fact, the Celts may have made no clear distinction between burial rites and sacrifice. For instance, were the human remains at Ribemont and Gournay simply the result of funerary practices or do they indicate ritual slaughter? It seems likely that many of the dead here were indeed ceremonial victims, prisoners of war, criminals, and perhaps even volunteers to be messengers to the gods (p. 97). Whatever the truth, these shrines must have been terrifying places, full of the stench of decaying flesh, and haunted by ravens and carrion crows.

The Celts dedicated both animals and humans to the gods. Pliny records the offering of two white bulls. But it was human sacrifice that held a particularly horrid fascination for the Greeks and Romans – and still does for us today. To the Classical world, it was one of the main reasons for thinking Gauls and Britons barbarous. When Caesar recorded Gallic human sacrifices, however, he neglected to mention that as recently as 114 BC Rome had sacrificed two Greeks and two Gauls to appease the gods – or that he himself paid for gladiatorial shows to spill human blood simply for the amusement of the crowds. And surely the ritual execution of his great Gallic foe Vercingetorix (pp. 126–27) after Caesar's triumph at Rome, was a human sacrifice?

A romantic nineteenth-century interpretation of Pliny's famous account of Druids gathering mistletoe.

PRIESTLY DUTIES: MISTLETOE AND MAGIC
'Having made preparation for sacrifice and a banquet beneath the trees, they bring thither two white bulls ... Clad in a white robe, the priest ascends the tree and cuts the mistletoe with a golden sickle, and it is received by others in a white cloak. They they kill the victims, praying that the god will render this gift of his propitious to those to whom he has granted it. They believe that the mistletoe, taken in drink, imparts fertility to barren animals, and that it is an antidote for all poisons ...'
Pliny, Natural History, 16, 95

LINDOW MAN: DEAD MEN DO TELL TALES

PUBLIC INTEREST in Celtic religion and sacrifice was reawakened recently with the discovery of the waterlogged, 'mummified' body of an ancient Briton, the apparent victim of a ritual killing, perhaps a Druidical sacrifice.

Discovery and investigation

In 1984 a remarkably well-preserved body was found during peat-cutting at Lindow Moss, 10 miles (15 km) south of Manchester. The body seemed to be in such good condition that police initially feared it might have been a modern murder victim. So, carefully lifting it in the enveloping block of peat, the excavators transferred the corpse to a hospital mortuary where experts could determine its age by radiocarbon dating techniques. The body proved to be ancient, nearly 2,000 years old, and was sent for scientific study to the British Museum. Lindow Man was a sensational discovery because his natural 'coffin' of waterlogged, partly rotted, oxygen-free vegetation had preserved the soft tissues astonishingly well, including not only skin but hair and even fingernails.

Bog bodies have been discovered in Ireland, Denmark and Germany, but this is the first to be found in Britain in modern times. Lindow Man lived around the end of the Iron Age, probably the first century AD, so for the first time we can actually look at the face of a Celtic ancient Briton. Yet the headlines were really made by the fact that he had met a violent and gruesome death.

What sort of person was he?

Scientists subjected Lindow Man to a painstaking series of investigations over a period of months. Removal of the peat in the laboratory revealed the remains of a bearded adult male, naked except for a fox-fur band around the left arm and a cord around the throat. Below the navel the body was damaged by the peat-cutting machine, but the severed portion has been largely recovered.

A small army of specialists commenced work on often minute traces of evidence. Analysis of the skeleton and teeth proved that this was the body of a healthy, well-fed young man, probably in his mid-twenties when he died. There were no signs of earlier injuries or disease, other than evidence from the stomach of intestinal worms. Electron microscopy of his fingernails has shown that he had a fine manicure. He clearly was not a labourer or agricultural slave, as his good health also suggests.

Death by violence

It is clear that this young man met a horrifically brutal end. He was struck twice or three times on the head by a narrow-bladed axe. He lost consciousness, but did not instantly die (although death would have followed within hours), because the wound swelled, indicating that his heart was still beating. Next a cord was tied about his neck (where it remains today), and then

Lindow Man under examination.

a stick inserted at the back and twisted to tighten what was in effect a garrotte. The strangulation was done with such violence that it broke his neck. This was the moment of clinical death, but Lindow Man's killer or killers had still not finished. His throat was now cut, and soon afterwards the body was pitched into a pool in the bog.

Why was he slain?

Quite clearly this was no casual killing, but an elaborate execution. Yet although we know how Lindow Man died, we cannot know for certain why: motives, being in the minds of the killers, leave no direct physical trace. The best guess is that he was the victim of a human sacrifice, a conclusion supported by the complexity of his death, and the deposition of the body in water. After the initial blow to the head he would have felt nothing: unlike other attested sacrifices this was not designed to inflict maximum suffering. Was he even a willing victim, a volunteer to serve as offering or messenger to the gods in some crisis, with a firm belief that his place in the afterlife was assured?

Perhaps the most tantalizing clue of all was the discovery in his stomach of a few grains of pollen from the mistletoe plant. No fragments of the plant itself were present: quite possibly a sprig of mistletoe had been dipped in his drink or brushed on to his food in a ceremony surrounding his last meal. Some have seen the death of Lindow Man as a Druidical sacrifice, for the Druids are often linked with mistletoe. Such an inference may indeed be correct, but we are unlikely ever to know for certain, any more than we can discover his name or the real reason behind his gruesome fate.

The peat of Lindow Moss may have more secrets to yield: further human remains, currently being studied, have subsequently come from the site. Lindow Man was probably not the only person to die in the midst of the marshes.

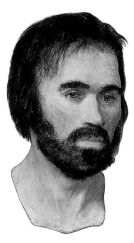

(Above) A reconstruction of Lindow Man's probable appearance. (Below) The body as it appeared during excavation from the enveloping peat, in which he actually lay face down.

THE TESTIMONY OF THE GRAVE

'Their funerals, considering the civilization of Gaul, are magnificent and expensive. They cast into the fire everything, even living creatures, which they believe to have been dear to the departed during life, and but a short time before the present age, only a generation since, slaves and dependants known to have been beloved by their lords used to be burnt with them at the conclusion of the funeral formalities.'
Caesar, *Gallic War,* 6,19

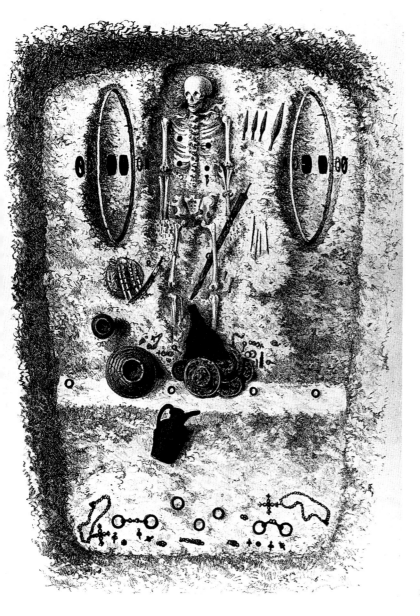

A fifth-century BC vehicle grave from Châlons-sur-Marne, France.

CEMETERIES WERE AN INITIAL KEY to the archaeology of the Celts and many of the greatest surviving La Tène treasures come from graves. The ancient Celts were frequently buried with personal effects, clothes, jewellery and sometimes other offerings, including foodstuffs. While these probably reflect a belief in the immortality of the soul and the progression to an afterlife, they also tell us about the status of the deceased and his or her family or community. A particularly lavish burial could advertise wealth and distinction on a grand scale. The burials provide us in addition with vital information about the lives of the people and trading and cultural contacts, as the Yorkshire cemeteries (pp. 100–2) and later southern British cremations (p. 103) illustrate.

The graves are the only surviving remnants of what must often have been elaborate funeral ceremonies, involving clan gatherings, feasting, processions and rites at the burial ground and elsewhere. Sometimes there was a preliminary cremation, followed by interment at another spot. In Yorkshire there are tantalizing hints of funeral banquets and evidence for the ritual hurling of spears into some graves (p. 102). Caesar records the Gallic practice of casting letters to the dead on to the pyre, as well as the immolation of favourite animals in lavish funeral ceremonies.

Burials, like so many aspects of Celtic life, show geographical diversity and change over time. The fashion for interment under square barrows or mounds was geographically widespread (although not very common) in the fifth century BC, from the Marne to Austria. Such barrows were constructed until the first century BC in the Champagne region, but elsewhere the pattern was different.

From around 400 BC, burial in 'flat cemeteries' became the most common funerary practice in central and western Europe. The intact body was laid stretched out in the grave, which was not marked by a barrow. Cremation was less usual, particularly in earlier times. Cemeteries were normally small and probably represented the burial grounds of farming communities in the

DEFLESHING THE DEAD

With the exception of east Yorkshire (pp. 100–2), there are very few formal burials anywhere in Britain before the late Iron Age. Perhaps the ancient Britons practised excarnation (defleshing), and subsequently used or disposed of the bones in some unknown way. Yet human bones have been discovered, at first sight carelessly abandoned, on settlement sites such as Danebury (photo, right). Human skulls – and sometimes whole skeletons – turn up in pits and ditches. Does this indicate human sacrifice? Quite possibly so, although it could equally represent a rite of passage for the dead, in which the bones, once defleshed, were returned to the place of living for a period of time, perhaps as part of an ancestor cult, before disposal. It has been suggested that the Celts may have deposited so many weapons in rivers not as offerings to the gods, but as part of prolonged funerary rites for the male aristocracy, involving the deposition of weapons and perhaps parts of the skeleton (specifically the skull) in the water.

THE IMMORTAL SOUL

'However, not only the Druids, but others as well, say that men's souls, and also the universe, are indestructible, although both fire and water will at some time or other prevail over them.'
Strabo 4,4,4

FINAL RITES

'The Vaccaei [of Spain] ... insult the corpses of such as die from disease as having died a cowardly and effeminate death, and dispose of them by burning; whereas those who laid down their lives in war they regard as noble, heroic, and full of valour, and them they cast to the Vultures, believing this bird to be sacred.'
Aelian, *De ora natura animali*, 10,22

(Below) A helmet from a fifth-century vehicle burial at La Gorge Meillet, Marne, France.

surrounding district. There was a gradual increase in preference for cremation but, puzzlingly, formal burials of any kind seem to have almost ceased by about 150 BC in central Europe and 100 BC in western Europe. What happened to the dead in subsequent centuries?

The mystery of the vanishing dead

Many areas – including wide tracts of the continent and most of the British Isles – have yielded almost no formal Iron Age burials at all. One explanation could be that the particular kinds of soil in some areas make it difficult for modern archaeologists to locate the evidence; some soils cause metal and bone to decay entirely. Or perhaps some regions were simply not settled very extensively during the Iron Age. But the most likely explanation for the absence of burials is the probable prevalence among the Celts of archaeologically undetectable rites such as exposure of the corpse (see box) or the scattering of cremated ashes.

Even in areas with rich cemetery remains, there are some intriguing anomalies in the evidence. Infants and children are absent or underrepresented, despite the fact that infant mortality would undoubtedly have been high, as it still is in societies without basic medical care. Perhaps some sections or classes of the community were excluded from formal burial altogether. Aelian records that among the (possibly Celtic) Vaccaei of Spain, those who died from disease were disposed of by burning while the glorious dead of war were fed to the vultures.

Notwithstanding such uncertainties, where cemeteries exist they do provide a wealth of information about the early Celtic populations.

THE CEMETERIES OF EAST YORKSHIRE

(Above) The location of the 'Arras culture' cemeteries (denoted by tint).

(Below right) Grave of an adult male from Kirkburn, interred with a joint of meat and a sword. (Below left) Detail of the reconstructed sword (see p. 112).

EAST YORKSHIRE in northeast England stands in stark contrast with the rest of the British Isles in that it has yielded literally thousands of Iron Age burials. Clustered together in cemeteries, these date mainly from the third to first centuries BC. Most of the graves are surrounded by a characteristic square ditch, the spoil from which was originally heaped up into a barrow or tumulus over the burial. Although a few still survive, most mounds have been ploughed flat, but the rich, moist soil filling the ditches favours plant-growth, making their positions visible from the air at certain times of year.

Many graves were explored in the nineteenth century, and some were found to contain vehicles, perhaps chariots. The finds were labelled the 'Arras culture', after the Yorkshire site of that name which produced three vehicle burials. New excavations took place from the 1960s to the late 1980s, especially in the parishes of Garton, Wetwang, Rudston and Burton Fleming. These have revealed some 700 graves, including five more vehicle burials, providing important information about the Iron Age population, its structure and ritual life.

The people of Iron Age Yorkshire

Archaeologists unearthed a substantial number of skeletons during the more recent excavations. A total of 95 bodies were identifiable as female and 107 as male (although the cemeteries were not completely excavated, and many bodies could not be 'sexed' due to poor preservation and other factors); men and women were not buried in segregated zones. Interestingly, there were hardly any child burials, even though there must have been many still-births and neo-natal or childhood deaths. Children, it seems, did not qualify for such formal burial.

We can tell a great deal about an individual from his or her skeletal remains. For instance, the bone lengths give us an idea of height, while we can estimate the age at death from the way in which the skeleton and teeth have developed and worn in life.

Analysis of the east Yorkshire material suggested that the mean height for adult males was 5 ft $7\frac{1}{2}$ in (1.71 m), and for females 5 ft 2 in (1.58 m). These heights are rather lower than the modern British figures, but we do not know whether this was a genetic difference; environmental factors such as poor diet and the physical stresses of living during the Iron Age were surely partly responsible.

The data on life expectance and pathology suggests that life was hard. Most males— provided they survived childhood – died in their twenties, thirties or early forties. Women were more likely to die in their late teens or twenties, largely due to the hazards of childbirth. The bones also preserve evidence of injury and disease. One man, probably a victim of polio, had an atrophied right leg. Osteo-arthritis of the spine was common, especially among women. The Yorkshire people generally had quite good teeth, although women were rather worse off than men, probably due to calcium deficiency caused by motherhood.

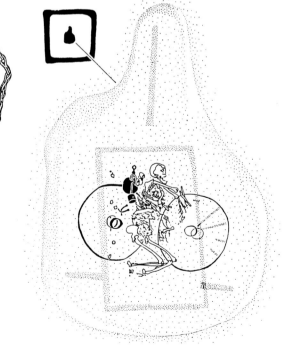

(Above) A reconstruction by Peter Connolly of the funeral rites culminating in a ?second-century BC burial at Wetwang Slack. The soil conditions in the Yorkshire cemeteries reduce organic materials like the wood of vehicles to no more than a dark stain, but such traces were carefully recorded and implied constructions like that shown here.

(Right) Grave of a woman interred with a dismantled vehicle at Wetwang Slack. The grave pit was probably once covered by a mound built from the spoil of the surrounding square ditch. Other objects buried with her included an iron mirror and the mysterious bronze 'bean can', of unknown purpose (above).

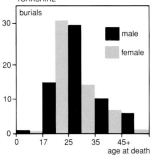

LIFE EXPECTANCY IN IRON AGE YORKSHIRE

Statistical analysis of the Yorkshire burials reveals that life expectancy was very low in comparison with today. New work on more recent skeletons has suggested that the age estimates may be inaccurate for maturity and middle-age: perhaps those labelled 17–25 were actually 17–30, and those labelled 26–35 were more likely 30–40, etc.

The predominant offerings in burials orientated north-south at Burton Fleming and Rudston were pots and brooches, but the graves at Rudston with different, east-west orientation betrayed different choices of offerings. (NB Individual graves often contained more than one category of object.)

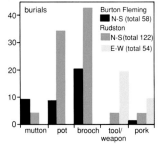

BURIAL RITES IN THE BURTON FLEMING AND RUDSTON CEMETERIES

The cause of death could also leave traces on the bones. Some skeletons, for instance, bore evidence of tumours, and two women apparently died in childbirth. Three males may have been killed by spear-thrusts: were they battle casualties, executions or sacrifices?

Burial rites

Beyond the common feature of burial under square-ditched mounds, careful study of the individual graves has revealed three groups with interesting variations in burial rite.

In the first group, the bodies were generally laid in the grave-pit curled up on their left side, head to the north, and facing east. About one in three possessed a brooch (presumably fixing a now-vanished garment), perhaps another offering such as a pot, and often had the bone from a joint of lamb or mutton. This was most commonly an upper left foreleg, suggesting a standardized funerary ritual, perhaps involving a banquet in which this particular joint was earmarked to accompany the deceased.

In the second type of grave the body was aligned east–west, and was generally unflexed. The offerings also differed: brooches were rare, but many contained iron tools, spears or swords. Instead of sheep-bones, there might be the halved skull and forelimb of a pig.

A third group was rather more diverse. Special offerings had been placed in these graves, such as vehicles presumed to be chariots, and very fine metalwork – including one of the earliest dated coats of iron mail. One of the vehicle burials contained a woman, with an iron mirror and a mysterious 'bean-can' (pictured on the previous page). There was also evidence of peculiar rites: spears had been hurled into a number of graves during the burial, often piercing the body (pathologists could distinguish these spear-thrusts from the ones that had apparently killed three men *before* burial – see above).

What is the significance of these groups? They may partly reflect changing burial fashions: the first group seems to date mostly to the second century BC, while the second is thought to belong largely to the following century. Ascribing an accurate date to these graves is difficult, however, in the virtual absence of datable imports.

There may be other distinctions. The third group, including the vehicle burials, may be spread throughout the period from the third to the first centuries BC. The groups tend to appear in different cemeteries (although there is overlap) and may represent varying traditions of discrete communities. Alternatively they could indicate differences in religious belief, or distinctions of rank (the chariots, with their other rich offerings, suggest that status was a factor in determining the type of burial). Indeed it is possible that all of these graves represent only certain segments of the community: perhaps even in east Yorkshire many people disposed of their dead in ways which leave no archaeological trace, like the majority of the contemporary British.

Continental connections?

These intriguing graves beg many questions, not least because, while within Britain they are peculiar to east Yorkshire, they echo early La Tène burial rites in eastern Gaul, where vehicle burials and square barrows have also been discovered. Links with the continent are apparently further implied by the fact that the people occupying east Yorkshire by the end of the Iron Age shared the name of Parisii with the Gallic tribe that eventually gave its name to the capital of France.

These observations have fuelled much speculation about the possibility of early migrations from Gaul to northeast England. But there are too many differences between the burial rites in the two areas to support such a view. The continental vehicles were buried complete, for example, and the body was laid out full length in the grave, whereas in Britain, the vehicles were dismantled and the bodies flexed. And if some of the Yorkshire burials were those of continental immigrants, why is there virtually no continental metalwork in the graves? Furthermore, in the territory of the Gallic Parisii there are no square barrows, and only two possible chariot burials have been identified.

There is evidently no direct continuity from Gaul to Yorkshire in these rites. Perhaps the identity of tribal names was a coincidence, and the Yorkshire fashion for vehicle burial was inspired by a bardic tale of events far away and long ago. The real nature of any link with the continent remains a mystery.

CELTIC CREMATION RITES

A NEW BURIAL RITE was introduced into Britain in the last decades BC, when Gaul was already under Roman dominion. The new rite consisted of cremation, followed by burial of the ashes. This was sometimes accompanied by substantial offerings, including iron fire-dogs, other fine metalwork such as bronze-decorated wooden buckets, imported pottery from Belgic Gaul, and even Roman wine amphorae and Italian bronze vessels.

Cremation graves have been found in Kent (Aylesford) and in the Thames Valley, especially in the heartland of the powerful Catuvellauni (pp. 128–29). The best-known example is the very rich burial from Welwyn Garden City, which included Roman amphorae and a silver wine-cup. Large cremation cemeteries are also known, as at King Harry Lane on the edge of the Catuvellaunian *oppidum* at Verulamium (St Albans).

The historical context of these graves is especially interesting. Cremation was becoming the standard funerary rite among the Gauls, and indeed across the Roman world, and graves very similar to the British examples are found in Gallia Belgica. Does the appearance of similar graves in Britain imply immigration or invasion? Certainly close political connections are historically attested earlier (p. 118). It is clear that

cultural exchange was taking place across the English Channel, resulting either from trade or maybe through kinship links between aristocrats. Perhaps refugees from Roman rule introduced the new rite.

It is not only the use of cremation, but other details of the graves which emphasize the Belgic connection. For example, several graves found at Goeblingen-Nospelt in Luxembourg are contemporary with the British examples, belonging to the latter part of the first century BC. They probably belong to prominent members of the Treveri, one of the most powerful tribes of eastern Gaul who prospered under the new Roman rule, and who were adopting many Roman ways (p. 140). The graves include Italian amphorae and bronze vessels, and one contained two buckets very similar to those from Aylesford, Baldock and elsewhere.

Besides being an interesting development in social and religious life in late La Tène Britain, the new cremations reflect the continued integration of the island into the wider Celtic world, while the Mediterranean imports suggest that a process of Romanization of habits was already underway.

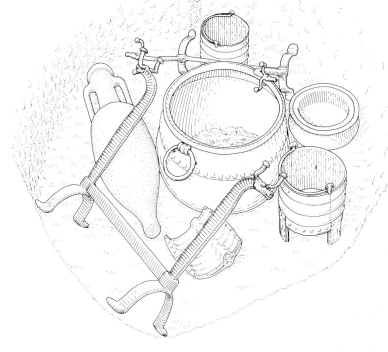

(Below right) Reconstruction of a mid-first century BC cremation burial from Baldock, Hertfordshire. The ashes of an adult male were placed in a bronze cauldron, surrounded by offerings that included bronze bowls, bronze-bound wooden buckets, an Italian wine amphora, a joint of pork and a pair of iron 'fire-dogs'. Such hearth-furniture is quite well known from the later Iron Age. (Below left) Detail of a stylized cow-head terminal from a fire-dog found at Welwyn.

LA TÈNE ART AND TECHNOLOGY

'... their lives were very simple, and they had no knowledge whatsoever of any art or science.'

Polybius 2,17,8, on the Gauls of northern Italy

IN CONTRADICTION to the words of Polybius, it is in the surviving treasures of artistry and artisanship that the brilliance of early Celtic societies can be most directly appreciated today. These objects, mostly metal, are frequently embellished in what modern scholars have labelled the La Tène style, often loosely called 'Celtic art'. La Tène-style art has rightly been described as one of the greatest glories of prehistoric Europe. This largely abstract style of curving lines represents an aesthetic sense fundamentally different from the Classical canon which has framed the Renaissance and modern Western conceptions of art. La Tène art therefore looks far stranger, more mysterious and less comprehensible to most modern people than Greek statues, Etruscan temples or Roman mosaics. Yet despite their very different courses of development, Classical and La Tène art share some common early Iron Age roots stretching across Europe to the eastern Mediterranean.

While certain Graeco-Roman commentators regarded the Celtic world as an artistic wasteland, the Classical world did come to appreciate and learn from Celtic technology – particularly ironworking. La Tène art also made some contribution to provincial Roman art, at least in the old Celtic lands. After surviving the Roman period in Ireland and northern Britain, Celtic art underwent a remarkable revival in post-Roman centuries, notably through the medium of the Irish church (pp. 172–75).

The fabulous Agris helmet, found in fragments in a cave in western France during the 1980s. It is made from iron with gold plating and bronze decorative strips, silver rivet heads and extensive coral inlay. Later fourth century BC.

THE ORIGINS OF LA TÈNE ART

(Above) A bronze bucket from Hallstatt, with the simple geometric and animal patterns characteristic of 'Hallstatt' art.

(Left) An impression from a metalworker's mould found at the Heuneburg, bottom, shown with the kinds of Classical metalwork which helped inspire it; above, a silver bucket handle, seventh century BC, Praeneste, Italy; centre, a figure from an unprovenanced bronze wine bucket.

(Right) The bronze flagon from Dürrnberg, Austria (see text).

THE LA TÈNE STYLE did not evolve in a vacuum: its roots can be traced to the art of the preceding Hallstatt culture of Europe north of the Alps, as well as to that of the Etruscans and Greeks, and thence to the Levant and Mesopotamia. Many Classical motifs, including lotus buds and animal figures such as the gryphon, can themselves be traced back to Assyrian and Persian prototypes.

From Hallstatt to La Tène

Hallstatt pottery and metalwork is often decorated with simple geometric elements such as chevrons, parallel lines and concentric circles. Representations of people or animals are rarer. Subsequently decorated metalwork and pottery from the Mediterranean began to be imported, exposing Hallstatt artisans to Greek and Etruscan patterns and figures. This inspired an entirely new aesthetic synthesis which appeared in the zone north and east of the Hallstatt chiefdoms, during the fifth century BC: the La Tène style.

Many of the earliest masterpieces of La Tène art have been found in graves alongside Etruscan and Greek imports, emphasizing the Classical influences on the new style. But the Celtic artisans were no mere imitators: they reinterpreted the designs they saw to produce a new form and decoration, as on the flagons from Basse-Yutz (Moselle: p. 31).

The early La Tène artists were selective in what they adopted from the Mediterranean. They picked up on vegetal elements, notably the palmette, lotus bud and blossom, and acanthus tendrils. However, while human faces were a popular motif, often distorted almost beyond recognition, complete human figures – so widely represented in the Classical world – were uncommon and heavily stylized. Perhaps human figures and scenes were taboo.

Where did La Tène art develop?

La Tène art arose across a wide area, in a number of early, experimental, regional styles. Many of the best early pieces are from the rich tombs in the Rhine-Moselle region, which outshine in wealth those of other developmental areas (notably the Marne and the zone from Switzerland to Bohemia). One of the finest examples from the region is the Schwarzenbach cup, from a Rhineland barrow, dated to 475–450 BC. The cup consists of openwork gold decoration on a wooden bowl, a pattern clearly derived from Classical palmettes and lotus-buds.

The earliest pieces from the Champagne region are highly geometric; Celtic artisans sometimes constructed their designs using compasses. Decoration was applied to scabbards and harness fittings, such as those in the Somme-Bionne grave (which also contained an Attic cup produced in about 420 BC).

Early La Tène art from Austria to Bohemia was also distinctly geometric (especially on stamped pottery). The local artisans employed fewer plant motifs and more animal patterns than their contemporaries in the Rhine-Moselle area. A fine early piece comes from Dürrnberg near Salzburg in Austria: a flagon which probably dates to about 450 BC, imitating but developing the form of an Etruscan wine-jug, embellished with early La Tène pattern.

During the later fifth century the early La Tène centres exchanged ideas and motifs, thanks to political and trading contacts, migrations, and perhaps the mobility of smiths. As a result many items, such as brooch types, became widely standardized

across the La Tène world during the later fourth and early third centuries BC. Celtic emigrants to the new lands took La Tène art with them: northern Italy became a zone of further artistic development, and the main area of contact with, and perhaps influence from, the Classical world. These cross-fertilizations resulted in the growth and widespread adoption of the 'vegetal style', which itself spawned the varied regional styles of later Iron Age Celtic art.

(Above left) The gold Schwarzenbach cup, found in a rich late fifth-century grave in Germany.

(Above right) The evolution of the palmette and lotus flower. Top to bottom: Etruscan version of the motifs; an early La Tène version added to an Etruscan flagon, Besançon; reduction of the palmette to three leaves on a gold drinking-horn mount from Eigenbilsen; inversion of the palmette, and simplification of the lotus, on the Schwarzenbach cup.

(Left) Analysis of the compass construction of a geometric bronze openwork mount from Somme-Bionne, Marne, fifth century BC.

(Right) A replica of the gilt-bronze flagon from the tomb of the Reinheim 'princess' (p. 69). Note the humanoid faces on the quadruped on the lid and at the base of the handle. Around the body of the flagon is engraved an intricate pattern derived from the lotus and palmette.

CELTIC ART STYLES

Some of the gold and silver/gold torcs from hoards excavated at Snettisham, Norfolk, in 1990. Spectacular additions to our knowledge of Insular British art, they were probably buried in the earlier first century BC, but some pieces appear to be considerably older in manufacture.

WITH THE EXCEPTION of the growing use of high-grade ironwork for scabbards and other arms on the continent, much La Tène metalwork was characterized by bright colour – from bronze, gold (silver was not widely used for decorative purposes), coral and red glass inlay, and later multi-coloured enamel in Britain. As with so many other aspects of the cultures of the Celtic-speaking world, diversity was more characteristic than standardization during the intricate history of La Tène art.

The experimental styles of the fifth and earlier fourth centuries BC gave rise, with some Classical influence, to the vegetal style (p. 107). In the later fourth century BC, the vegetal style formed a common mode of artistic expression across much of the expanding Celtic world, but the early third century BC saw fragmentation into a range of derivative regional styles (including distinctive variants in Britain and Ireland), and divergent traditions among black-smiths and those working in bronze or gold. For the next two centuries there was little or no further influence from the Classical world: Celtic art developed under its own impetus.

The vegetal style

The objects in the grave from Waldalgesheim, near Mainz in Germany, date to about 350–325 BC. They are decorated in a characteristic new vegetal style, that is plant-derived pattern, again with Classical inspiration. The only import in the grave was an Italian bucket bearing the Classical motifs which were adapted into the new style: yet other than the Waldalgesheim bucket few imports reached lands north of the Alps to inspire the new style there. This may suggest that the vegetal style arose in the zone of contact in Italy, and was then transmitted to other parts of the Celtic world where it was further developed into the many strands of later La Tène art.

(Left) Italian bucket from Waldalgesheim, with a detail of the palmette design (far left) clearly echoed in the 'vegetal' pattern on the gold torc from the tomb (below left).

(Right and, detail, below right) The Battersea shield, a red-glass inlaid bronze shield-facing from the Thames. The central circular boss is characteristically British. The shield could date from any time during the third to late first centuries BC.

(Above) Eastern sword style on an iron scabbard from Batina, Croatia (third century BC).

Examples of plastic style on a bronze anklet from Klettham, Bavaria (below), and on the extraordinary bronze mounts from a wooden flagon from Maloměřice, Brno, Czech Republic (right and far right).

Sword style and plastic style

Modern art historians have focused mainly on two major derivatives of the vegetal style: the sword style (basically incised decoration, found largely on iron scabbards) and plastic style (three-dimensional embellishment on torcs, bracelets, anklets and other items, mostly in bronze or sometimes gold). The differences between the two may have developed largely for practical reasons. The style of decoration was probably dictated both by materials used and the function of the object; for instance, embellishment in the round is more difficult in iron and unsuitable, moreover, for scabbards. Differing traditions between blacksmiths and bronze/gold workers may also help to account for the evolution of the two distinct styles. There were also more local developments. For example, several regional 'schools' or traditions of sword decoration have been identified.

Britain and Ireland

La Tène art was introduced to Britain by 300 BC, and by 200 BC to Ireland, although for unknown reasons it failed to penetrate Spain significantly. Objects of the vegetal style are rare in Britain and Ireland, but nevertheless inspired insular La Tène styles. British artisans tended to work bronze for many of the items that their continental counterparts would have made from iron, notably scabbards and shield bosses, as well as full shield-facings – a British speciality – such as those from Battersea and Witham (p. 115).

Both islands became centres of innovation, and insular art became the finest branch of later Iron Age La Tène style.

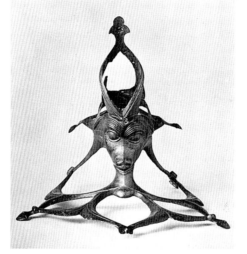

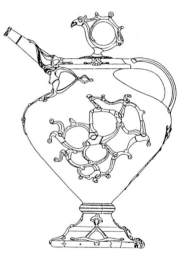

Bronze plaque from the lake deposit at Llyn Cerrig Bach, Wales.

DEPOSITION AND SURVIVAL

Most of what we have left of the art of the last four centuries BC consists of metalwork. Of textiles, commented upon by Classical writers, only a handful of faded fragments survive (p. 66). Wooden vessels at Glastonbury suggest curvilinear decoration may have been quite common on such containers (p. 114), but they are rarely preserved.

Among the metalwork particular items tend to have survived in particular places. Weapons, for example, turn up in water-courses and sources (e.g. the scabbards from the River Bann in Ireland, and the range of arms from the Witham and Thames in England). In contrast, in Britain mirrors occur in graves (as sometimes do weapons), but not in water. Torcs are rarely found in either, occurring more often in hoards (whereas on the continent, torcs do appear in graves).

These patterns of discovery reflect the belief systems of the early Celtic societies. Water deposition and burial in graves were partly religious in nature, but also linked to the common human desire for pomp and ostentatious consumption of wealth. Hoards are more enigmatic and motives for their deposition more diverse. Why were they not recovered in antiquity? Were they buried for fear of invaders? or for secure storage of bullion and raw materials? Perhaps they were simply offerings to deities. The motives may not have been mutually exclusive: hoards whose practical purpose was storage of wealth for the future, may have been placed under the watchful eye of the gods, in holy ground.

TECHNOLOGIES OF FIRE: METAL, GLASS AND POTTERY

SMITHS were probably accorded relatively high status in early Celtic society, as they were later in Ireland, thanks to the importance of their product and the mystery of their art. As well as the many finished masterpieces of metalwork that we possess, archaeology has recovered smiths' tools, crucibles, ingots, kilns and smelting hearths. An important deposit of bronze-manufacturing debris was found in a pit on a British farmstead site at Gussage All Saints, Dorset. Scientific analysis of such industrial waste not only tells us about the composition of materials used but also reveals something of the techniques employed to work them.

Blacksmiths did not have the technology to melt iron for casting: instead it was forged (i.e. heated and hammered), using techniques quite adequate for producing very effective tools and weapons. Centuries of experiment resulted in remarkable virtuosity, and a good empirical understanding of how to produce and work different qualities of metal for different jobs. La Tène swords and other blades were often very well made, strong and flexible. Some blades were wrought from strips of alloys with different properties, with mild steel cutting edges welded on. 'Makers' marks' or magical symbols are sometimes found stamped or inlaid into sword blades.

Smelting and forging

Experiments simulating Iron Age smelting and forging techniques have underlined the huge investments of time, energy and skill required to produce even small quantities of metals, particularly iron – let alone to work them into usable condition and turn them into objects. This is perhaps best seen in the production of iron mail, probably invented by Celtic smiths around 300 BC (p. 77).

The actual manufacture of metalwork was the last stage in a long series of preparatory steps. Foresters managed woodlands to provide timber for woodworking, domestic fuel and to make the charcoal needed to smelt metals. The ores had to be mined and smelted, and frequently had to be moved long distances to their markets.

While iron was widely available, the best ores came from a few particular areas. For example, the mines of Noricum in Austria were said to produce some of the best iron; Cornwall had long exported the tin needed to make bronze; and goldmines were worked in the Cevennes and Pyrenees. There were other sources too, and we must not forget that bullion was plundered, traded, or earned (through military service) in the Mediterranean.

Inlays, enamelling and glass

From the beginning of the La Tène period, smiths embellished their wares with surface decoration, inscribing designs, modelling in the round, and inserting inlays. Red glass and coral already ornamented the Basse-Yutz flagons, and both materials were used throughout the pre-Roman period. In the later Iron Age, especially in Britain, craft workers learned how properly to fuse glass on to the surface of copper alloys – true enamelwork – and adopted a variety of colours in addition to the favourite red.

Glass was also worked in its own right. Beads were widely worn, and glass bangles were popular, for example, among many Gaulish women in the third century BC. The Celts seem to have found cobalt blue particularly appealing, with yellow or white decoration. Archaeologists have as yet unearthed no traces of the manufacture of

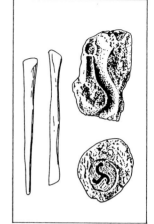

(Above) Evidence of the bronzesmith's craft from Gussage All Saints. Left: small bone modelling tools (remarkably like modern plastic versions) to shape the wax originals for making moulds. Right: fragments of the clay mould for making part of a horse-bit, and the decorated end of a wheel retaining pin.

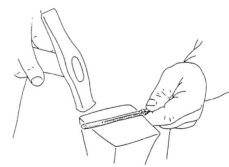

(Right) The end of the billet has been stretched into a rod, and is wound round a rod to make the complex spring which tensions the pin when it is hooked into the catchplate, just like a modern safety pin.

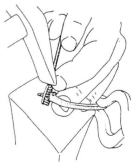

(Left) Making a bronze brooch. The smith hammers out a thin billet of metal. Repeated reheatings keep the metal pliable as it is shaped into the bow of the brooch.

ANATOMY OF A MASTERPIECE: THE KIRKBURN SWORD

In 1987, excavators investigating a grave at Kirkburn in east Yorkshire unearthed a spectacular sword, dating to the third century BC, decorated from one end to the other with scarlet enamel. Careful study by archaeologists and restoration work by conservators at the British Museum in London have revealed the secrets of a splendid example of Celtic craftsmanship.

The iron blade possessed a hilt assembly and scabbard of great complexity and artistic beauty. It was crafted from over seventy components, each made with great skill and finished to the highest standard.

The hilt was constructed mostly from iron, with decorative iron and bronze studs. These were covered with scarlet 'enamel' or glass, which also filled the patterns cut into the grip. The guard and pommel were of organic material, probably horn, with enamelled iron binding strips.

Iron also formed the main structure of the scabbard, but the front plate was of copper alloy, probably golden in colour. This plate was decorated with an elaborate pattern chased into the surface. At some stage the metal split along one of the scribed lines, and the carefully riveted repair can still be seen. Again the assembly was secured and decorated with large rivets, and both these and the iron scabbard plates were also enamelled.

The sword was suspended by a belt running through the iron loop on the back of the scabbard. Curiously, this is very low, and must be near the point of balance; the sword must have tended to tip upside down when worn. Exactly how it was worn remains a mystery.

Overall length 27½ inches (697 mm); blade about 22½ inches (570 mm).

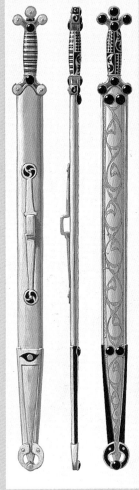

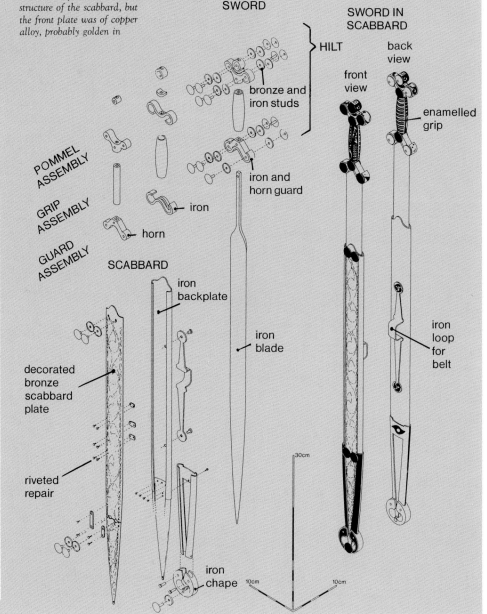

SWORD

HILT

bronze and iron studs

iron and horn guard

POMMEL ASSEMBLY

GRIP ASSEMBLY

GUARD ASSEMBLY

iron

horn

SCABBARD

iron backplate

iron blade

decorated bronze scabbard plate

riveted repair

iron chape

SWORD IN SCABBARD

back view

front view

enamelled grip

iron loop for belt

30cm

10cm

10cm

(Below) The complex assembly of the ceremonial bronze shield recently discovered in the bed of the River Thames at Chertsey (see p.72).

To the axial spine assembly, left, were added the two large plates forming the shield-board, and the carrying handle, centre. Finally trimming strips and an edge binding were added, right.

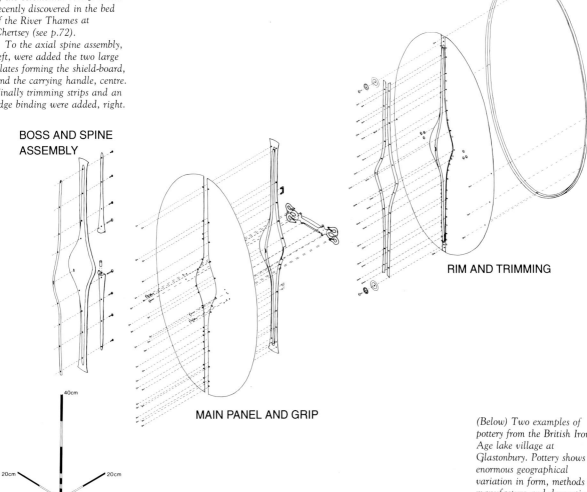

BOSS AND SPINE ASSEMBLY

MAIN PANEL AND GRIP

RIM AND TRIMMING

(Below) Two examples of pottery from the British Iron Age lake village at Glastonbury. Pottery shows enormous geographical variation in form, methods of manufacture and decoration.

raw glass, leading some to conclude that this commodity was imported from the Classical world. Colourless glass, which is technically difficult to make, was used later.

Pottery

Potters threw vessels on the wheel from the start of the La Tène period on the continent, firing them in quite sophisticated kilns which permitted the control of the oxygen flow around the pots. By varying the amount of oxygen, the potter could choose the colour of the vessel, from reddish to grey or black.

Early Iron Age pots from the eastern Celtic lands were stamped with animal and other designs. Later, Gaulish potters painted their vessels with bands of red or white and black patterns such as cross-hatching, by applying slip (liquid clay) before firing. Another interesting technique they used was to add graphite to the clay to achieve a metallic appearance.

The potter's wheel was not used across the English Channel until the end of the Iron Age: British vessels were made by hand and tended to be much coarser. The north British and Irish used very little pottery at all, most probably preferring wooden\or metal vessels.

While Roman techniques and fashions displaced many native pottery traditions after the conquest, some survived and even flourished: the manufacture of 'black burnished' ware of southwestern England, for example, expanded under Roman rule. These pots have been found in some quantity as far north as Hadrian's Wall.

CRAFTS: WORKING IN WOOD

A remarkably well-preserved wheel under excavation from the silts at La Tène. The quality of construction and excellent finish of Celtic wheels is evident.

'they make their ships with broad bottoms, high sterns, and high prows; they make them of oak ... and this is why they do not bring the joints of their planks together but leave gaps; they stuff the gaps full of seaweed ... so that the wood may not ... become dry when the ships are hauled up, because the seaweed is naturally rather moist, whereas the oak is dry and without fat.'

Strabo 4,4,1

CRAFTS were important in the Celtic world, and they are important to us, for studies of them provide a rich picture of how the Celts dressed, cooked, travelled, transported goods and built their homes. Most craft items were made from perishable organic materials such as wood, textiles, leather or basketry, so we must seek evidence in environments with special conditions of preservation e.g. the salt-mines of Hallstatt or the waterlogged bogs at Glastonbury and the lake-bed at La Tène. We can derive some details of leatherworking techniques from surviving tools and depictions of leather goods such as shoes; few actual examples have survived. But we do have a fine sample of wooden objects, ranging from small statues to vehicles and parts of buildings, and these allow us to reconstruct the art of the carpenter.

Woodworking

Wood was enormously important to early societies for buildings, equipment and fuel. Surviving wooden objects indicate that Celtic carpenters were as skilled as the smiths.

Foresters would fell trees with axes, and probably split them into planks and balks using wooden wedges. At La Tène, constructional timbers up to 40 feet (12 m) long were recovered, along with a variety of woodworking tools, including small saws. Adzes are also known.

Joints were not especially complex – mostly mortises and tenons, or pegged joints – but this was also true of much Roman carpentry. Classical sources mention the construction of wooden bridges in Gaul, and there are archaeological traces of elaborate gate structures and the *murus gallicus* defences of Gaulish settlements (p. 121). Normally only the foundations of Celtic buildings have survived, but even these can tell us a fair amount about construction methods (pp. 57–59).

Celtic carpenters also produced a fine range of portable objects. Their skills are readily apparent, for instance, from the widely known stave-built vessels, especially metal-bound buckets, or the barrel of Alpine silver fir found at Manching in Germany. They also evidently used lathes to turn tool-handles and wooden bowls. But perhaps the most spectacular achievement of Celtic carpentry was the manufacture of vehicles.

Ships and vehicles

Caesar describes Gaulish sea-going vessels in the English Channel as tall, tough, sailing ships, with leather sails and anchor cables of iron chain. In fact, we have to rely heavily on his written accounts for shipbuilding, because archaeology has so far revealed details about river craft only – such as a huge dugout from Hasholme in east Yorkshire (third century BC).

We have more information about land vehicles. Smiths and carpenters cooperated closely in the manufacture of these vehicles, and nowhere is this collaboration better exemplified than in Celtic wheel construction, which displays great precision and knowledge of the properties of different wood types. Gaulish wheelwrights learnt to make the wooden felloe or outer circle of the wheel from a single piece of wood. Blacksmiths would then drop a heated iron tyre over the assembly which would shrink on cooling, thus binding all the components together without the need for heavy iron nails. The result was a technical *tour de force* unmatched by the Classical world, where the felloe was made in sections.

(Right) Reconstruction of an elegantly decorated wooden bowl from Glastonbury lake village.

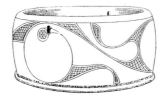

WHAT WAS LA TÈNE ART FOR?

DID THE EARLY CELTS consider the masterpieces which are so admired today to be works of art as we understand the term? The richest La Tène art is concentrated on items of personal adornment (jewellery, mirrors, elaborate weapons), on transport (horse and vehicle harness), and on equipment for aristocratic feasting. Most of it was designed to be seen on or immediately about the person, and it is probable that the display of the wealth and taste of the owner was its principal *raison d'être*. Indeed the idea of art for art's sake, as something separate and independent, is an unusual and largely modern conceit.

La Tène is almost entirely a *portable* art, in stark contrast to the major art of Greece and Rome which was distinctly immobile. Powerful Romans preferred to display their wealth in the form of private houses, public buildings, and statuary. They regarded gaudy personal appearance as barbaric and effeminate. Caesar was thought eccentric for wearing long sleeves!

Yet Celtic and Classical art shared much in common. Artists in both cultures were closely linked with the lifestyles and aspirations of the ruling classes. Indeed it is likely that most of the finest La Tène metalwork and the greatest Roman architecture existed only because nobles commissioned and paid for it. A similar undercurrent of patronage and power is to be found in many societies: the Sistine Chapel is as much a monument to the earthly power and aesthetic taste of a pope as it is to the glory of God and the genius of Michelangelo.

The close connection between art and the ruling nobilities in areas such as Gaul and southern Britain is dramatically illustrated by the fate of La Tène when these regions fell under Roman rule: the manufacture of La Tène masterpieces, already declining, effectively ceased within a generation. Celtic aristocrats, wooed into a Roman lifestyle by the imperial authorities, quickly diverted their wealth into Roman status symbols such as architecture (p. 132).

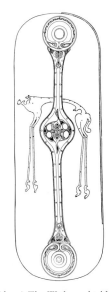

(Above) The Witham shield bears the outline of a boar, a symbol of ferocity; ?second century BC. (Left) The Elmswell casket-mount, mixing Roman pattern with one of the last major examples of la Tène pattern from Roman Britain, late first century AD.

CRAFTSMANSHIP?

How far is it legitimate to speak of craftsmen in ancient Celtic societies? It is easy to assume, for example, on the basis of parallels with the Classical world and many other societies, that the working of metal was a specialist industrial craft and that smiths were male, and that other productive activities – notably vitally important textile production – were domestic crafts and therefore the responsibility of women. Yet for most early Celtic societies we do not even have good evidence that domestic tasks were specifically regarded as women's work!

The need for sheer physical strength may have made smithing, carpentry and other such activities largely male preserves. But pottery production, for example, was in some areas virtually a specialized industry, in others a low-technology domestic activity. Can we assume that the former was a male preserve, the latter part of women's household duties? It is possible that domestic potmaking was not a gender role at all, but the responsibility, for instance, of slaves of either sex.

However, if the pattern of gender roles in crafts was very different from that of other contemporary peoples, we would expect Greek or Latin authors to comment on it, as the place of women in Celtic society was a favourite theme.

(Left) A warp-weighted loom, similar to Celtic types.

(Right) Potmaking at Butser.

THE CELTS AND THE CLASSICAL WORLD

'Formerly the Allobroges kept up warfare with a myriad of men, whereas now they till the plains and the glens that are in the Alps, and all of them live in villages, except that the most notable of them, inhabitants of Vienne ... have built [their settlement] up into a city.'

Strabo 4,1,11

THE CELTIC WORLD reached its greatest territorial extent in the third century BC, with the establishment of Galatian power in Asia Minor. But by the end of the century, decline was under way, and by 100 BC, Celtic Italy had ceased to exist, the Celtiberians of Spain were virtually broken, and the Galatians of Turkey were about to receive fatal blows.

North of the Alps the pattern was somewhat different. In the last two centuries BC, Gaul (and to a lesser extent Britain) began to import Roman goods on a large scale. When Julius Caesar invaded Gaul in the 50s BC, he found a land dominated by a group of early states, dotted with settlements he called towns (*oppida*). Clearly some of the northern Celts were moving towards an urban pattern of life well before the Roman conquest.

Contrary to popular belief, the conquest did not signal the immediate death of Celtic culture. Under Roman rule, many Celtic-speaking regions maintained much of their identity for a surprisingly long time, and achieved a degree of political stability and material prosperity far beyond that of the Iron Age. Because so many aspects of our culture are based on Graeco-Roman models, we tend to see Gallo-Roman and Romano-British societies in terms of how Roman they were. But to better understand them we need also to see how *Celtic* they were. These were vigorous hybrid cultures in which the Celtic cultural heritage was an essential (if often hidden) element, instrumental in shaping the Roman West.

Detail of the 'Dying Gaul', actually a Galatian of Asia Minor (see p. 40).

THE CHANGING WORLD OF LATE IRON AGE GAUL

BACKWARD BARBARISM OR PARALLEL DEVELOPMENT?

Modern commentators, as well as Classical writers, usually emphasize the differences between Iron Age Celtic societies and Graeco-Roman civilization: but Celtic cultures (particularly in central Gaul and the zone stretching east to Bohemia) in fact had many features in common with the Classical world.

For example, the Celtic pattern of population growth, dispatching of migrants and the eventual development of centralized urban states is broadly similar to the evolution of Greece just a few centuries earlier. And social organization in late Iron Age Gaul was similar to that in contemporary republican Rome, where society was dominated by great noble houses which exerted influence through a system of clients and patrons. Rome had a militaristic ethic and – until the middle republic – Roman generals like their Gallic counterparts behaved in 'heroic' manner, engaging Celtic chiefs in single combat (p. 82). Even the political struggles faced by the central Gallic states (as depicted by Caesar) resembled those of the Roman republic, itself a constitutional government vainly trying to check overmighty noble warlords – of whom Caesar himself proved the most dangerous.

Remembering also the comparable technological and other achievements between the two cultures, it is clear that the contrast drawn between Celtic barbarism and Classical civilization is much exaggerated.

'*All Gaul is filled with traders, is full of Roman citizens. No Gaul does any business without the aid of a Roman citizen; not a single sesterce in Gaul ever changes hands without being entered in the account books of Roman citizens.*'
Cicero, *Pro Fonteio*, 33

THANKS TO CAESAR, we have a fairly comprehensive picture of several Gallic societies in the mid first century BC, including details of their political and social structures, their domestic policies and their external relations. The later Iron Age Celts of central Gaul had evolved quite sophisticated states, ruled by kings or elected magistrates, some of which dominated their neighbours to form substantial competing power-blocs.

Gallic politics were highly volatile, with widespread factional strife both between and within these political units. Diplomatic links between such groups were forged through a series of alliances. Caesar records the great political influence of the Aedui (one of the most important Gallic states), and that of a rival powerbloc under their enemies the Sequani; the Aedui held as allies or clients a number of other tribes, including the powerful Bituriges and Senones, the Belgic Bellovaci, and lesser groups including the Aedui Ambarri, Segusiavi, Ambivareti, Aulerci Brannovices, Blannovii, and some newly-arrived Boii. Such links were cemented by the giving of hostages. But by the early first century BC, alliance networks had also been extended beyond the frontiers of the Celtic-speaking world: the Aedui were allied to Rome (p. 46), while Diviciacus of the Suessiones held power over parts of Britain. Later, certain German tribes were coopted into Gallic politics as mercenaries.

Political development was not an even or universal process. The Aedui, and a number of neighbouring states, had in recent decades undergone profound changes, while other peoples, for example in Belgica, retained more traditional patterns. Thus, a variety of political formations existed on the eve of the Roman conquest, and changes continued to occur.

Rulers, patrons, clients and trade

Tribes such as the Suessiones were still ruled by a king or high chief. Others, like the Eburones, had two rulers (perhaps reflecting the coalescence of two earlier tribes – or maybe the division or duplication of duties, like the two Roman Consuls). But among the Aedui, and some others, kings had been replaced by elected magistrates, drawn from the aristocrats. According to Caesar, the aristocracy dominated the mass of the free people, who had but little to say in affairs. The power of the nobility appears to have grown greatly, cutting across the older structures of family and clan ties. Individuals, especially those who had fallen on hard times, could place themselves under the protection of a powerful noble patron, who in return demanded their loyalty. Accumulation of such clients provided the patron with political muscle.

To maintain their clients and position, ambitious nobles needed wealth and prestige. However, the development of state governments may have curtailed the traditional opportunities to acquire fame and by private war. Perhaps this is one reason for the growing importance of trade with Rome. As in earlier times, this tended to concentrate on luxuries, particularly wine, which the aristocracy could employ to enhance their standing.

Some nobles built up such a powerful personal retinue of clients and retainers that they endangered the stability of the state – as they doubtless intended. Dumnorix, for instance, managed to gain control of the entire tax and customs system of the Aedui: no one dared bid against him for the (apparently annual) contract, and the wealth it brought him was the basis for a virtual take-over of the state. An equally outstanding example is that of Orgetorix of the Helvetii (see box p. 121). Gallic politics were unstable and violent.

Wider changes and the appearance of towns

Alongside the documented developments in political organization, much greater changes were taking place, including major population growth and probably a concurrent rise in farming production (now well attested in Britain at least). Growing wealth-

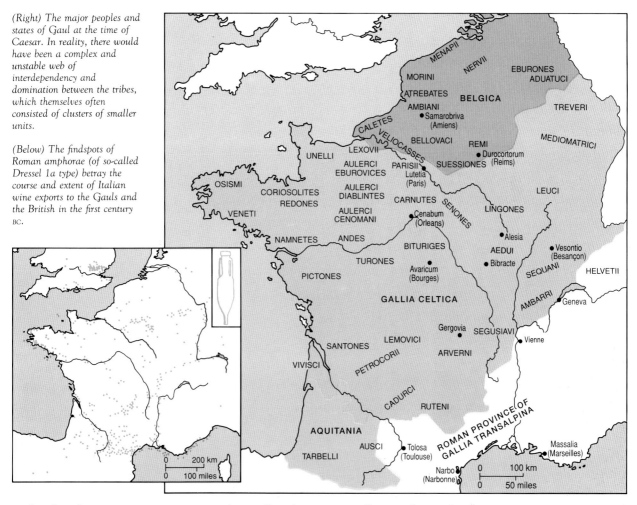

(Right) The major peoples and states of Gaul at the time of Caesar. In reality, there would have been a complex and unstable web of interdependency and domination between the tribes, which themselves often consisted of clusters of smaller units.

(Below) The findspots of Roman amphorae (of so-called Dressel 1a type) betray the course and extent of Italian wine exports to the Gauls and the British in the first century BC.

and class-distinctions were intimately related to these developments. From the third century BC, the Gauls increasingly adopted coinage, and there is also some evidence of literacy (texts in Greek characters are known in southern Gaul by the second century BC, while by Caesar's time coins with Latin script were being minted further north).

New types of settlement began to appear too, especially large proto-towns that Caesar referred to as *oppida*. In fact this blanket term disguises the range of large settlements which appeared from the second century BC in a band from Bohemia to central France. Later they also developed in northern Gaul and eastern Britain. Why these sites developed is unclear, but they are connected with increasing wealth and organization, allowing societies to support specialist craftsmen, and growing interregional trade.

Oppida were typically sprawling agglomerations of buildings and enclosures with streets and elaborate defences. One of the best-known *oppida* is the 900-acre (380-ha) site of Manching in Bavaria, on the south of the Danube Valley, which developed in the second century BC – apparently on the basis of local trade. Some of these towns – e.g. Bibracte, chief *oppidum* of the Aedui – are situated on hills, but many are in valley locations, like Villeneuve-St Germain near Soissons which is partly protected by river meanders.

Evidence from *oppidum* interiors reveals industrial activity, notably metalworking, and coin production – which may indicate the presence of governmental and legal institutions (an idea confirmed by Caesar's description of the public places and activities at Bibracte). The Celts further east – for example at Stradonice, the most important *oppidum* in Bohemia – evidently engaged in

HEAVY DRINKERS

'The Gauls are exceedingly addicted to the use of wine and fill themselves with the wine which is brought into their country by merchants, drinking it unmixed, and since they partake of this drink without moderation by reason of their craving for it, when they are drunken they fall into a stupor or a state of madness. Consequently many of the Italian traders ... believe that the love of wine of these Gauls is their own godsend. For these transport the wine on the navigable rivers ... and through the level plain on wagons, and receive for it an incredible price; for in exchange for a jar of wine they receive a slave.'
Diodorus Siculus 5,26,2–3

Magistrates. *While some
tribes were still ruled by kings,
others (e.g. the Helvetii and
Aedui) were governed by
magistrates. Among the Aedui
the 'Vergobret' or chief
magistrate was head of state,
wielding power of life and
death over the citizenry. He
was elected to serve for a year,
and was forbidden from
leaving state territory during
his term of office. The law
apparently decreed that no one
could hold the office during the*
*lifetime of a previous
incumbent from the same
family, suggesting not only the
development of a legal system
and constitution but also
perhaps reflecting the
competition for power among
the eligible noble families, and
attempts to regulate it and
maintain political stability.
The election mechanism is
unknown, although in times of
civil strife the Vergobret was
appointed by the priests.*

The senate. *This was the
council of senior noblemen; in
the case of the Nervii, it
consisted of 300 members. The
growing power of the nobility
was reflected in the increasing
importance of the senate (and*
*declining role of the popular
assembly). The Aedui
attempted to contain the power
of individual families or clans
by restrictions on eligibility to
the chief magistracy.*

The popular assembly. *Large
assemblies – probably of free
adult males with enough
wealth to own arms – did
meet, in all likelihood simply
to approve the decisions of the
council and magistrates (or*
*king). Assemblies had their
own procedures: 'if a man
disturbs the speaker and
heckles him, the sergeant-at-
arms approaches him with
drawn sword, and with a
threat commands him to be*
*silent; if he does not stop, the
sergeant-at-arms does the same
thing a second time, and also a
third time, but at last cuts off
enough of the man's cloak to
make it useless for the future'
(Strabo 4,4,3).*
*Some groups were excluded
from the political and
legislative process altogether:
these included women and
girls, boys below arms-bearing
age, slaves, and foreigners.*

similar activities. The presence of wine amphorae and other Classical imports in Gallic towns supports the view that these places were important centres of trade and exchange: Caesar mentions that Italian merchants were resident at *oppida* in the 50s BC. But despite the rambling, chaotic appearance of these settlements, the *oppida* fulfilled many of the functions of a typical Classical town: they housed administrative, political and residential institutions, as well as trading, agricultural and storage facilities (e.g. communal grain stores).

The engine of change

The Gauls were moving towards social and political structures which in some ways strikingly paralleled the Classical world (see box p. 118), particularly in the regions adjacent to the Graeco-Roman enclave of southern Gaul. Further Classical influences seem to be at work in the use of Greek coins as prototypes for Gallic ones, the adoption of Greek and Latin writing, some religious innovations (p. 92), the rediscovered taste for wine and perhaps the institution of magistracies. Does this suggest, then, that all the changes taking place in Gallic society in the last centuries BC were the result simply of exposure to the 'civilized' Graeco-Roman cultures to the south?

Not necessarily. Powerful states like the Arverni and Aedui existed before the Roman conquest of the Rhône Valley in the second century BC, as did the earliest *oppida* in Gaul, while towns were growing in areas like southern Germany and Bohemia which show no signs of Classical

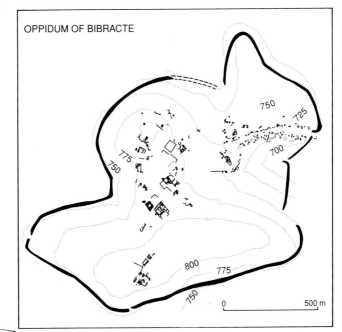

(Right) The great oppidum of the Aedui at Bibracte – now Mont Beuvray – sprawls over 320 acres (135 ha) of a large hilltop, 2,600 ft (800 m) above sea level. The site was occupied from the later second century BC until about 12 BC, when the Aedui established a new urban centre at Augustodunum – Autun – 12 miles (20 km) to the east. Excavations at Bibracte have revealed buildings of the early Roman period, including workshops near the main entrance, and large aristocratic houses of Roman form in the interior. New excavations currently underway should reveal much more about the site in its pre-Roman heyday.

OPPIDUM OF BIBRACTE

ORGETORIX: AN OVERMIGHTY SUBJECT
Frequently, the personal ambitions of individual nobles threatened the stability of the state. One such noble was Orgetorix, a prince of the Helvetii of Switzerland. Seeking to be king, Orgetorix conspired c. 61 BC with other nobles, including Dumnorix of the Aedui and other outsiders; these private alliances were cemented through marriages. Orgetorix planned to win power by leading the people in a migration westwards, but his attempt to subvert the Helvetian constitutional government was betrayed, and he was summoned by the ruling magistrates to stand trial for treason.

Orgetorix, however, had already amassed a considerable following. He was able to resist arrest by assembling a private army of 10,000 men plus 'all his clients and debtors, of whom he had a great number': the total population of the Helvetii and their allies at the time was under 400,000, of whom Caesar says 92,000 could bear arms, underlining the scale of Orgetorix's personal power. In the event the Helvetian state weathered the crisis, due to Orgetorix's sudden and mysterious death.

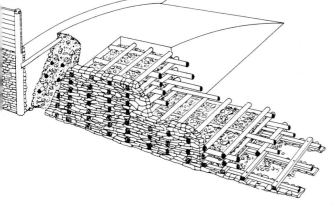

(Left) Manching was surrounded by a defensive wall about 3 miles (5 km) long, made of timber, stone and earth. Due to the interlacing and nailing together of thousands of huge beams, these so-called murus gallicus *('Gaulish wall') defences were extremely resistant to assault by battering ram.*

contact at the time. Thus the changes responsible for the appearance of urban states were probably triggered by a variety of local stimuli, including population growth, innovations in farming, subtle ecological changes and other factors such as the increasing threat from the Germans (p. 125).

The Graeco-Roman cultures nevertheless acted as a catalyst for change. Rome and Marseilles (Greek Massalia, known in Roman times as Massilia) provided models, for example of government, to meet the developing needs of the nascent Gallic states. Likewise, as the need for literacy grew (e.g. for the state censuses mentioned by Caesar or for private accounting), the available Greek and Latin alphabets were adopted. Rome also established trade and diplomatic links with the Gallic aristocracies, and in so doing became enmeshed in the web of Gallic alliances.

This cultural exchange had two significant and related results. First, central Gaul (and later southern England) became partly Romanized. Secondly, Rome became increasingly aware of Gaul's growing wealth *and* vulnerability (following the development of centralized institutions and fixed centres of power). Gaul had become ripe for conquest – not because it was markedly less 'civilized' than Rome, but because it was rich, complex, and already sufficiently *similar* to the Classical world to be absorbable. Thereafter, the development of the western Celtic heartlands was diverted on to a different, albeit parallel, track: that of Classical urban civilization.

ROMAN CONQUEST: ITALY, IBERIA AND GALATIA

Situated on a hill overlooking the River Duero in Spain, Numantia was occupied from ancient times, but in the third century BC the powerful Celtiberian tribe of the Arevaci developed it into a substantial defended town, covering over 50 acres (20 ha). A well-defined street grid divided up blocks of stone-founded, mud-brick buildings.

Numantia became the focus of the epic Celtiberian resistance to Roman conquest in the second century BC. Twenty years of fighting culminated in a siege of the town by the Roman general P. Cornelius Scipio, in 133 BC. The city finally succumbed to starvation, was razed, but then reoccupied under Roman rule.

Legionaries of the late republic depicted on the Altar of Domitius Ahenobarbus. Note their mail shirts, short swords, horsehair plumes and their enormous body shields or scuta.

'... of the four divisions into which the Celtiberians have been separated, the most powerful, generally speaking, are the Arvacans [Arevaci] ... and they have a city of very great renown, Numantia. They gave proof of their valour in the Celtiberian War against the Romans, which lasted for twenty years; indeed, many armies, officers and all, were destroyed by them, and at the last the Numantians, when besieged, endured till death, except a few who surrendered the fortress.'
Strabo 3,4,13

AFTER INITIAL CLASHES with the Gauls of the Po Valley in the fourth century BC, Rome was gradually drawn into deeper conflict with the Celts as she absorbed Etruria (p. 35). Outright conquest of Gallia Cisalpina had already begun when the process was interrupted by Hannibal's daring invasion of Italy over the Alps in 218 BC, following a spectacular march from Spain. The ensuing Second Punic War between Rome and Carthage had drastic consequences for the whole Mediterranean world, and with it much of Celtdom. Rome emerged from the life-or-death struggle as a world-class military power; Carthage was a broken reed. This stimulated Roman conquests in Spain, leading to the subjection of the Celtiberians, and intervention in Gaul (p. 46).

The Second Punic War also helped draw Rome into the labyrinthine politics of Greece and the Greek kingdoms built on the ruins of Alexander's empire, leading to a clash with the Galatians of central Turkey (p. 41).

'Decelticization': the conquest of Gallia Cisalpina

The critical moment in Italy came in 225 BC, when the Gauls launched an attack on Roman Etruria. The conflict culminated in the Battle of Telamon (pp. 84–85) where the Gauls suffered a terrible defeat. Over the next few years, the subjugation of Gallia Cisalpina was all but completed; the Boii were overrun in 224, the Insubres in 222. Roman military colonies were established at Placentia and Cremona, showing Rome intended to stay.

Then came Hannibal's invasion. The ensuing struggle devastated Italy for years. Hannibal allied himself with the Gauls, and a new generation of Celtic warriors grew up in Carthaginian service. Hannibal's final defeat at Zama in 202 BC, however, left the battle-hardened Romans free to resume the conquest of the north, and the Boii and the Insubres were eventually subdued in the 190s. It was said that the Gauls were all but exterminated or expelled, but substantial numbers did in fact remain in the region, as names on later inscriptions reveal – they were gradually absorbed into Roman society.

Victory over the Celtiberians

Roman armies entered Spain to attack the Carthaginians there: Spain was the source of Hannibal's strength. The establishment of Roman provinces in eastern and southern Spain inevitably led to conflict with the peoples of the interior. The Celtiberians were among the toughest of Rome's foes; a long series of wars took place between the two peoples (from 197 to 179, and 154 to 133 BC), which showed the worst side of Roman character. Frustration and ruthlessness led to treachery and brutality. After a prolonged struggle most of Iberia was subjected, culminating in the final capture of Numantia in 133, after several abortive attempts (see box). Fighting continued in parts of Iberia for generations – the Roman emperor Augustus campaigned there, 26–19 BC – but the peninsula was destined to become a thoroughly Romanized land, in which it is hard to discern anything which may be labelled Celtic. Inscriptions and other evidence show that the Celtic language continued to be spoken into the imperial period, but it gradually disappeared.

The fall of Galatia

Rome found the Galatians a useful source of instability serving Roman interests in Asia Minor (p. 41). But catastrophe struck in 88 BC when Mithridates VI of Pontus revolted against Rome, attacking all Rome's allies. Mithridates invited sixty Galatian chiefs (presumably the five officials of each of the twelve tetrarchies) to meet him at Pergamon, where he subsequently massacred them: only three escaped. He also killed their families, which suggests that he perceived a strong hereditary element in Galatian government.

For the rest of the war – until Mithridates' final defeat in 66 BC by the Roman general, Pompey – the Galatians were Rome's allies. In 64 Pompey reorganized the Galatian government, establishing for each of the three tribes a single ruler, who (showing the power of tradition over logic) was still called a tetrarch. Deiotarus of the Tolistobogii became the most prominent of the tetrarchs, and was sufficiently enamoured of things Roman to train an army in legionary style. Eventually the Romans regarded him as sole king of Galatia. However, he picked the wrong side in the Roman civil war which erupted in 49 BC, supporting Pompey whom he surely regarded as his patron. Happily, this wily old Celt survived his trial before Caesar, thanks to the advocacy of Cicero.

The history of the Galatian state ended with the death of his son Deiotarus II, after which Galatia was incorporated into the empire as a province. In AD 74 it was subsumed into Roman Cappadocia, but even before this it was losing its Celtic character: St Paul's letter to the Galatians was not written to Celtic aristocrats, but to people of Hellenistic Greek culture. Nonetheless, it does appear that Celtic language, and probably other aspects of Celtic life, survived in Galatia for centuries – St Jerome (AD 331–420) wrote: 'The Galatians have their own language and it is almost the same as that of the Treveri [of eastern Gaul]'.

New threats

In the second century BC then, Celtica was everywhere under threat from Roman expansion. Moreover, in the north it was beginning to come under pressure from the Germans, while in the Danube basin it faced assimilation and, in the first century, the new power of Dacia. The Boii of Bohemia were smashed by the Dacians in 60 BC, and soon replaced, expelled or subsumed by migrating German groups. By the time Rome absorbed the Danube basin, culminating in Trajan's conquest of Dacia (AD 101–6), little of identifiable Celtic character survived in the region.

The huge siegeworks around Numantia, built in 133 BC by the Roman general Scipio Aemilianus and manned by 60,000 Roman and allied troops. The Numantines were finally starved into surrender. The town was destroyed, and the survivors sold into slavery. Inset: the mouth of a pottery trumpet in the shape of a wolf's head, from Numantia.

A defeated Galatian warrior commits suicide. Roman marble copy of a third-century BC statue from Pergamon.

JULIUS CAESAR AND THE CONQUEST OF GAUL

THE ROMAN PROVINCE of Gallia Transalpina developed slowly, and not altogether peacefully. The Allobroges in particular remained rebellious, and Roman armies were destroyed there by the Cimbri and Teutones in 105 BC. The province became notorious for corrupt administration, a place where governors made fortunes by fair means or foul. Among the most infamous were Fonteius (governor *c*. 74–72 BC), indicted for extortion, and Caepio, who looted the shrines of the Tolosates in 107 BC (p. 94). Nevertheless the province provided access to the heart of free Gaul, and led to increasing Roman interest there.

Prelude to conquest

Given the expansionist nature of the Roman state in the last centuries BC, it was inevitable that a rich neighbouring land like Gaul would eventually be invaded. However, the fact that it was conquered by Julius Caesar was almost an accident: Gallia Transalpina was only assigned to his governorship on the unexpected death of another man. Caesar – an aristocrat, but an opportunistic and ruthless politician – needed military glory and above all wealth to survive, let alone achieve the power he aspired to. The Roman senatorial nobility were in increasingly cut-throat competition for power (on a scale even greater than that of the Gallic aristocrats) and, as in Gaul,

much of the wealth necessary to finance lordly ambitions came from activities outside their own lands. In the case of the great Roman warlords, it was largely acquired by conquest and extortion. Caesar, as consul in 59 BC, was subverting the state in unconstitutional alliance with Pompey the Great, leading soldier of the day, and the financier Crassus. He was the weakest of the three, lacking both Pompey's military prestige and Crassus' wealth (Caesar was hugely in debt). Following his consulship, Caesar was desperate for a provincial command to escape his creditors and political foes (government office conferring immunity from prosecution), and to build up his position.

Caesar's responsibility was the administration and security of Gallia Cisalpina, Illyricum and Gallia Transalpina. In practice this also meant dealing with allies and potential threats beyond his frontiers. He did not have the sanction of the senate to embark on unprovoked wars of conquest, but Caesar was never one to let mere laws stand in his way.

The Helvetii: pretext for intervention

Caesar found himself confronted by the planned migration of the Helvetii, a large Celtic tribe dwelling in Switzerland, who intended to move westwards in search of

CAESAR: STATESMAN AND WARRIOR

Gaius Julius Caesar (depicted left) was born in 100 BC, a blue-blooded senatorial noble. The republic was already in the grip of strife between warlords: Caesar had family connections with the radical Marius, which nearly cost him his life. Caesar developed a ruthlessness and cunning audacity which outstripped his rivals, stunning them by becoming pontifex maximus (highest priest) in 63 BC, followed by the praetorship in 62, and then governorship of Further Spain – where he discovered his talent for war.

Aligning himself with the

general Pompey and the financier Crassus to jointly manipulate the state, he became consul in 59 BC, departing for Gaul in 58. His subsequent conquests were technically illegal (he had no such instructions from the government), but as an astute politician he was aware of the importance of a semblance of legality, and needed to maintain favourable public opinion. It is to this need for self-justification (and indeed publicity) that we owe the publication of his Gallic War.

After the death of Crassus in 53, tensions with Pompey

grew, until Caesar precipitated war, and his final bid for sole power, by crossing the River Rubicon from Cisalpine Gaul into Italy in 49. He defeated Pompey in 48, but the civil war rumbled on until 45. In 44 BC Caesar was declared dictator for life, but later that year, on the Ides of March, he was assassinated by a group of senators.

The renewed civil strife thus unleashed ended with the Battle of Actium in 31 BC. Caesar's adopted son, Augustus, was established as first emperor soon after.

new lands (p. 121). Such a migration would have threatened the stability of central Gaul and, consequently, Roman allies and interests – even if Rome's own province in southern Gaul was not itself under threat. Caesar leapt at the excuse to intervene, and in 58 BC turned the Helvetii back by force. On his own figures this resulted in the slaughter or starvation of more than a quarter of a million people, before the shattered remnants got home.

The pattern of conquest

Once in Gaul, Caesar was quickly able to find further motives for involvement and opportunities for glory and loot, especially through the Aedui, Rome's long-standing allies. One such pretext was provided by the Sequani, allies of the Arverni, who had brought in German mercenaries under Ariovistus: having decimated the Aeduan aristocracy, the Germans were now running amok, attacking their erstwhile employers. Caesar quickly manoeuvred Ariovistus into war, even though the German had been hailed as a friend by the Roman senate, and was not keen to fight. In a battle near the Rhine, Ariovistus was routed.

Having annihilated the Germans, Caesar became increasingly involved in the labyrinthine politics of Gaul, in a series of campaigns which the Gauls realized were taking on the aspect of a formal conquest. Some tribes, such as the Aedui and the Remi, became firm allies of Caesar, treating him as their patron, but others resisted with heroic ferocity. The fighting strength of the Nervii was almost wiped out (p. 73), while

the Eburones ceased to exist as a people. By 55 BC, Roman legions had overrun most of Gaul, permitting Caesar to launch his two expeditions to Britain in that and the following year. But the Gauls were not broken. In secret conference during the winter of 53–52 BC, they plotted rebellion, a last bid for freedom.

(Right) A statue of a first-century BC Gaulish warrior from Vachères in France. Caesar's legionaries faced men like this on the battlefields of the Three Gauls. He wears a long tunic with sleeves, an iron mail shirt, a heavy cloak and a tubular torc. A long sword hangs at his right hip, and he leans on his shield in characteristic Gaulish fashion.

(Below) The course of the Roman campaigns in Gaul and Britain. In 58 BC, Caesar frustrated the westward migration of the Helvetii, and smashed Ariovistus' Germans. The years 57 and 56 BC were spent fighting the Belgae and reducing the Veneti. Further campaigning against the Belgae and across the Rhine into Germany opened the way for the expeditions to Britain in 55 and 54 BC.

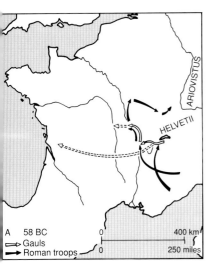

A 58 BC
⇨ Gauls
➡ Roman troops

0 ———— 400 km
0 ———— 250 miles

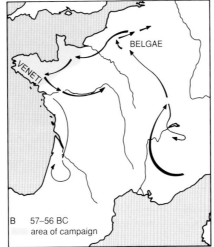

B 57–56 BC
area of campaign

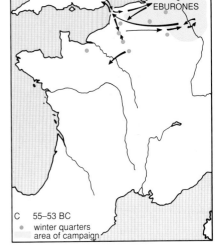

C 55–53 BC
● winter quarters
area of campaign

THE REVOLT OF VERCINGETORIX

THE CELTIC WARLORD: VERCINGETORIX

Vercingetorix, son of Celtillus, was a young nobleman of the Arverni, one of the most powerful tribes of central Gaul. His father had been killed by the tribal authorities for plotting to seize personal power, and in the midst of Caesar's invasions, Vercingetorix tried too: he was more successful. Through his wealth, eloquence and formidable powers of leadership he was chosen to lead the great Gallic revolt against Caesar in 52 BC.

It is unclear why Vercingetorix was appointed supreme commander of the joint rebel forces with such apparent ease, as he seems to have been young and untried. But the choice proved to be an inspired one. His generalship in leading huge and unwieldy armies, both instilling fear and inspiring courage, caused Caesar great difficulties, until Vercingetorix was trapped and besieged at Alesia. After his defeat he languished for several years as a prisoner at Rome, until Caesar had the leisure in 46 BC to stage a formal triumph through the city; Vercingetorix marched in the procession. Caesar did not exercise his famous mercy in the case of his great enemy: after the celebrations Vercingetorix was ritually executed, in accordance with Roman tradition.

In recent centuries Vercingetorix has been rediscovered as a symbol of French national consciousness, and resistance to invaders.

'Vercingetorix summoned a council, at which he stated that he had undertaken that campaign, not for his own ends, but for the communal liberty; and as they must yield to fortune he offered himself to them for whichever course they pleased – to give satisfaction to the Romans by his death, or to deliver him alive.'
Caesar, *Gallic War*, 7,89

THE RESISTANCE of the Belgae, especially the courage of the Eburones under their wily leader Ambiorix, helped to inspire the spirit of resistance which flared up across Gaul in the winter of 53–52 BC. Events at Rome gave the Gauls further reason to hope for success in destroying or expelling the invaders, for tension was growing between Caesar and Pompey (pp. 124–25). Caesar was wintering in northern Italy so that he could stay in touch with affairs at Rome when suddenly almost the whole of Gaul erupted in revolt, trapping the legions in their bases, separated from their general. Hardly any of the Gallic peoples remained loyal to Rome: even the Aedui were persuaded to put their Gallic identity first.

Opening moves

The leader of the revolt was an Arvernian named Vercingetorix. The Arverni had escaped serious damage in Caesar's earlier campaigns: he had thought, wrongly, that they were pacified. Vercingetorix showed himself to be a very capable general, leading his confederate army in some strategically sophisticated operations which stretched Caesar's talents considerably.

Vercingetorix's first move was an invasion of Gallia Transalpina, near Narbonne. A blow against the enemy in his own territory was good for morale, but it was mainly a delaying tactic: Vercingetorix was hoping to engage Caesar in the south while the Roman legions were overrun in central and northern Gaul. Caesar, however, was too quick for him, sweeping into the province and bundling the invaders out. Then, exhibiting his decisiveness and famed speed of movement, Caesar forced a passage through the snow-laden Cevennes to threaten Vercingetorix's homeland. Taken by surprise (the mountains were thought impassable in winter), the Gallic leader

hurried home, only to be bypassed by Caesar marching northwards to join the legions. The first round had gone to Rome.

Blow and counterblow

The war which followed during 52 BC did not consist of pitched battles: Vercingetorix was too cautious. Instead it became a war of sieges like a vast game of chess, as the protagonists attacked each other's supply bases and allied *oppida*. Vercingetorix also executed a scorched earth policy to deny the legions supplies. Caesar's anxiety is reflected by his frequent references to supply difficulties in his *Gallic War*. His main counterblow was an attack on Avaricum (Bourges), capital of the Bituriges. Despite skilled counter-siege warfare by the defenders, who undermined the Roman siege works, Avaricum fell in fire and massacre. Despite this disaster, Vercingetorix's hold on his army did not weaken. Caesar then besieged the Arvernian *oppidum* of Gergovia, but failed to take it due to the strength of its defences, while Vercingetorix's army hovered menacingly on the surrounding hills. At that moment the Aedui defected, leaving Caesar isolated in hostile land without a source of supply. Vercingetorix must have expected Caesar to withdraw into the Roman province, but his opponent took the bolder course, striking north to join up with his lieutenant, Labienus. Nevertheless it was a humiliating

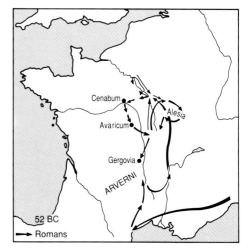

THE GALLIC ORDER OF
BATTLE AT ALESIA
*According to Caesar's account
(Gallic War 7,75), the Gallic
army sent to relieve
Vercingetorix at Alesia in 52
BC was to be composed of the
following tribal contingents:*

Aedui and	
dependants	35,000
Arverni and	
dependants	35,000
Sequani	12,000
Senones	12,000
Bituriges	12,000
Santoni	12,000
Ruteni	12,000
Carnutes	12,000
Bellovaci	10,000
Lemovices	10,000
Pictones	8,000
Turoni	8,000
Parisii	8,000
Helvetii	8,000
Suessiones	5,000
Ambiani	5,000
Mediomatrici	5,000
Petrocorii	5,000
Nervii	5,000
Morini	5,000
Nitiobriges	5,000
Aulerci	
Cenomanni	5,000
Atrebates	4,000
Veliocasses	3,000
Lexovii	3,000
Aulerci	
Eburovices	3,000
Rauraci	2,000
Boii	2,000
Armorican	
states	30,000
Total	281,000

reverse for Caesar, and a great fillip to Gallic morale.

Caesar wins the initiative

On re-establishing contact with the Romans, Vercingetorix risked a cavalry fight, probably hoping that the destruction of the Roman horse would hinder Caesar's ability to monitor Gallic movements and make foraging harder. But the Gauls were routed, and recoiled into the hilltop *oppidum* of Alesia to recover and replenish their cavalry. It was a catastrophic mistake, for Caesar seized his chance and laid seige, beginning the final, epic struggle for the control of Gaul.

The siege of Alesia

Caesar's detailed description of the siegeworks at Alesia was verified by excavations at the site during the nineteenth century. In a month, within an outer rampart some 13 miles (22 km) long, Caesar's army built several defended camps, and a continuous inner wall, strengthened with wooden towers and fronted by ditches and traps. The defenders soon began to starve. The

last hope of the besieged Gauls came in the form of an enormous relief force, almost a quarter of a million strong (compared with Caesar's army of no more than 50,000 men). For days the Gallic forces vainly battered the Roman positions, suffering huge casualties, but they eventually gave up and dispersed. Left without hope, Vercingetorix surrendered.

Casualties and plunder

Plutarch recorded that a million men died during the Gallic wars (including the fighting against the British and Germans), and a further million were enslaved. Caesar left Gaul at peace, but it has been justly observed that it was the quiet of the cemetery. The land was devastated and stripped of its gold – this financed Caesar's bid for power at Rome, until his murder in 44 BC.

Caesar's conquest of Gaul was greeted with enthusiasm at Rome: no doubt the lingering *terror Gallicus* overcame any qualms about Caesar's naked aggression. With the emperor Augustus' later annexation of the Alpine tribes, Gallic independence was gone forever.

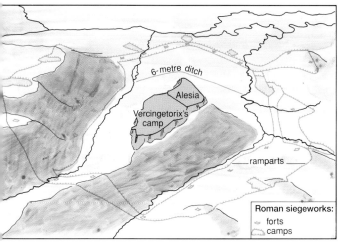

(Far left) Caesar's movements during the Gallic revolt.

The siege at Alesia. (Top) A section of the Roman siegeworks, reconstructed at Beaune, France. The original rampart was built of turf, earth and timber. Pit-traps, ditches, and other obstacles were designed to disrupt any attempt to break through, while attackers would be exposed to a hail of arrows, stones and catapults from the rampart and towers. (Left) The layout of Caesar's encampments, which trapped Vercingetorix's army.

In the event the Bellovaci did not send their full contingent, but if Caesar's figures are to be believed, he faced a total Gallic strength of about 350,000 men, including the trapped army which was fighting to escape. It is remarkable testimony both to the scale of Gallic manpower and to the battlefield superiority of the vastly outnumbered Roman legions.

BRITAIN FROM CAESAR TO HADRIAN

'We, the most distant dwellers upon earth, the last of the free, have been shielded till today by our very remoteness and by the obscurity in which it has shrouded our name. Now, the farthest bounds of Britain lie open to our enemies ... Pillagers of the world, [the Romans] have exhausted the land by their indiscriminate plunder, and now they ransack the sea ... To robbery they give the lying name of "government"; they create a desolation and call it peace.'

Imaginary speech of Calgacus (general of the Britons at Mons Graupius in AD 84), Tacitus, *Agricola*, 30

LATE IN THE SUMMER of 55 BC Caesar led an expedition to Britain in reprisal for British aid to the Gauls, but equally to test Roman public opinion regarding further operations, this time across the Channel. It caused great excitement in Rome and added further to Caesar's prestige, although it was militarily ineffective and nearly cost him his fleet in a storm. Caesar repeated the exercise on a greater scale in 54 BC, and this time penetrated into the interior, encountering fierce resistance from a coalition under Cassivellaunus, apparently a tribal ruler from the south Midlands. Despite effective guerrilla resistance and skilful use of chariotry which hampered Caesar's reconnaissance patrols, Cassivellaunus' stronghold was betrayed and he had to sue for peace. Anxious to leave as the bad weather of autumn approached, Caesar demanded hostages and tribute and imposed an agreement that Cassivellaunus would not attack the Trinovantes on his eastern border – a tribe that had sued for Roman protection.

After Caesar

When Caesar departed it may have appeared that permanent occupation was imminent, yet it was almost a century before the legions returned. Henceforth Britain was on the fringes of the empire which now stretched to Boulogne, and there were extensive cross-Channel contacts which we may expect ranged from the personal to the diplomatic. Besides trading links there must still have been family and tribal ties (for example Commius, king of the Gallic Atrebates, established himself in Britain, and surely maintained contacts with Gaul). The continental fashion for cremation burial was adopted in Britain from this period (p. 103). Political contacts were perhaps intermittent, especially during the civil wars before and after Caesar's assassination in 44 BC. Rome nevertheless maintained some links with the British petty dynasts, several of whom fled to seek imperial assistance in their internal squabbles, and Britons are recorded conducting sacrifices in Rome.

With the return of peace in the empire after the Battle of Actium in 31 BC, Britain was high on the list of targets for further expansion. Augustus, the first emperor, considered invasion several times, but devoted most of his energies to the abortive conquest of Germany. When this ended in military disaster in AD 9, the ageing emperor turned his back on conquest, and decreed that the existing frontiers should be maintained, a policy followed by Tiberius who became emperor in AD 14.

The reign of Cunobelinus

The leading state in southern Britain between Caesar's invasions and Claudius' conquest in AD 43 was the kingdom of the Catuvellauni, which seems to have been growing in power, most notably by the incorporation of the Trinovantes. During the AD 10s the Trinovantes were ruled by the Catuvellaunian prince Cunobelinus (Shakespeare's Cymbeline). Cunobelinus

The political geography of Britain on the eve of Roman invasion. The Catuvellauni dominated the southern Midlands, and effectively absorbed the Trinovantes. Much of their wealth derived from lucrative trade with Roman Gaul, and probably from supplying the imperial garrisons along the Rhine. Some of the developing towns or oppida are also shown.

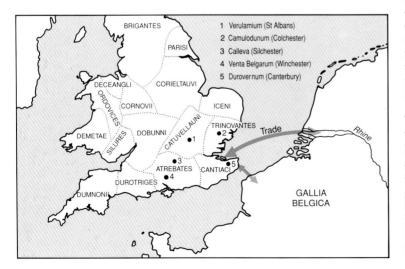

1 Verulamium (St Albans)
2 Camulodunum (Colchester)
3 Calleva (Silchester)
4 Venta Belgarum (Winchester)
5 Durovernum (Canterbury)

BRIGANTES
PARISI
DECEANGLI
CORIELTAUVI
ORDOVICES
CORNOVII
ICENI
DEMETAE
SILURES
DOBUNNI
CATUVELLAUNI
TRINOVANTES
Trade
Rhine
ATREBATES
CANTIACI
DUROTRIGES
DUMNONII
GALLIA BELGICA

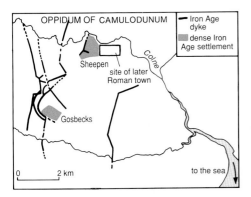

(Above) Latin graffiti on pots at Braughing, including the name Graecus, suggest the presence in Britain of Italian or Gallo-Roman traders before the conquest.

(Left) The sprawling oppidum of Camulodunum.

(Above) Roman-style coin of Cunobelinus.

later succeeded to the rule of all Catuvellaunian territory, although he continued to be based at the old Trinovantian centre at Camulodunum (Colchester) – close to the Thames estuary and hence good cross-Channel communications with Gaul in general, and Belgica and the Rhine in particular. One major source of Catuvellaunian wealth and power may have been control of continental trade, for a major new market had appeared in the Low Countries: the Roman army. The geographer Strabo records the importance of British exports, probably for Roman garrisons on the Rhine. Significantly, besides hunting dogs and slaves, he mentions cattle, hides, and grain: agricultural produce suitable for an army. In Roman times, it was easier to move bulk goods by water from Britain than overland from central Gaul.

The Britons were evidently affected by this long-term exposure to Roman culture. Imported Roman pottery has been discovered at their settlements, Roman amphorae and metal vessels have been found in their graves, and inscriptions in Latin letters appear on tribal coinages. Contacts with Romanized kin in Belgica may also have brought familiarity with Roman ways. This trend towards what may be termed proto-Romanization parallels the situation in central Gaul a century earlier, and it must surely have been a factor in the rapid and relatively successful integration of the tribes of southern Britain into the Roman empire after AD 43.

Oppida in Britain

Southern Britain was part of that wide swathe of Celtic Europe which saw the appearance of oppida, one symptom of a deeper restructuring involving the appearance of centralized states. After Caesar,

most of the southern British tribes developed proto-towns e.g. at Verulamium (St Albans, also in Catuvellaunian territory), Silchester, Chichester, Winchester and others. These British oppida were somewhat different from their continental counterparts, being less regularly organized and less densely occupied. As in Gaul, Rome had at least a catalytic role in the widespread development of British oppida.

Collapse of the status quo

It appears that during the first decades AD, cross-Channel relations were basically friendly, especially between Rome and the

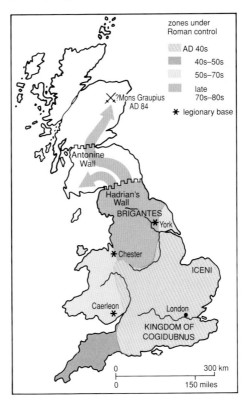

(Left) The course of conquest. The British tribes were absorbed piecemeal, some retaining a degree of autonomy for a while as nominal allies or dependent 'client kingdoms', freeing troops for further conquests. For Claudius, the venture was a success, providing him with the military prestige he desperately needed. He exploited it to the full, as this gold coin testifies (above). It depicts a triumphal arch built to celebrate the victory.

THE BRITISH STRONGHOLD AT MAIDEN CASTLE

Archaeological evidence of the actual conquest is seen no more dramatically than at the most spectacular hillfort in England, Maiden Castle in Dorset. The future Roman emperor Vespasian is recorded to have attacked twenty 'towns', presumably hillforts, in and around the territory of the Durotriges – probably under orders from the emperor Claudius (above). Maiden Castle appears to have been one of these, according to the famous excavations by Sir Mortimer Wheeler in 1934– 37. To Wheeler, the clearest traces of the Roman assault were the hastily-buried bodies bearing weapon wounds in the so-called 'war-cemetery'. Ten of these had sword-cuts to the skull: one still had a javelin-

head in his spine. Today the evidence does not look quite so clear-cut: some of the wounds showed signs of healing, indicating no hasty battlefield clearance, but more formal use of an established cemetery on the spot. Similarly, the substantial traces of burning around the entrance to the for

are now thought to result from long-term industrial activity rather than a Roman assault. Nevertheless it is clear that a number of people died violent deaths at or near the site around the time of the conquest, and an assault by Vespasian's troops remains likely.

Maiden Castle was later abandoned, probably eclipsed by the new Roman town of Durnovaria nearby. However, the impressive earthworks still dominate the landscape, and their significance was not forgotten: in later Roman times, a small pagan temple was constructed on the site.

Catuvellauni under Cunobelinus. However, on his death in AD 40–41, a struggle for power between three of his sons, Caratacus, Togodumnus and Adminius, led to Adminius' flight to Rome. Tiberius had recently been succeeded by the unstable Gaius Caligula, who craved military adventures. Caligula set his sights on Britain. In the event, his planned invasion ended in farce on the beaches of Gaul (the garbled accounts suggest disaffection in the legions). But the abortive attempt indicates that the long

status quo between Britain and Rome had ended.

The Claudian invasion

In the summer of AD 43, a massive invasion force was dispatched across the English Channel on the orders of the new emperor, Claudius. It achieved tactical surprise: the Britons had been forewarned of an assault but, after news of a mutiny in the invasion force, had assumed the danger had passed and dispersed to their homes.

Hadrian's Wall, looking eastwards towards the fort of Housesteads (behind the trees). This spectacular monument runs for 76 Roman miles (113 km), from sea to sea. It was just one part of a deep defensive zone, and was not designed to withstand major attacks; these would have been tackled in the field. Instead, it served as a visual expression of Roman military power, and (rather like the Berlin Wall) also controlled movement and communication between the Roman province and the unconquered lands to the north. Yet, for all its grandeur, it was a manifest admission of the Roman failure to complete the conquest of the island.

THE CAPTURE OF CARATACUS

Resistance to the Romans was led in AD 43 by the Catuvellaunian princes Caratacus and Togodumnus, sons of Cunobelinus. Togodumnus died in the fighting, but his brother fought on for nine years as war-leader of the Welsh tribes. He was finally betrayed by Queen Cartimandua in AD 52, and sent to Claudius in Rome. He pleaded for his life: 'Had my lineage and my rank been matched by my moderation in success, I should have entered this city rather as a friend than as a captive; nor would you have scorned to admit to a peaceful league a king sprung from many famous ancestors and holding sway over many peoples ... I had horses and men, arms and riches: what wonder if I lost them with a pang? For if you would rule the world, does it follow that the world must welcome servitude?' (Tacitus, Annals 12,27).

Unusually (and shrewdly on the part of Claudius), he was spared, becoming a living monument to the emperor's triumph.

The Roman forces engaged a hastily reassembled tribal coalition in a hard-fought two-day battle at an unnamed river before breaking through to the Thames. Here they awaited the arrival of Claudius, who nominally commanded the legions at the capture of Camulodunum (Colchester). He then departed, leaving instructions for further advance and the establishment of a new province.

The immediate reason for the invasion had nothing to do with Britain, although the flight to Rome of an Atrebatic prince, Verica, provided the pretext necessary to convince Roman public opinion. The main motive was that Claudius desperately needed the prestige of a military victory. He had not been a popular choice for the throne, especially among the Senate, and the army did not know him: although he was a member of Augustus' family, physical handicap had kept him out of public life. Claudius thus seized the opportunity to win army support.

FROM HILLFORT TO PRINCELY VILLA

At Bagendon, in the Gloucestershire Cotswolds, massive earthworks define the entry to a valley once thought to hold an oppidum of the Dobunni, whose lands stretched from Wiltshire across the Severn Valley. Archaeologists now believe the earthworks may have been merely the outer façade of the true heart of the complex which lay further up the valley at the small hillfort known as The Ditches. Covering some 10 acres (4 ha), the fort was founded in the first century BC, and elaborated with a second ditch in the first century AD. The presence of Gallic pottery, Roman amphorae and evidence for gold coin production suggest that this was an important place, especially in the conquest period, when the Dobunni were friendly with Rome and close to the active frontier in Wales. Probably between AD 45 and

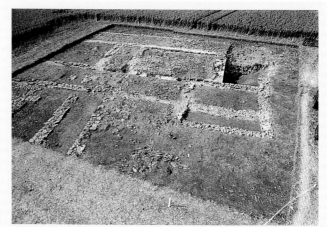

55 the defences were slighted, and then or immediately afterwards a plain Roman villa was constructed in the centre of the enclosure. This building is remarkably early (most Cotswold villas date to a century or more later), and in a very un-Roman location on a draughty hilltop, rather than in the shelter of the valley below. The best explanation for these anomalies is that we see here

the residence of a British noble, perhaps a prince of the Dobunni, who – in demolishing the Iron Age earthworks and building a villa – is exchanging Celtic cultural symbols for Roman. The Romanization of the aristocracy is well attested in Gaul, and seems also to have occurred in Britain.

But what, then, of Bagendon? Perhaps the best

comparison is to be made not with the urban oppida to the east, but with the royal sites of Ireland (pp. 156–57). According to this scenario, the valley below the hillfort may indeed have been an important centre for the Dobunni, but it was only seasonally occupied – when people gathered together for religious festivals, markets and political assemblies.

BRITISH CLIMATE THROUGH ROMAN EYES

'Most of the island is flat and overgrown with forests, although many of the districts are hilly ... Their weather is more rainy than snowy; and on the days of clear sky fog prevails so long a time that throughout a whole day the sun is to be seen for only about three or four hours round about midday ...'
Strabo 4,5,1

PRE-CONQUEST CONTACTS

'[Caesar] brought back hostages, slaves, and quantities of booty. At present, some of the chieftains there, after procuring the friendship of Caesar Augustus by sending embassies and by paying court to him, have not only dedicated offerings in the Capitolium, but have also managed to make the whole island virtually Roman property.'
Strabo 4,5,3

The strategy of conquest

After initial resistance, the British tribes were overcome piecemeal by an army of about 40,000 men. By AD 50, the tribes of the south and the Midlands were under Roman control, although some – notably the groups under King Cogidubnus (presumed successor to Verica), and then the Iceni under Prasutagus and the Brigantes under Queen Cartimandua (p. 67) – were nominally independent allies.

Rome appears to have developed a broad but effective strategy in the conquest of the hardier tribes of the western and northern uplands. By quickly advancing to the Bristol Channel at Gloucester and the sea in the Liverpool area, Rome divided the opposition into three blocs: the north, Wales and the west country. The southwest was quickly absorbed in the 40s and early 50s, after which the Romans focused on conquering the tribes of Wales. But first (to avoid war on two fronts), they diplomatically neutralized the dangerous northern power of the Brigantes under Queen Cartimandua, securing the right flank.

After years of bitter fighting in Wales, Roman plans were disrupted by the terrible

Boudican revolt in East Anglia of AD 60 or 61 (p. 139), and then by civil war among the Brigantes. The Romans intervened with a series of rapid attacks (AD 71–73), but no garrison was yet installed in the north: Wales remained top priority, and was finally subdued by the governor Agricola, who then turned north, carrying Roman arms far into Scotland. His victory over the Caledonian tribes at Mons Graupius in AD 84 was the high tide of conquest. There were insufficient troops to hold all the territory, and a slow withdrawal presaged the establishment of a deep zone of garrisons, stretching from the legionary bases of York and Chester into southern Scotland. During the 120s under Hadrian the famous stone wall was built along the Tyne and Solway valleys, but Roman outposts remained to the north. There were further attempts to advance into Scotland – notably under Antoninus Pius, whose generals constructed the short-lived Antonine Wall on the Forth-Clyde line (roughly AD 140s–160s) – but ultimately Rome was unable to complete the conquest of Britain, and Hadrian's Wall became the approximate limit of empire.

WHY NOT SCOTLAND OR IRELAND?

'Ireland, lying between Britain and Spain, and easily accessible also from the Gallic sea, might serve as a very valuable link between the provinces ... I have often heard Agricola say that Ireland could be reduced and held by a single legion with a fair-sized force of auxiliaries: and that it would be easier to hold Britain if it were completely surrounded by Roman armies, so that liberty was banished from its sight.'

Tacitus, Agricola, 24

MOST OF THE CELTIC LANDS had been absorbed by Rome by the second century AD – but not all of them. Caledonia remained outside the empire, and Roman arms were never carried to Ireland at all. This is surprising, because the Romans clearly knew that Britain would be much more easily held if 'liberty was banished from its sight'. Had the necessary force been applied to complete the conquest of Britain, the process of pacification and Romanization would have freed troops to conquer Ireland. Ultimately, the absorption and successful Romanization of all the British Isles would have liberated huge resources for service on the continent: in the mid-second century AD, over 50,000 troops – one eighth of the entire armed strength of Rome – were tied down in Britain. Even these were apparently insufficient to hold the province and quell the Highlands; yet more would have been needed to conquer Ireland, at least for a few decades. They never became available, due to growing pressures on other frontiers.

The prerequisites of conquest

Rome was caught in a trap. She had reached the limit of her ability to expand. She could only easily absorb societies with a good agricultural base and centralized political institutions. Such societies were more vulnerable to attack, could support invading armies, and were more easily Romanized. Sparsely peopled, loosely organized lands, especially those with difficult terrain, were much tougher to swallow. This distinction can be seen within Britain, where the good lands and centralized states of the south were overrun in two or three years, whereas mountainous Wales and Brigantia took a generation to absorb. It may be that western

and northern Britain and Ireland formed a cultural zone not amenable to conquest at the time. Rome ran out of suitable societies to conquer, and the continuous expansion of her manpower, economy and military resources petered out in the highlands of Scotland, the African deserts, the Asian steppe, and the forests of Germany. She switched permanently on to the defensive, and thereafter her armies were too busy defending the major frontiers to complete the conquest of Celtica.

Had Rome not run out of military steam, the Celtic languages might have become completely extinct, and the ethnic identity of the Celts lost as thoroughly as that of the Etruscans.

Detail of an inlay from a bronze statue found at Volubilis, Morocco. It shows a trophy (a stand bearing captured weapons) flanked by two captives. The one on the left probably represents a Caledonian, cloaked, barechested, and wearing chequered trews. It perhaps alludes to one of the various Roman campaigns in Scotland, all of which ultimately failed to absorb the region into the Roman world.

THE ROMANIZATION OF GAUL AND BRITAIN

The following verses were sung everywhere:
'Caesar led the Gauls in triumph,
led them to the senate house,
then the Gauls took off their breeches,
and put on the laticlave* ...'
The senator's toga, with a broad purple stripe.
Suetonius, *Caesar*, 80,2

The splendid temple of Augustus and Livia at Vienne, France. It is in the Corinthian order, and stands on a raised podium in Italic style. Dedicated initially to the cult of Rome and Augustus, it manifests the thorough Romanization of Gallia Narbonensis. The extension of the dedication to Augustus' wife Livia followed her deification by Claudius in AD 41.

'*[Caesar] showed equal scorn of traditional precedent by ... admitting to the Senate men of foreign birth, including semi-civilized Gauls, who had been granted the Roman citizenship*'
Suetonius, *Life of Caesar*, 76,3

GAUL WAS INITIALLY SLOW to adopt Roman ways, due no doubt to the diversions of the imperial civil wars, and the time it took to recover from the devastation of conquest – not to mention the strain of paying 400,000 gold pieces annually as tribute.

Yet under Augustus (emperor from 27 BC), Romanization became rapid, at least among the ruling classes. Cities blossomed, especially in the south, and the first real wave of assimilation swept Gallia Comata (newly conquered 'hairy' Gaul).

Traditional ways of gaining and expressing wealth and power – e.g. raiding and military display – were removed: the *pax Romana* forbade private war. Celtic nobles

needed to express their position in new ways. Aspects of *Romanitas* (Roman lifestyle) were already fashionable (pp. 118–19), and presumably many die-hard traditionalists had been eliminated in the conquest. The Roman authorities encouraged the Celts to adopt the ways of the Mediterranean urban aristocracies; the Gallic nobility thus inherited a new cultural mantle: Roman citizenship, Classical learning, art and access to a wider imperial world.

And so Gallic (and later southern British) aristocrats adopted the status symbols of their overlords, favouring fine architecture instead of weapons and gold jewellery; feasting was partly displaced by Roman entertainments. But the outwardly Classical forms may be deceptive: in Gaul and Britain, for instance, theatres are often found adjacent to temples associated with native Celtic cults. Perhaps these Romanized structures were simply built to accommodate continuing Celtic social gatherings and religious activities.

The Gauls and the House of Augustus

The Gauls probably saw Julius Caesar as their supreme chief, by right of war. The allegiance to Caesar of leading aristocrats from favoured states such as the Aedui, Arverni and Remi (and through their clientage networks the rest of the Gallic states) was probably the earliest mechanism of imperial social control in Gaul. This personal connection was apparently inherited and understood by Caesar's adopted son, Augustus. He made several extended visits to Gaul, and also sent imperial princes – including his heir designate, Marcus Agrippa, who effectively acted as viceroy.

Demilitarization and civil development

Augustus was intent on conquering Germany, and in the 10s BC moved the forces stationed in Gaul to the frontier with Germany, thus bringing to an end the years of military government in the interior of Gaul. This aided the development of local government, returned limited power to strictly supervised aristocracies, who, by

(Right) Augustus, the first Roman emperor, was an astute politician who well understood how to deal with the disparate peoples of a world empire, not least the Gauls. This statue, from Prima Porta near Rome, is a masterpiece of propaganda, portraying him as a militarily strong but benign world ruler. He claimed divine ancestry, and was worshipped in the provinces as a god.

(Below) The famous Pont du Gard carries an aqueduct across the Gardon gorge. This spectacular structure, 160 ft (50 m) high, is but one part of a 30-mile (50-km) channel which wound along the contours of the Cevennes from the source at Uzès, carrying over 20,000 tons of water a day to the burgeoning Gallo-Roman city of Nemausus (Nîmes, France). The ambition of the scheme well represents the confidence and wealth of early imperial Gaul.

UP IN ARMS: THE GAULS REBEL

In AD *21, revolt broke out in Gaul. The causes were apparently corrupt government, high taxes and aristocratic debt – some nobles had probably been spending beyond their means on the new Roman lifestyle. The main leaders were two very Romanized Gauls, Julius Florus (a Treveran) and Julius Sacrovir (an Aeduan), both Roman citizens and commanders of Gallic auxiliaries. Each tried to seize power in his own state. Florus was quickly rejected by the Treveri, and although Sacrovir took the new Aeduan capital of Augustodunum, he too was rapidly defeated by the legions. Both killed themselves.*

Later in the century Julius Vindex became a governor, probably of Lugdunensis. Claiming descent from Aquitanian kings, he was the son of one of Claudius' Gallic senators. In AD *68 he revolted*

against Nero. Significantly, he behaved in a thoroughly Roman manner: he wanted a better emperor, not a free Gaul. Equally significantly, the legions on the Rhine reacted as though he were a Gallic rebel, and smashed him.

Over the following three years imperial civil wars prompted further risings, in connection with the revolt of the Batavian king, Civilis, in what is now Holland. Gallic nobles again tried to take over their civitates, and Civilis declared an 'empire of the Gauls', but most of Gaul was unenthusiastic. This revolt, also, was crushed in AD *70.*

The course of these revolts indicates that there was no strong movement for independence: Florus and Sacrovir met with very limited support, and most civitates did not come out for Vindex, or Civilis' Imperium Galliarum.

Indeed, the very name 'empire of the Gauls' suggests that Roman ideas about political organization and expression were generally accepted. Gaul was at least acquiescent, and much of the nobility was enthusiastic about the imperial

order. However, the fate of Vindex shows how strong Roman fears of Gallic power continued to be, even a century after the conquest. Captured Gaulish arms from the arch at Orange, southern France, are pictured above.

Detail from the Altar of Peace at Rome, depicting the imperial family at a sacrifice. The child with a torc may be a fostered Gallic prince.

serving as magistrates, acquired Roman citizenship. The seal was put on the new order on 1 August, 12 BC when the imperial prince Drusus dedicated the Altar to Rome and Augustus at the new capital of Lugdunum (Lyon), the natural gateway from the Rhône Valley to the interior.

Within a generation, Gallic aristocrats were not only Roman citizens, but members of the equestrian order (the second rank of Roman citizens). The speed of this assimilation is no surprise: some nobles, on being granted Roman citizenship, were already wealthy enough (i.e. owned property worth 400,000 sesterces or more) to qualify for equestrian rank. Caesar even appointed some Gauls from Gallia Transalpina as senators. Strong underlying traditions and the strain of adapting did lead occasionally to revolt (see box above), but remarkably rarely.

The Three Gauls, the Germanies and Britain

Gallia Comata was organized into three provinces in about 27 BC. The new province of Gallia Belgica had some *civitates* (see below) added to it from Caesar's Gallia Celtica; Aquitania was also greatly

increased, to include all tribes south of the Loire; the rest of Celtica was renamed Gallia Lugdunensis, after the new capital at Lugdunum. (The 'fourth Gaul', the old province of Gallia Transalpina, was renamed Gallia Narbonensis after its capital, Narbo.)

The three new provinces were roughly equal in size, and it is no accident that three especially powerful Gallic states, the Arverni, Aedui and Sequani, were allotted to separate provinces. Nevertheless, the Romans did foster some sense of Gallic unity in the imperial cult at Lugdunum (see p. 138).

There were later adjustments, especially along the Rhine, where in the AD 80s the military zone was reorganized into the two provinces of Upper and Lower Germany. While the Germanies were being organized, Roman expansion in Britain also reached its greatest extent (p. 132). The first capital had been at the old *oppidum* of Camulodunum (Colchester), site of a great temple of the imperial cult which echoed that at Lyon. However, the administration was soon relocated to the new site of Londinium, at a major junction of river- and seaways with the military road network.

The framework of Romanization

Initially the Celtic lands posed a problem for the Roman administration, for they did not consist of the city states with which Roman government was designed to deal (see box, right). Augustus imposed a pragmatic solution in Gaul: the tribal units were already described in Latin as *civitates*, which can mean both city and state (the two being inextricably linked in Roman eyes), and they were treated as though each was a city – even though they were essentially rural, and mostly far larger in area and more populous than Mediterranean city states. The same approach was adopted in Britain.

Romanization was undoubtedly helped by the fact that many tribes were urbanizing, and some were already governed by elected magistrates (p. 120). It was then relatively easy to relabel existing institutions in Roman ways, to remodel tribal councils into new city councils, while (in many of the *civitates*) the prize of Roman citizenship – with its status, tax exemptions and political opportunities – was offered to those who took on magistracies.

Map of the Gallic provinces.

The change from Gallic to Roman administrative structures was rapid, citizenship leading to adoption of Roman personal names among the aristocracy; but the transformation was uneven and piecemeal. Old institutions, such as the Vergobret of the Aedui, survived for some time, while the curious post of *magister pagi* ('master of the pagus', a subtribe or district) makes an appearance in some areas. Presumably a

---

HOW ROMAN WAS ROMAN? EVOLVING AESTHETICS

Gaul and Britain are often measured against the material culture of Italy. Britain in particular is often seen to fall far short of 'standards' set in Italy: its towns are small and relatively poor, inscriptions are rare, and Romano-British art often looks naïve in comparison with the sophistication of Rome.

But such comparisons are based on a largely false idea of what constituted Roman taste at the time. We tend to assume that the Romans all subscribed to Classical Greek conceptions of artistic taste and proportion: in reality, this was confined to a small élite with the education and wealth to pursue it. Even in Roman Italy, much art was far simpler, 'cruder' or more 'primitive' than the select pieces which graced the homes of the rich – or today's museums. Yet this more popular art is just as typically Roman. Indeed, by AD 300 artistic taste even among

wealthy Italians was moving away from that of the Greek world, eventually to become the stylized aesthetic of the medieval Romanesque.

We thus see the art of Roman Britain as a reinterpretation of a range of Italian and Gaulish artistic tastes. The people commissioning it were presumably quite happy with

it: for them, this was Roman art. Indeed, by the latter days of empire, the definition of 'Roman' was determined as much by the citizens of Britain, Gaul and the other provinces as it was by Italians.

Water-nymphs from High Rochester fort, Northumberland.

Part of a Roman bathhouse under excavation at Huggin Hill in the City of London in 1988. The building was demolished in antiquity, leaving only the foundations of the walls, and the bases of the tile stacks which supported the raised floor. The hot gases from the fire circulated between the stacks, warming the floors and watertanks above. By comparison with many Gaulish cities, even the provincial capital of Britain was relatively undistinguished in terms of size and monumental buildings. Nevertheless it possessed a very large forum, and a busy harbour.

The Mediterranean and Celtic worlds met at Lugdunum (Lyon). On the high ground around the Gallic shrine to Lug, an imperial palace, temples and theatres were built, while at Condate (the Confluence, to the right of the picture) the federal shrine of the Gauls was established, dedicated to Rome and the emperor, complete with an enormous altar and oval amphitheatre. On the low ground between the river courses developed the river port, attracting traders from all over the empire. Lyon became a highly cosmopolitan city.

response to the subdivided structure of the Gallic states, the post is unique to Gaul; the Roman system clearly needed a good deal of adaptation to fit local conditions. We know less about the process in Britain, but we can nevertheless discern a similar general pattern.

The new local administrative structures in Gaul and Britain were very much a façade, at least at first, simply a new set of labels and symbols for existing institutions. The underlying patterns of society were apparently little changed for many generations to come. The façade was especially flimsy in Britain, partly because it was poorer than Gaul and Romanization had begun several generations later here. The huge Roman garrison stationed in Britain (p. 133) imposed martial law on local areas, which probably inhibited civil development there – a problem not suffered in most of Gaul.

The growth of Classical-style cities

Continuity from the Iron Age past into the new Romanized societies is emphasized by the fact that many of the finest cities of Gaul and Britain grew directly from *oppida* (Toulouse, Orleans, Paris, Bourges, Colchester, Silchester, Verulamium). Bibracte was succeeded by a new site on ground more suitable for a Classical city. It was called Augustodunum (Autun), itself an interesting hybrid Romano-Celtic name, 'stronghold of Augustus'.

In Britain, some early Roman towns acquired distinctly unRoman-looking earth bank 'defences' in the first century; most towns featured these earthworks by the later second century. Do they in fact represent the survival of the ancient British tradition of surrounding their most important sites with banks?

The evolution of 'barbarian' tribe to Romanized city state was not necessarily quick and easy everywhere. The Roman administration, more rigorously policed by the emperors than it had been under the republic, was often still corrupt and brutal. Perhaps the most difficult aspect for the Celtic aristocracies to adjust to was the removal of the right to bear and use arms in private war, hitherto the mark of free manhood. This was largely offset, however, by the possibility of military service.

Gauls in the army

A major factor in the success of Romanization was undoubtedly the demand for soldiers for the Roman army, which young Gallic nobles gladly fulfilled. Restless spirits were able to pursue adventure and fortune in the wars of Augustus and his dynasty; the conquered Gauls probably regarded the Roman emperors as their overlords, who consequently had every right to demand military service. Mercenary service was also a time-honoured Celtic tradition, so serving the emperor for pay was no affront to Gallic honour. Early auxiliary regiments were often little more than the armed retinue of particular Gallic princes such as the Treveran Julius Indus, whose squadron developed into the regular cavalry unit, the *ala Indiana*.

During military service, Celtic princes were immersed in Roman culture; assimilation was further enhanced once they were discharged, for then they acquired Roman citizenship. Most such nobles took the imperial family name of Julius, resulting in hybrid names such as Julius Togirix.

BOUDICA'S REVOLT

'Boudica rode up to each tribe in a chariot with her daughters in front of her. "We British", she cried, "are used to women commanders in war. But it is not as the descendant of mighty ancestors that I fight now, avenging lost kingdom and wealth; rather as one of the people, avenging lost liberty, scourging, and violation of my daughters ... But the gods are at hand with a just revenge ... Think of the number of our troops, think of why you fight – and you must either win on this battlefield or die. That is my resolve, and I am a woman; men may live and be slaves."'

Tacitus, imagining a speech of Boudica
(Boadicea), *Annals*, 14,35

THE REVOLT of the East Anglian Iceni in AD 60 or (more probably) 61 was one of the greatest internal shocks the Roman empire faced in the first century AD. Prasutagus of the Iceni had allied with the Romans, and remained a nominally independent client king. When he died, according to contemporary Roman practice the treaty lapsed, and the Iceni were to be absorbed into the province. Prasutagus had named his wife Boudica and his daughters joint heirs with the emperor Nero, apparently in the hope that part of the patrimony would remain with the family.

Bungling to disaster

The Roman procurator's undisciplined staff carried out the 'provincialization' with stunning brutality, raping the princesses and flogging Boudica. These outrages triggered the pent-up fury of the Iceni, and also the Trinovantes (suffering at the hands of Roman veterans, in the new colony at Camulodunum, modern Colchester). Bent on revenge, a huge force of Britons led by Boudica descended on Camulodunum, on the new port of Londinium, and on Verulamium (St Albans), burning and slaughtering in a determined effort to drive out the Romans.

The Roman governor, C. Suetonius Paulinus, was campaigning in north Wales, and the legions were dangerously dispersed. Paulinus marched southeast at top speed, collecting forces as he went. The acting commander of legion II Augusta at Exeter, lost his nerve and refused to march, compounding the peril.

The revolt is crushed

The opposing forces met at an unknown site in the Midlands. As so often, the sheer size of the Celtic force was its undoing: when the front lines recoiled from the determined attacks of the Romans, they were trapped by the wagons at the rear, on which the women and children stood to watch the hoped-for slaughter of the invaders. In the ensuing massacre, 80,000 Britons are said to have died, in addition to the 70,000 Romans and pro-Roman Britons slaughtered by the rebels. Boudica died, probably by her own hand, soon after.

Aftermath

Slaughter was followed by famine, as the governor embarked on savage punitive actions; thousands more perished. But eventually Paulinus was removed (following intervention by the new procurator, Classicianus, p. 140), and subsequent governors pursued a policy of peace-making, encouraging Romanization. Military expansion stopped for a decade.

The story of the revolt is a classic case of crass misgovernment and officials out of control. However, it underlines the general success of Roman administration elsewhere, for overall, such major rebellions were rare.

Boudica and her daughters in a chariot: a romanticized statue group erected in 1902 on the embankment opposite the Houses of Parliament in London. The scythes are merely fantasy.

The course of the revolt. The exact site of the decisive battle is unknown.

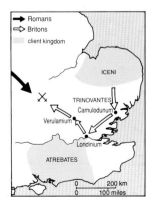

GAULS IN TOGAS

The historian, Pompeius Trogus (lived first century BC), took pride in his descent from the Gallic Vocontii (around modern Vaison-la-Romaine). His grandfather had won Roman citizenship from Pompey the Great – hence the name Pompeius – for service as a cavalry commander in Pompey's campaign against Mithridates of Pontus. His father served Caesar. This family history is a good illustration of how Gallic aristocrats achieved Roman citizenship through service with prominent Romans.

Sextus Afranius Burrus (died AD 62), also a native of Vaison, reached the highest post open to men of equestrian rank: commander of the Praetorian Guard. He and Seneca were joint tutors to Nero.

> *'"If you review all our wars, none was ended in a shorter time than that with the Gauls. Thenceforth there has been an unbroken and loyal peace. Mingled with us as they are now, in their way of life, in their culture, and by intermarriage, let them bring us their gold and wealth rather than keep it in isolation." ... [Claudius'] address was followed by a decree of the senate, and the Aeduans were the first to obtain the right to enter the senate.'*
>
> Tacitus, *Annals* 11,2

CAESAR AND AUGUSTUS offered the Gallic nobility access to the empire's power structure through citizenship, and limited membership of the equestrian order and even the Roman senate. This hastened the process of Romanization, and the remarkable integration of Gallic society into the wider imperial world by AD 70.

Names reveal recent enfranchisement: the new Roman citizens adopted the name of their 'sponsor', for example Pompeius, Cornelius (from the Roman dictator L. Cornelius Sulla), Domitius (from the conqueror of Narbonensis), and of course large numbers of Julii, from Caesar or perhaps Augustus.

Heavily Romanized Gallia Narbonensis produced many notable figures who, judging from their names, were only recently enfranchised, but how Celtic were they?

(Left) A thoroughly Romanized tomb monument of a family of Gaulish Roman citizens who took the name Julius. Glanum, France, 40s BC.

(Below) Tomb of C. Julius Alpinus Classicianus from London – a wealthy Roman equestrian official, almost certainly of Gaulish (probably Treveran) ancestry.

Some examples are fairly clear, for instance Pompeius Trogus (see box). Others could have been of Italian origin from veterans settled as colonists in cities. The senator Valerius Asiaticus, consul in AD 35, came from Vienne, capital of the Allobroges; Domitius Afer, consul in AD 39, was from Nîmes. The Roman colony of Forum Julii (Fréjus) produced the equestrian Cornelius Gallus (69–26 BC), prefect of Egypt, and Gnaeus Julius Agricola, a senator and governor of Britain (p. 132) whose career was recorded by his son-in-law, the historian Cornelius Tacitus. Tacitus, another senator, came from Narbonensis or Gallia Cisalpina.

These thoroughly Romanized southerners, of Celtic origin or not, fitted smoothly into Roman society. The more certainly Celtic newcomers from the three Gauls provoked some xenophobia.

Claudian triumph, Neronian disaster

After the relative neglect of Gallic affairs under Tiberius and Caligula, Claudius (reigned AD 41–54) reverted to a policy of Gallic advancement. Born at Lugdunum (Lyon), Claudius felt particularly close to the Gallic aristocracy, and in AD 48 overcame opposition to elect important Aedui to the senate.

Under Nero (AD 54–68) events conspired to end this remarkable experiment in integration. The revolts of Vindex, and the attempt by the Batavian king Civilis to establish a bogus 'empire of the Gauls', renewed Roman fears about Gallic power (p. 136).

Nero's suicide (and the consequent extinction of the Julio-Claudian house) precipitated the civil wars of AD 69. The victor, Vespasian, crushed Civilis. The new imperial dynasty lacked links of patronage with the Gauls, and recent rebellions in Gaul had made the ruling authorities in Rome highly suspicious of them. Henceforth, there were few senators from Gaul outside Narbonensis. Consequently it is perhaps not surprising that Britain, newly-conquered, never produced any major Roman figure of native origin either, despite the spread of citizenship there.

The Three Gauls and Britain subsequently developed their own particularly local flavours of *Romanitas*, distinct from those of the rest of the empire.

Gaul: powerhouse of the Roman West

The zenith of empire in the second century AD ironically saw the triumph of the provinces, which surpassed Italy as the economic foci of the empire: the new economic centres were Egypt, Syria and western Turkey, Africa, Spain and Gaul. Gaul was perhaps the most spectacular success of all, strategic linchpin of the Roman West, providing communications between Spain, Britain, Italy and the Danube.

Narbonensis was part of the Mediterranean world, virtually an extension of Italy, but the Three Gauls belonged to the northern world and, with the two Germanies and Britain, went much their own way, developing a regional *Romanitas* and becoming a distinct economic and administrative bloc within the empire. Lugdunum was the meeting place of these two worlds. Its name was Celtic, but it was a cosmopolitan Roman city; the Rhineland region, too, was highly Romanized, with many troops garrisoned there, and Claudian colonies at Cologne and Trier.

Gaul developed into a substantial economy, aided by the massive civil and military market on the Rhine. It may be that the extra 2.5 per cent tax Rome levied specifically on trade with Gaul reflects the shift of economic power. It is surely a significant measure of the growth of the northern markets that the manufacturers of the fashionable glossy red 'samian' tableware (pottery also known as *terra sigillata*) based at Arezzo in Italy opened a branch factory at Lugdunum in about 10 BC. La Graufesenque in southern Gaul then took over as the main centre of production until about AD 100, when it was supplanted by new kilns in central Gaul and the Rhineland itself. Since transport costs were high, it is likely that these moves in part reflect shifts of the industry closer to its major markets in the Rhineland. This kind of pottery was nevertheless found all over the western empire: a crate of newly-arrived samian ware from La Graufesenque was buried at Pompeii in the eruption of Vesuvius in AD 79.

Samian production was actually a tiny part of the economy of the Three Gauls, but happens to be archaeologically highly visible. Other industries also developed considerably, for instance glass production in the Rhineland. An increase in industrial manufacture evidently occurred in Britain too, which saw its own short-lived samian production. With the expansion of mineral extraction, and above all the growth of agriculture, the northern provinces witnessed remarkable changes.

(Above) Buying wine from a bar. Note the metal jugs hanging over the counter. Detail from a stone relief, Dijon. Many such depictions, often from tombs, provide important insights into Gallic daily life.

(Left) A jeweller's stall bedecked with bracelets, necklaces, and trays of smaller objects, probably rings (very fashionable in Roman times). Note the typical Gallo-Roman male dress of long tunic and heavy cloak. Funerary relief from Metz.

ROMANO-CELTIC RELIGION IN BRITAIN AND GAUL

'Among the gods, [the Gauls] worship Mercury. There are numerous images of him; they declare him the inventor of all the arts, the guide for every road and journey, and they deem him to have the greatest influence for all money-making and traffic. After him they set Apollo, Mars, Jupiter and Minerva. Of these deities they have almost the same idea as all other nations: Apollo drives away diseases, Minerva supplies the first principles of arts and crafts, Jupiter holds the empire of heaven, Mars controls wars.'
Caesar, *Gallic War*, 6,17

ONE HALLMARK of Roman imperialism was the respect the conquerors manifested towards the religions of the vanquished. This was born both of superstition and deliberate policy: the Romans had learned that their subjects could be most effectively integrated by allowing existing society slowly to adapt to Roman rule – it was thus deemed prudent to conciliate both the people and their gods. And from the Celtic point of view, worship was probably one way in which traditional political and social groups could still express themselves without breaching Roman law. The Romans arrived with not only their own gods but a variety of exotic deities which had spread along the arteries of empire from other provinces. The process of identifying Roman gods with local ones (the

(Above) The remains of a huge Romano-Celtic temple, the so-called Temple of Janus, at Augustodunum (Autun), France. This lofty brick and concrete structure was the central tower-like shrine room of a building similar in form to the small Romano-Celtic temple reconstructed at Beaune, France (right). Note the ambulatory – which may sometimes have had solid walls or a half-height wall and dwarf columns – around the central shrine. Most such temples, often in clusters, were of this more modest size.

so-called *interpretatio Romana*) is widely attested in inscriptions. The result was a polytheism of bewildering complexity, which is perhaps at its richest in Gaul.

There were exceptions to this picture of tolerance and religious interplay, however, and one of the most striking was the assault on Druidism.

Priesthoods and the suppression of Druidism

Poorly documented attempts were made by Augustus, Tiberius and Claudius to eradicate the Druids, ostensibly because of their association with human sacrifice, but more probably arising from the fear that such a supratribal organization might foment rebellion. This, and the equally infamous clashes with Judaism and persecutions of the Christians, arose from political concerns as much as religious scruples. How effective the suppression was is unclear: people calling themselves Druids – and Druidesses – appear later, but this may simply have been the adoption of an evocative name by self-styled priests.

However, the numerous cults of Roman times needed priests, and many were served by Roman-style part-time officiants, largely drawn from the local privileged classes. Such services were both a social duty and a mark of status, part of the culture of public service which formed the prestige system of the Roman empire. (Certain priesthoods were even reserved for prosperous ex-slaves, who could not aspire to magistracies.)

(Above) The native water shrine of the god Glan (at Glanum in southern France) was much embellished with Classical temples. The columns are the remains of a small temple dedicated to the goddess of health by Marcus Agrippa.

(Left) The Celtic horse goddess Epona on a relief from Beaune, France.

(Right) A stone carving of a three-faced god from Soissons, France. The beards consist of ears of wheat. A ram and a cock (both sacred to Mercury) are carved below, suggesting that this strange god was identified with the Roman deity.

(Left) An altar to the Matronae Aufaniae, a triad of mother goddesses peculiar to Roman Germany. It was set up by Quettius Severus, a magistrate in Cologne. The high quality of the carving and the prominence of the dedicator reveal the reverence shown for native cults, even by the rich.

Rome also introduced oriental cults to the Celtic lands, including Christianity. (Right) A head of the saviour god Mithras, from a Mithraic temple excavated in London.

coming Romans were identifying Celtic gods with their own, the Gauls and Britons reciprocated, continuing to worship Celtic gods but in socially and politically fashionable Roman ways. The Gauls worshipped a vast spectrum of deities, from the purely Roman such as the cult of Rome and the emperor, to the purely Celtic, e.g. the antlered Cernunnos. Some gods were worshipped under double-barrelled Romano-Celtic names (e.g. Mars Toutatis, Apollo Belenos, Sulis Minerva), but others, for instance Epona the horse-goddess, had no equivalent Classical deity. Reliefs such as those depicting the Three Mothers, and the many figurines of 'Venus' in Gaul and Britain, may represent significant aspects of popular religion which did not receive the lavish architectural investment of other cults, but which may nonetheless have been very important to major sections of the population, perhaps especially to women.

Places of worship

The conquest of Gaul and Britain reinforced the existing trends towards building shrines to the gods, and making anthropomorphic representations of deities. The very construction of masonry houses for the deities itself implies the adoption of Classical ideas, art and technology. Celtic artisans increasingly sculpted their shrines and statues of gods from stone instead of wood, while many other aspects of Classical religious expression, such as the use of stone altars and the cutting of inscriptions, were widely adopted. Yet it is at many temple sites that the hybrid nature of Romano-Celtic culture is most readily apparent, for a new form of temple evolved,

LEAD CURSE
'A memorandum to the god Mercury from Saturnina a woman concerning the linen cloth she has lost. Let him who stole it not have rest until he brings the aforesaid thing to the aforesaid temple, whether he be man or woman, slave or free.

'She gives a third part to the aforesaid god on condition that he exact those things which have been written. A third part from what has been lost is given to the god Silvanus on condition that he exact this, whether the thief is man or woman, slave or free.'
From Uley temple, Gloucestershire

Romano-Celtic religion and the *interpretatio Romana*

Rome brought with her all the gods of the Graeco-Roman pantheon, from the state cults (p. 134) to the long train of minor deities. The Celtic provinces were also recipients of eastern 'mystery' cults, initiation into which offered a more emotionally satisfying religious experience than traditional Roman religion. Christianity reached Gaul in this way. These religions – such as Indo-Persian Mithras, or Egyptian Isis – did not penetrate much beyond the upper and urban classes, which, with the army, were the main foci of Romanization.

Yet despite the arrival of so many foreign cults and the widespread adoption of Roman ways of worship, the underlying Celtic structures remained. While in-

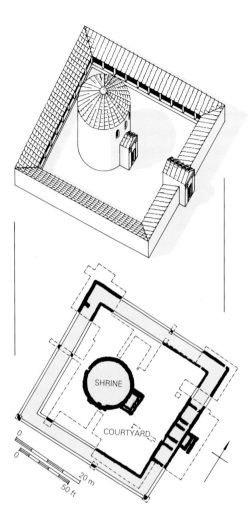

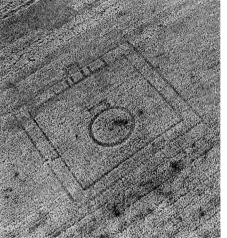

(Left) The grain growing in a field on Hayling Island, off Britain's south coast, reveals the outline of a buried Romano-British temple. The stony foundations stunt the growth of grain along the lines of the walls. Excavations at the site (below) indicated that the elaborate building of the early Roman period overlay a native Iron Age shrine of essentially the same shape. (Far left) Plan and suggested reconstruction of the Roman-period temple.

SHRINE

COURTYARD

0
0
20 m
50 ft

presumably specifically adapted to the different needs of Celtic liturgy but built with varying degrees of Romanization. These Romano-Celtic temples were usually of concentric square or polygonal plan and occur right across Europe, from Britain to Budapest; they are often associated with theatres, both in urban areas (Verulamium) and rural settings (e.g. Gosbecks, near Colchester).

Continuity is detectable at many Iron Age sanctuaries, for example Hayling Island temple in Hampshire, and in Gaul where a Romano-Celtic temple was built at Gournay. Some developed into very elaborate Gallic rural shrine complexes, known as *conciliabula*, as did Ribemont-sur-Ancre. Perhaps such places were community foci for the *pagi*, that is, rural centres for the subunits of the *civitates*.

THE COUNTRYSIDE: CONTINUITY, CHANGE AND CONFLICT

(Below) The Gauls ingeniously invented the vallus *or harvesting machine, depicted here on a stone relief. It seems to have been used for a considerable period, but only in Gallia Belgica.*

'From cereals are also made beverages: zythum in Egypt, caelia and cerea in Spain, cervisia and several other kinds in Gaul and in other provinces; the froth from these is used by women as a cosmetic for the face.'
Pliny, *Natural History*, 22,82

THE CHANGED FACE of the landscape in much of Gaul and Britain – the roads and cities, the villas with mosaics and other luxurious appointments of the Classical good life – has led to a widespread assumption that Rome revolutionized agricultural techniques in the Celtic lands. Modern research shows that this is much exaggerated. Villas, for instance, do not represent a major influx of immigrant 'improving' landowners from Italy. Instead they reflect the growing Classical taste of native landowners, and their increasing willingness – and ability – to invest in Roman-style houses.

Farming regimes

This is not to say that no agricultural innovations took place at all. In Gaul, the Roman period saw the first wine vintages of Burgundy, Bordeaux, the Moselle and the Rhineland. The grape-vine was also introduced in Britain, as perhaps was horticulture, maybe linked with the needs of new urban populations. Fruits including the cherry, plum and some types of apple, and vegetables ranging from peas and broad beans to cabbage, carrots, turnips, parsnips and radishes, were apparently first grown in Britain at this time too.

But many aspects of traditional Classical agriculture were inappropriate in temperate climates: most notably, the olive will not grow in the north. Indeed, existing Iron Age farming regimes were already well adapted to local conditions (pp. 54–56), and production was increasing before Rome arrived. A basically Iron Age agricultural system, with access to Roman markets, was sufficient to generate the wealth to build the villas which carpeted Picardy and other areas of Gaul. Conversely, many other areas – both poor uplands and the rich Fenlands of eastern England – lacked villas, and show relatively little sign of Roman influence at all.

Expanding farms and populations

The pattern of agriculture in Gaul and Britain in the early empire is a mixed one: some important but regionally localized innovations, combined with continued intensification – more farms (whether villas

COMMAND ECONOMY, AD 301

The emperor Diocletian tried to halt inflation in the later empire by issuing a detailed edict specifying maximum prices. Carved in stone in major cities, many fragments have survived, revealing fascinating details of the goods traded from the Celtic provinces. A selection is given here, with some other items for comparison: Gallic goods were often expensive, but of high quality. The high figures show the effect of many years of monetary inflation, but give an interesting idea of relative values.

Falernian wine (Italian), 1 Italian pint	30 denarii
Ordinary wine, 1 Italian pint	8 denarii
Cervisia (Celtic beer), 1 Italian pint	4 denarii
Egyptian beer, 1 Italian pint	2 denarii
Pair of Gallic shoes for farm workers, double-soled, men's	80 denarii
Birrus Nerbicus (hooded cloak, made by the Nervii), shaggy (?), first quality	15,000 denarii
Birrus Britannicus	6,000 denarii
Tapete Britannicum (a type of rug)	5,000 denarii
Tapete Britannicum, second quality	?4,000 denarii
Gallic shirt	1,250 denarii
Cloak with brooch (fibulatorium), from the Treveri	8,000 denarii
Cloak (sagum), Gallic, that is, from the Ambiani or Bituriges	8,000 denarii
Cloak, African	500 denarii

or, more commonly in Britain, native-style establishments), more marginal land drained, more livestock, more crops and more people. Recent estimates suggest a population of 3–4 million in Britain, and about 8 million in Gaul at the conquest, perhaps rising to 12 million in the late Roman period.

Increasingly intensive farming and population growth, continuing the trends of the later Iron Age, may have been accelerated by the growth of urban markets, and especially the need to grow cash crops to pay taxes and to meet the demands of the army (which in Gaul alone consumed about 25,000 tons of grain per year). Economic expansion was aided by improvements in communications – by the new roads and, equally importantly, by access to waterways for shifting bulk produce.

By the third century AD, the northwestern provinces were more populous and wealthier than ever before, with extensive grain production and woollen industries of high repute. It was a period of renewed innovation: for example, evidence from Britain suggests that new forms of heavy plough appeared, indicating that important developments were taking place in arable farming. Farmers were also making improvements to their livestock, with larger varieties of cattle, sheep with finer fleeces, and a continuation of the late Iron Age trend towards greater emphasis on cattle both to work the land and to be slaughtered for food.

Living in the countryside

On the whole the old settlement patterns survived, especially in Britain. Despite the attention-grabbing total of nearly 1,000 villas, there are estimates that up to 100,000 native-style farmsteads and hamlets existed in the province. The pattern in much of Gaul is somewhat different, with great numbers of villas, but the flimsy homes of the mass of the rural poor probably still await discovery.

Only an estimated 5 per cent of the population in Britain lived in towns or villas. While the percentage may have been higher in Gaul, these were still fundamentally rural societies, consisting of Celtic-speaking peasant families for whom the Roman conquest brought few changes, except perhaps access to more manufactured goods.

Rich and poor

Did this wealth filter down to the poor? In Gaul there is a mix of massive luxury dwellings and quantities of medium-sized villas. Was this a society of some great landowners and many lesser ones? Or were the smaller villas dwellings of tenants, clients of great nobles, with all the land in the hands of the few? According to the Classical texts, the gulf between the rich and poor was widening, which ultimately led to conflict. As early as the 180s, one Maternus led an army of brigands all over Gaul. This is the first of a long series of rural disturbances which show that behind the magnificent facade of the Romanized good life in the villas, there was great distress and serious social tension in the Gallic countryside.

Air photograph and reconstruction of a villa complex at Estrées-sur-Noye, Somme, France. Note the long approach to the main house.

CIVIL WAR AND CRISIS IN THE EMPIRE

(Right) A grave relief depicting a pot-seller from Bourges, France.

(Below) Tomb of a smith, here shown with the tools of his trade: hammer, tongs, and diamond-shaped anvil. From Sens, France.

GAUL was caught up in the Roman civil war after the murder of the emperor Commodus in 192, and became the battlefield between the contenders for the throne – Clodius Albinus (governor of Britain) and Septimius Severus (governor of Pannonia). The decisive battle was fought at Lyon. The city, and the leading aristocrats of Gaul, suffered from the victorious Severus' confiscations, but it was a passing horror, and is not now thought to have been the body-blow to Gaul it once appeared. The cities and economy continued to grow, and even the demise of the samian pottery industry in the third century may have resulted from a change in fashion rather than political or economic crisis.

Some even see this as the time of a Gallic revival, when the regional identity and self-confidence of Gaul, with its strong Celtic undercurrent, reached its zenith. Gaul had its own peculiar local flavour (reflected to a large degree in Britain), with characteristic temple styles, villa types, curious hybrid theatre/amphitheatres, and regional fash-

ions in costume, not least cloaks such as the *caracallus*, much favoured by the elder son of Septimius Severus, known by the nickname Caracalla.

How far was Gaulish still spoken? In Gaul there are about 10,000 known inscriptions in Latin, and only twenty or so in Celtic, but this simply reflects the fact that Gaulish was not favoured as a written language – on stone. However, the third-century Roman jurist Ulpian declared that, alongside Latin and Greek, Gaulish was an accepted testamentary language – proof that Gaulish was still widely spoken and indeed officially endorsed at the imperial level as a first language. Latin did not completely supersede it, even among the propertied classes.

At much the same period, the Gallic *leuga* (league) prevailed over the Roman mile as the official unit of distance in the Gallic provinces. Once again we can trace continuity in the local pre-Roman traditions and tolerance of these ways on the part of the imperial authorities.

We must not exaggerate any resurgence in Celticity, however. Most of the institutions of the Gauls remained very Roman in form, albeit interpreted and modified to accommodate Celtic culture. However, the strength of Celtic identity probably increased as one looked down the social scale, for the poor had less to gain from Romanization than their power-thirsty aristocratic counterparts. Many pre-Roman social patterns continued to underpin life in Gaul, and even more so in Britain, at the time the Roman empire began to run into serious trouble.

The third-century crisis and after

The third century was a time of crisis, of unending civil wars, and of invasion by Germans and other 'barbarians' on the Rhine and Danube.

Gaul was raided by the Germans in the 250s, and Rome subsequently abandoned territory beyond the Rhine. The disaster of 260, when the emperor Valerian was captured by the Persians, led to civil war and further German attacks. Gaul looked to its own defences, and established a

LANGUAGE LOANS

The influences operating between cultures are never entirely one-way, and the situation in Gaul was no exception. Latin absorbed a number of words from Gallic, particularly agricultural and technical terms. Some of these are listed right.

Alauda	lark (Caesar's Gallic-raised legion was known as V Alaudae, perhaps after the feather crests in their helmets; modern French *alouette*)
Bracae	trousers (c.f. 'breeches')
Caracallus	hooded cloak
Cervisia or **cervesia**	beer (modern Spanish *cerveza*)
Leuga	league (1½ Roman miles)
Reda	four-wheel carriage
Sagus (later **sagum**)	a popular type of cloak

(Above) A Roman sword-belt fitting from Dura-Europos, Syria, AD 250s. The decoration is British, part of the Celtic legacy to the Roman empire.

(Left) A Gallic school scene. A youth reads from a book, while a late arrival with his wax writing tablets greets the teacher. Relief from Neumagen, Germany.

THE LATE ROMAN COUNTRYSIDE

The late empire was not all doom and gloom; many areas saw generations of peace and plenty. Ausonius, whose life spanned the fourth century (c. 310–94), wrote a famous poem describing the Moselle Valley, near the imperial capital at Trier, in the 370s. It is very romanticized, but vivid nonetheless:

'Hail, river, blessed by the fields, blessed by the coloni, to whom the Belgae owe the imperial honour which graces their city [Trier]; river, whose hills are o'ergrown with Bacchus' fragrant vines ... ship-bearing as the sea, with sloping waters gliding as a river ...

'The people, happy in their toil, and the restless coloni are busy ... exchanging shouts in boisterous rivalry. Here the wayfarer trampling along the low-lying bank, and there the bargeman floating by, troll their rude jests at the loitering vine-dressers; and all the hills, and shivering woods, and channelled river, ring with their cries ...

'these splendid dwellings in the Belgic land ... these lofty villas ... set beside verdant meadows, their trim roofs resting upon countless columns ... their baths, contrived low down on the verge of the bank, which smoke when Vulcan, drawn by the glowing flue, pants forth his flames and whirls them up through the channelled walls, rolling in masses the imprisoned smoke before the scorching blast!'
Ausonius, *The Moselle,* 10,17–340

separate 'Gallic empire' under Postumus, consisting of the northern provinces and Spain. Unlike most power-hungry usurpers, Postumus was content to rule over Gaul and did not attempt to extend his dominion over Italy or the rest of the Roman empire.

Gaul was re-annexed by Rome in 274, but the most disastrous German invasion yet followed soon after. Cities were sacked, and many villas abandoned, perhaps through economic dislocation as much as German destruction. But longer-term social changes were at work, with effects more profound than the frightening but transient invasions.

Citizenship and class

In 212 the emperor Caracalla decreed all free-born inhabitants of the empire to be Roman citizens, a striking symbol of integration. Yet at the same time, distinctions of rank and class were becoming more rigid, as extremes of wealth and poverty grew. Consolidation of land-ownership in the hands of the aristocracy through clientage and debt-bondage reduced the Gallic peasantry to virtual serfdom as *coloni*, peasants tied to the land. It was the culmination of a process reaching back into the Iron Age (p. 71).

It is against this background of rural distress that we see the risings of the *bagaudae*, perhaps dispossessed peasants who, from the third century, so terrorized Lugdunensis that the army had to mount campaigns against them.

By the reign of the reforming emperor Diocletian (284–305), and that of Constantine, the first Christian emperor (306–337), the old *terror Gallicus* was forgotten and the Gallic nobility was totally Romanized and integrated into the imperial system. Indeed, the aristocrats were ultimately more dependent on the Roman authorities than on the loyalty of the peasantry. Thereafter – partly due to the proximity of the imperial capital recently established at Trier – men such as Ausonius, a native of Bordeaux, were permitted to serve at the highest level, their Gallic blood no longer a cause of suspicion. Ausonius became Praetorian prefect of Gaul, and consul. But the cost of this rapprochement was the virtual breakdown of social ties between rich and poor in Gaul – and with it the death of the last vestiges of the old Celtic social order.

(Left) The Porta Nigra at Trier. The city became a rich imperial capital in the fourth century AD.

THE GOLDEN AGE OF ROMAN BRITAIN

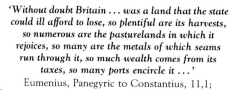

'Without doubt Britain ... was a land that the state could ill afford to lose, so plentiful are its harvests, so numerous are the pasturelands in which it rejoices, so many are the metals of which seams run through it, so much wealth comes from its taxes, so many ports encircle it ...'
Eumenius, Panegyric to Constantius, 11,1;
c. AD 300

Reconstruction of the façade of a fourth-century Roman basilica-shaped villa building recently excavated at Meonstoke in southern England. The upper part had fallen in one piece and revealed vital details about the windows and roof.

The range of settlement types in late third-century Britain. While most people still lived in modest establishments close to Iron Age traditions e.g. at Burradon, Northumberland (below left), a few possessed substantial villas like Gadebridge Park, southern England (below right).

IN SOUTH AND EASTERN Britain, the first and second centuries AD saw the rapid development of Romanized cities, around and between which other, smaller towns also grew. This suggests that urbanism and other aspects of Roman life really were taking root, an impression reinforced by the appearance (at first slow but by the third and fourth centuries in increasingly large numbers) of villas.

In contrast, much of the far west and north shows very little sign of Roman-style life, partly due to the inhibiting presence of the army, but perhaps also because differences in social organization rendered the inhabitants of these regions less receptive to Romanization than those of the south and east (p. 133). In these areas, traditional Celtic social structure seems to have survived the Roman occupation.

Largely insulated from war by the sea, Britain enjoyed a period of relative prosperity during the third century. Part of the Gallic empire, Britain broke away again under the curious 'British empire' of Carausius (287–296). This was not a nationalist movement: Carausius sought recognition from Diocletian, but the island was forcibly re-annexed.

The fourth century is often described as the Golden Age of Roman Britain. Some really luxurious villas were built at this time, probably a manifestation of an empire-wide process, with aristocrats turning away from building in the towns to embellishing their country estates. These changes also suggest that the social polarization witnessed in Gaul and elsewhere (p. 149) was occurring in Britain too.

The reason for this rural prosperity may have been that the aristocracy benefited from the disruption of agriculture in Gaul. As a secure source of supply, easily accessible by water, Britain may have become the granary of the Rhineland cities and soldiers. Gaul's tragedy was Britain's opportunity.

Unquiet coasts

Britain did not escape entirely unscathed, however: she suffered coastal raiding from the Saxons (from Germany) on one side and the Irish on the other, with further trouble from a new north British confederation, the Picts (p. 170). A 'barbarian conspiracy' of several of these groups invaded in 367, bringing chaos, and has been blamed for initiating the province's decline. However, the scale and impact of this aggression have been exaggerated: a small expeditionary force from the continent, probably of no more than 4,000 troops, was enough to restore order. Life continued, although there are signs of economic decline towards the end of the fourth century.

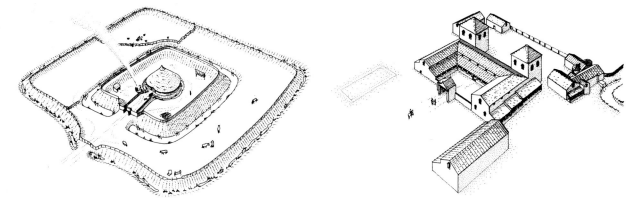

THE FALL OF ROMAN GAUL AND BRITAIN

IN LATE ROMAN GAUL, less and less can be identified as Celtic: the last vestiges of the old social structure were disappearing by AD 300, followed, probably by AD 500 by the extinction of the Gaulish language. The nobility became monoglot Latin-speakers. But why did Gaulish vanish among the lower classes? The influx of German settlers (mainly Franks) after the frontier collapsed in 406–7 was probably a key factor: Latin dialect developed as, literally, the lingua franca in an ethnically mixed land, later evolving into French. In contrast, there was considerable continuity in the institutions of Gaul, as – during the fifth century – the western empire crumbled and Christian imperial rule gave way to Christian Germanic government. Many Gallo-Roman aristocrats were absorbed into the new socio-political synthesis, and excavations of cemeteries have revealed a process of 'Frankization' of the people in early medieval times.

Britannia vanishes

The most remarkable aspect of the end of Roman Britain is the speed and totality of its collapse. Imperial rule ceased about AD 409, and within a generation almost all traces of Roman life – and in the east, Celtic culture too – had vanished. What happened?

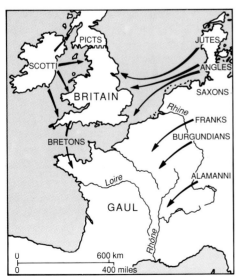

It is now clear that Romano-Celtic society in Britain did not perish by German (Anglo-Saxon) swords in the fifth century: a couple of generations elapsed between Roman collapse and the main period of German settlement. One possible explanation is that the Romanized aristocracy, so dependent on imperial power, rapidly withered after contact with Rome was lost. Pagan Saxon princelings then moved into the power vacuum. Perhaps some British aristocrats 'Germanized' themselves to gain admittance to the new power structure, just as their ancestors had Romanized. There is evidence for an important British component in early England: the Britons were not all killed or driven out.

Yet as British and Latin gave way to Old English in the east, in the un-Romanized west and north of Britain the old Celtic patterns were re-emerging (p. 166).

Retrospect: the Celts under Rome

In Gaul a Romanized Germanic political structure was built on the ruins of the old administration. By the tenth century even the name of Gaul was no more, while much of Britannia had become Germanic-speaking England.

But, in looking at the centuries of Roman government of Celtic Europe, who really conquered whom? Gauls and Britons, and many other peoples across the empire, had taken Italian *Romanitas* and transformed it to meet their own needs. In the process most of Celtic Europe lost its identity: but Roman culture was similarly moulded by contact with the Celts and others, Rome's old identity being lost in a welter of powerful new regional forms.

(Left) Portchester Castle was built in the late third century AD, one of a growing chain of fortified naval bases defending the south and east coasts of Britain from the threat of Saxon sea-raiders.

(Below left) Raids and migrations of the late Roman period.

(Below right) The great dish from Mildenhall. The largest item in a treasure found in Suffolk during the 1940s, it is 2 feet (60 cm) across and made of some 18 lb (8.3 kg) of silver. Several such late Roman treasures have now been found buried in eastern England, including a vast hoard discovered at Hoxne, in Suffolk in 1992, consisting of about 200 gold and silver objects and over 15,000 silver and gold coins. These attest the great wealth and artistic taste of the ruling classes of late Roman Britain.

THE CELTS
OF IRELAND

*'Súaltaim came to Emhain and called out to the men of
Ulster: "Men are slain, women carried off, cattle driven
away!"'*

Táin Bó Cúailnge 3423–25

APART FROM THE HIGHLANDS and Islands of Scotland,
Ireland was the only part of the Celtic world to
escape conquest by Rome. The earliest recorded
Irish history barely pre-dates the coming of St Patrick
in the fifth century; before this there are magnificent but
shadowy legends and tales, such as the *Táin Bó Cúailnge*
(the 'Cattle Raid of Cooley'). The extract above, Súaltaim's call to arms, typifies the image of early Ireland as
a land of heroic war and plunder. The Irish were feared
in fourth-century Britain as sea-raiders, their name a
byword for savagery. But the Irish Sea linked as well as
divided, bringing not only war but trading, kinship and
settlement. Such contacts allowed Ireland to participate
in the civilization of early medieval Europe on a scale
never seen in Roman or earlier times. Moreover, the
introduction of Christianity from overseas had one
crucial result: early Irish clerics – Christian but proud
of their heritage – wrote down many traditional stories,
epics, and poems, including the *Táin*. These are precious
survivals of Celtic mythology and oral literature of a
kind which has been largely lost elsewhere.

Many see the early Christian period as Ireland's finest
hour. By AD 800, with threats all around from the
Vikings, she had become one of the chief centres of
literate civilization and Christian religion in western
Europe, and was justly known as the Isle of Saints and
Scholars.

*Aerial view of the spectacular 'fort' of Dun Aengus on the isle of
Inishmore, Ireland. Now interpreted as a ceremonial site, it could have
had a theatre-like function (note the square 'stage' on the cliff edge) for
events such as sacrifices or royal inaugurations.*

IRELAND IN THE ROMAN IRON AGE, AD 1–400

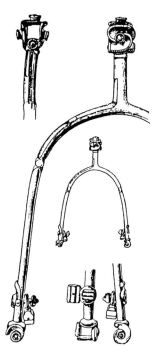

'In soil and climate, and in the character and civilization of its inhabitants, [Ireland] is much like Britain; and its approaches and harbours have now become better known from merchants who trade there...'

Tacitus, *Agricola*, 24

LITERARY EVIDENCE indicates that Ireland was a very complex society, with many kings and sub-kings of the tribes or peoples (*tuatha*). Each *tuath* had its nobility and esteemed 'men of art', represented in the tales by legendary figures such as Culann the smith, and Cathbad, Druid to King Conchobar of Ulster. Touchy warriors avenged insults and responded to challenges, competed for renown, but feared the barbs of the satirist. As elsewhere in the Celtic world, noblewomen were prominent and fiercely proud.

The society which emerges into the light of historical record from the fifth century was undergoing change, but still possessed many features characteristic of earlier continental Celtic societies. Irish society was held together by ties of mutual obligation and dependency: clientage was important, as was slavery. Wealth was largely portable, and measured in units such as head of cattle and female slaves.

Before the fifth century AD, the political shape of Ireland is obscure. It seems to have been divided into four 'provinces':

Ulaid (Ulster), Connachta (Connaught), Laigin (Leinster) and Mamu (Munster). A fifth may have existed, because these provinces were known as 'fifths' (*coiced*). Kings struggled for supremacy over the many sub-kingdoms or chiefdoms within each province. How often High Kings of all Ireland managed to establish themselves, and how far their power actually extended, is unknown.

Art and archaeology

Like Britain, Ireland in the last centuries BC developed her own insular brand of La Tène culture, blending surviving Bronze Age traditions with imported ideas. There is little evidence for any Celtic invasions (p. 49), although some immigration probably took place in the later Iron Age, if only arising from trading contacts. Furthermore, refugees from British or Gallic internal conflicts, and especially from the Roman conquests, may have found their way to Ireland: such refugees are documented crossing the English Channel in both directions. But most La Tène material in Ireland is best understood as a local adaptation of imported ideas. In the early centuries AD, Irish La Tène art reached a peak, and developed both its own style and new types of object, including enigmatic Y-shaped bronze mounts.

Metal artifacts dating from 50 BC to AD 200 include bowls, disks, torcs, horse-

(Above) A bronze 'Y-shaped mount'. This enigmatic type of object was peculiar to Ireland: perhaps it was attached to a horse's bridle.

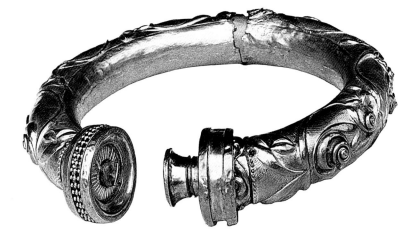

(Left) The gold torc from the Broighter hoard, with a drawing of its decoration shown straightened out. Tubular torcs like this seem to be of Gallic origin, but this example is Irish in stylistic detail. It was found in 1896 with a model boat and other items in gold near the shores of Lough Foyle, Co. Derry. Probably first century BC.

harness fittings (especially snaffle-bits) and a few brooches – a range curiously different from the scabbards and spear-butts of the earlier Irish La Tène. The most famous find of this later period is the hoard from Broighter, Co. Derry: a gold torc of local style found with imported continental bracelets, betraying foreign contacts around the end of the last century BC.

There are signs of growing British and Gallic influence in later La Tène times, with bridle bits, *fibulae* and other imported forms appearing at about the same time refugees were probably fleeing the Roman conquest. Items possibly of Irish manufacture were found in the Llyn Cerrig Bach hoard on Anglesey, suggesting that goods moved in both directions across the Irish Sea. Whatever the details, Ireland and north Britain were the areas where La Tène art survived the Roman period.

Roman contacts, first to third centuries AD

After Tacitus' account of merchant traders (see opening quotation), the Classical writers had little to say about Ireland, but archaeology provides evidence of continued contacts between north and eastern Ireland and coastal districts of Britannia. Such ties may well have underlain the flight to Britain of an unnamed Irish prince, 'expelled from his home by rebellion', whom Agricola considered using as a pretext for an expedition to Ireland. Irish tales reflect the frequency of Irish visitors to Britain: the Ulster hero Cú Chulainn is said to have spent time in *Alba* (North Britain).

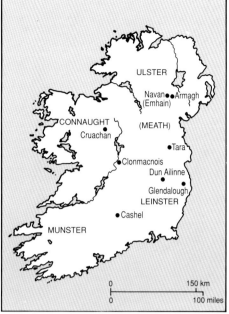

The provinces of Ireland during the early centuries AD.

In Ireland, unambiguous traces of Roman trade or British immigration are elusive. For although small quantities of Roman coins, brooches and pottery have been found (and a Romano-British style cremation grave of a woman at Stonyford, Co. Kilkenny – perhaps a refugee or the wife of a trader), the Irish seem not to have been interested in Roman art or style. Instead, surviving artifacts suggest an artistically independent, talented society.

It was only towards the end of the Roman period that outside influences and internal developments brought dramatic changes to the island.

GAELS AND GAULS
'Gaelic' is the adjective for – and the language traditionally spoken by – the Irish and the Scots of the Highlands and Islands (Scots pronounce it 'Gallic'). The word comes not from 'Gaul', as one might expect, but from 'Gael', originally Goidel, itself probably derived from Gwyddel – the early Welsh word for the Irish!

THE CALENDAR AND FESTIVALS

Irish evidence suggests that the Celts annually celebrated four main festivals, each apparently associated with fertility and the changing seasons. But the feasts reflect more than just the annual cycle of farmers and herders: they also relate to the political and religious life of Irish communities. For example, the annual assembly of the Ulaid was held on the days either side of Samhain.

1 February

Imbolc
Said to be linked to the lactation of ewes. In Ireland sacred to the goddess Brigid (Christian feast of St Brigid), a mother-goddess and patroness of childbirth.

1 May

Beltain
'Good fire', connected with the sun's warmth and the consequent fertility of crops and cattle. We are not certain it was celebrated outside Ireland, but it was perhaps associated with the sun god Belenos, who was worshipped in Gaul, Italy and the Alps.

1 August

Lughnasa
Harvest festival, associated with the god Lugh. A major festival was held in Lugdunum, 'stronghold of Lug' (Lyon) on that day.

1 November

Samhain
The most important festival, perhaps marking the start of the Celtic year. Celebrated on the eve and day of 1 November, it coincides with the modern Hallowe'en. At Samhain, the barriers with the Other World came down. The Gaulish Coligny calendar (p. 90) records it as Samonios.

155

FORTS, FARMS AND ROYAL RESIDENCES

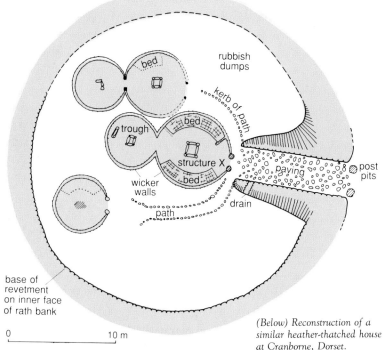

(Below) The rath at Deer Park Farms, Glenarm, Co. Antrim. Note the double wattle house-walls.

bed

rubbish dumps

kerb of path

trough

bed

structure X

paving

post pits

wicker walls

bed

path

drain

base of revetment on inner face of rath bank

0   10 m

(Below) Reconstruction of a similar heather-thatched house at Cranborne, Dorset.

THE IRISH LANDSCAPE is thickly studded with thousands of abandoned settlement sites dating from prehistoric to post-medieval times. Some settlement types, notably ring-forts, appear to have been very long-lived, spanning the Iron Age and early medieval periods and beyond.

Raths and cashels

The most common sites are the small fortified ones, the so-called ring-forts, mostly enclosed farmsteads, of which it has been estimated that 30,000–40,000 were built from Iron Age to post-medieval times. Called variously raths (earthwork forms), cashels (stone examples) and duns (more heavily fortified sites, probably from *dunum*, 'stronghold'), most contained a central round-house. Some of these sites were occupied for long periods, gradually building up into mounds like that of the early Christian period rath at Deer Park Farms, Co. Antrim.

Crannogs and souterrains

Crannogs are artificial islands built in shallow lakes, partly for defensive purposes. Tree-ring dating suggests that these house-platforms were actually a late introduction to Ireland, the earliest constructed in the early Christian period, i.e. the sixth and seventh centuries. Scholars now believe that the fashion for crannogs was imported from Scotland, where many date back over 2,000 years. Other possible British imports are the so-called souterrains: stone-built, underground chambers of strange shapes and uncertain purpose. Confined in Ireland to Ulster, their only known parallels are the rather differently constructed souterrains of northern Britain.

Hillforts and promontory forts

Fifty or more hillforts are known from Ireland, the majority probably of Iron Age date, although their chronology and function are obscure. Promontory forts comprise another distinct category, exemplified by the spectacular Dun Aengus (pp. 152–53), now thought to be a ceremonial site. Contacts down the Atlantic coast could have brought Spanish or western

French influence in earthwork design. Details such as the stone obstacles at Dun Aengus, however, may well have been inspired by wooden versions at contemporary Irish forts built in areas where timber was the traditional building material.

Places of kingship

The early Irish tales mention a number of special places associated with kingship and communal gatherings. Many of these are still visible as earthworks, which betray great variety of layout. Some are surrounded by 'ramparts' which evidently had no defensive function since the ditch lies inside the bank.

The most famous of all the so-called royal sites was Ráth na Ríogh (Fort of the Kings), at Tara, Co. Meath. Traditionally seen as the seat of Irish high kingship, Tara may have been the centre of Mide (Meath), the fifth province, although the province's status is disputed: it may only have arisen with the dynasty of Uí Néill in the fifth century. Another famous seat of royalty was Navan (Emhain Mhacha), capital of

Ulster, whose early development we discussed on p. 49. Occupation at Dun Ailinne (Knockaulin, Co. Kildare), the main royal site of Leinster, may have been seasonal, perhaps around major festivals. It was also a place of burial. At Rathcroghan lie the earthworks of the principal centre of the kings of Connaught, a complex of monuments covering about 4 square miles.

The royal sites were probably the focus of many activities associated with power, government, exchange, ceremonial and religion. As such they may be compared with the *oppida* of Britain. Rathcroghan was the site of a great annual fair, revered also because it was believed to be one of the entrances to the underworld. Several royal sites incorporate much earlier monuments suggesting that these places had long been the object of veneration. Were they permanent royal residences? Perhaps not: the kings (and queens?) may well have been constantly on the move, collecting dues in the form of hospitality rights from their vassals, visiting the royal centres only at certain ceremonial times of the year.

An aerial view of the ancient royal centre of Tara, Co. Meath. The large enclosure, the Ráth na Ríogh (Fort of the Kings), is hardly defensive: the ditch is inside the bank. It surrounds the 'Mound of the Hostages' (actually a Neolithic tomb) and two inner ringworks, one of which contains a stone structure known as the 'Stone of Destiny' – supposedly linked with kingly inaugurations. Tara has produced Roman objects of the first three centuries AD, attesting both the use of the site and foreign contacts during that period.

MYTHS AND LEGENDS OF IRELAND

THE VISION OF DUBTHACH

'A wonderful morning for a battle, a wonderful time when armies will be thrown into confusion, kings will be overthrown, men's necks will be broken and the sand will be red with blood ... Heroes will be slain. Hounds will be checked. Horses will be destroyed ... '

Táin, c. 3527–40

SLIABH GCUA

'Sliabh gCua, haunt of wolves, rugged and dark, the wind wails about its glens, wolves howl around its chasms; the fierce brown deer bells in autumn round it, the crane screams over its crags.'

Anonymous; ?ninth century

ON MAEL MHURU THE POET

'The choice earth has not covered, there will not come to the towers of Tara, Ireland of the many fields has not enfolded a man like the pure gentle Mael Mhuru.

'There has not drunk bravely of death, there has not reached the fellowship of the dead, the cultivated earth has not closed over a sage more wonderful than he.'

Anonymous; AD 887

THE EARLY IRISH CHURCH was a highly scholastic and artistic institution, its numerous achievements including the production of exquisite religious manuscripts (pp. 172–75). But we owe particular thanks to the monks for preserving so many traditional Irish tales – our only record of the oral literature of a Celtic people unconquered by Rome.

Today, scholars tend to concentrate on a group of tales called the Ulster Cycle. The most famous of these is a long prose epic, the *Táin Bó Cúailnge* or 'Cattle Raid of Cooley'. The *Táin*, like the *Iliad* or *Beowulf*, reflects the world of warrior aristocrats where honour, fame and combative prowess are more important than life, and where wealth is gained by plunder. The stories centre on the legendary king of Ulster, Conchobar mac Nessa, whose seat was at Emhain Mhacha (Navan, p. 49). Like King Arthur, or King Hrothgar in *Beowulf*, Conchobar was surrounded by a retinue of warrior lords and noblewomen, and youths in fosterage at his court. The most prominent warrior was the youthful hero Cú Chulainn (the 'Hound of Culann'). Many fables were written about this mythical court, and about the old gods who, in Christian times, were transformed into heroes or even saints. Stories about Cú Chulainn in particular continued to be composed, like the tales of Arthur, until the end of medieval times.

The story of the *Táin*

The men of Connaught – with allies including exiled Ulstermen commanded by Cú Chulainn's foster-father Fergus – were led by King Ailill and the treacherous Queen Medb ('she who makes drunk', originally a goddess) on an expedition into Ulster to seize the divine Brown Bull of Cúailnge. All the Ulstermen but Cú Chulainn were struck down by a mysterious malady, leaving the young hero to fight off the invaders with help only from his faithful charioteer. The epic is a long series of heroic episodes in which Cú Chulainn displays superhuman feats of arms, to delay the invaders until the Ulstermen recover. It ends with a great battle and a final conflict between the Brown Bull of Cúailnge and the White Bull of Connaught.

A window on the Iron Age?

The story of the *Táin* was perhaps first written down in the ninth century, but it has been thought to reflect an early Irish society contemporary with the Roman world. Indeed many of the modern ideas about La Tène Europe derived in part from the *Táin* and other early medieval Irish literature. The parallels are often striking: the Champion's Portion ws a ritual known in both Ireland and Gaul (pp. 70–71). Nevertheless, such comparisons should not be taken too far. Ireland underwent tremendous internal changes in the fifth century, long before the *Táin* was written down, and much of the detail in the epic is early medieval, not Iron Age, in origin. Pagan religious themes may have been censored (see box, p. 161). Nevertheless, the surviving Irish tales are as close to the ancient Celtic world as we can get.

Extracts from the *Táin*

The Chief Episodes of the Táin

The Hard Fight of Cethern mac Fintain
The Tooth-fight of Fintain
The Red Shame of Mend
The Bloodless Fight of Rochad
The Humorous Fight of Iliach
The Missile-throwing of the Charioteers
The Trance of Aimirgin
The Repeated Warning of Súaltaim

The Mustering of the Ulstermen
The Trance of Dubthach
The Trance of Cormac Con Longes
The Array of the Companies
The Final Decision in Battle
The Fight of the Bulls
The Adventures of Dub Cúailnge on the Foray
(*Táin*, c. 3155–60)

Fergus describes his foster-son, the Ulster hero Cú Chulainn

'You will not encounter a warrior harder to deal with, nor a spear-point sharper or keener or quicker, nor a hero fiercer, nor a raven more voracious, nor one of his age to equal a third of his valour, nor a lion more savage ... nor doom of hosts, nor one better able to check a great army. You will not find there any man his equal in age like unto Cú Chulainn in growth, in dress, in fearsomeness, in speech, in splendour, in voice and appearance, in power and harshness, in feats, in valour, in striking power, in rage and in anger, in victory and in doom-dealing and in violence, in stalking, in sureness of aim and in game-killing, in swiftness and boldness and rage.'

(*Táin Bó Cúailnge*, 381–92)

How the 'Hound of Culann' won his name

When Culann the smith prepared a feast for Conchobar, king of Ulster, he asked that the king bring only a few retainers, since he earned his wealth from his smithy, and did not have an estate rich enough to feed a great host. Conchobar therefore took with him only fifty of his bravest nobles.

As Conchobar departed he saw a little boy (one of many fostered at his court) performing feats of skill and courage on the playing fields, against three times fifty other boys. He beat them all at ball-games and at wrestling. Conchobar, marvelling at the boy's strength and skill, invited him to the feast.

The boy replied: 'I have not yet played enough, master Conchobar, but I shall follow you later.'

When Conchobar arrived at the feast, his host Culann asked him if anyone else was to follow. Forgetting the boy, Conchobar said 'no', and so Culann unleashed his enormous hound to guard the fort and its cattle.

At that moment the boy came in sight, and to the horror of Culann and his guests the hound ran to attack him. The little boy, unconcerned, threw aside his ball and

hurley, seized the mighty hound with his bare hands, and smashed it to fragments against a stone.

The Ulstermen ran to the boy and took him to Conchobar, who was greatly relieved, for the boy turned out to be Sédanta mac Sualtaim, his sister's son. Culann the smith formally welcomed him, but mourned the loss of his great dog, for it was the strong defender of his home and cattle.

The little boy replied: 'I shall raise a puppy of the same breed for you, and until he is ready to serve you, I shall protect you and your cattle myself.'

'Then you shall be called the Hound of Culann [Cú Chulainn]' said Cathbad the Druid.

(Abridged paraphrase of *Táin Bó Cúailnge*, 540–605)

Cú Chulainn offers Fergus hospitality

This is a ritual offering of hospitality and safe conduct, but somewhat spartan as Cú Chulainn was on campaign.

'Welcome, master Fergus,' said Cú Chulainn. 'If fish swim in the estuaries you shall have a salmon and a half; or else if a flock of birds fly over the plain you shall have a barnacle goose and the half of another; or you shall have a handful of cress or seaweed, a handful of laver, a drink from the sand. I shall go to the ford to encounter an opponent if he challenges you and you shall be guarded until you have slept.'

(*Táin*, c. 1312–16)

Touchy warrior pride

'Maine Aithremail [emissary of the king of Connaught] ...went first to Láeg [Cú Chulainn's charioteer].

"Whose vassal are you?"

Láeg did not address him. Maine asked him the same question three times.

"I am Cú Chulainn's vassal," said Láeg, "and do not plague me lest perchance I strike your head off."

"What a bad tempered fellow!" said Maine ... So then Maine went to speak to

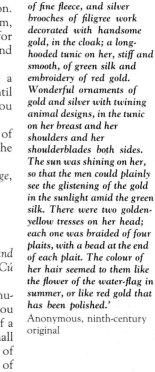

Cú Chulainn ... Maine asked him three times ... whose vassal he was.

"Conchobar's vassal, and do not plague me. If you bother me any more, I shall cut off your head as the head is cut off a blackbird."

"It is not easy to speak to these two," said Maine.'
(*Táin, c.* 1572–84)

The rage of Cú Chulainn

'Cú Chulainn took up position at the mound in Lerga ... and his charioteer, Láeg mac Ríangabra, kindled a fire for him in the evening of that night. Cú Chulainn saw afar off, over the heads of the four provinces of Ireland, the fiery glitter of the bright gold weapons at the setting of the sun in the clouds of evening. Anger and rage filled him when he saw the host, because of the multitude of his foes and the great number of his enemies. He seized his two spears and his shield and his sword. He shook his shield and brandished his spears and waved his sword, and he uttered a hero's shout deep in his throat. And the goblins and sprites and spectres of the glen and demons of the air gave answer for terror of the shout that he had uttered. And Némain, the war goddess, attacked the host, and the four provinces of Ireland made a clamour of arms round the points of their own spears and weapons so that a hundred warriors among them fell dead of fright and terror in the middle of the encampment on that night.'
(*Táin, c.* 2076–88)

The battle-distortion of Cú Chulainn

'Then a great distortion came upon Cú Chulainn so that he became horrible, many-shaped, strange and unrecognizable. All the flesh in his body quivered ... He performed a wild feat of contortion with the body inside his skin. His feet and his shins and his knees came to the back; his heels and his calves and his hams came to the front ... Then his face became a red hollow. He sucked one of his eyes into his head ... The other eye sprang out onto his cheek ... He drew back his cheek from his jawbone until his inward parts were visible. His lungs and liver fluttered in his mouth and throat ... The hero's light rose from his forehead ... As high, as thick, as strong, as powerful, and as long as the mast of a great ship was the straight stream of dark blood which rose up from the very top of his head and dissolved into a dark magical mist.'
(*Táin,* 2245–78)

Other Irish writings: Poems and tales

May-time

'May-time, fair season, perfect in its aspect then; blackbirds sing a full song, if there be a scanty beam of day ...

'Summer brings low the little stream, the swift herd makes for the water, the long hair of the heather spreads out, the weak white cotton-grass flourishes ...

'Bees, whose strength is small, carry with their feet a load reaped from the flowers; the mountain allures the cattle, the ant makes a rich meal.

'The harp of the wood plays melody, its music brings perfect peace; colour has settled on every hill, haze on the lake of full water ...

'A timid persistent frail creature sings at the top of his voice, the lark chants a clear tale – excellent May-time of calm aspect!'
(Author unknown, ninth–tenth century)

The dream of Oenghus

One night Oenghus [Angus], son of the Dagda and of Boann, goddess of the river Boyne, dreamt that the most beautiful girl he had ever seen approached him. He went to her, but she vanished. The same happened the next night, and the next, for a whole year, so that Oenghus, sick for love of her, began to waste away.

Of all the physicians of Ireland only Fíngin, doctor of King Conchobar, diagnosed the cause: love for an absent girl. He counselled that Oenghus should send to his mother, to scour Ireland for a girl to match his vision, but the year-long search was in vain. They consulted Oenghus's father the Dagda, who might know something as king of the fairy hills (the earthen barrows where dwelt the gods and fairies). But he did not: and so they went to Bodhbh, king of the fairy hills of Munster, and asked him to search. He sought her for a year, and found her at last, with three times fifty maidens, at Loch Bél Dragon in Connaught; her name was Caer Ibhormheith. Oenghus met his parents at Newgrange mound to tell them his news, and the Dagda promised to go to King Ailill and Queen Medb of Connaught, to seek the girl's hand for their son; but they had no power to grant it. They summoned Ethal Anbhuail, the girl's father, but he refused to come; and so they attacked the fairy hill, and brought him captive. But still even he could not give his daughter to Oenghus, for her magic power was greater than his; but he revealed that at the approaching Samhain she would be at the loch in the shape of a bird, with three times fifty swans about her.

At Samhain Oenghus went to the lake, and called to her, and she came. He put his arms about her, and they fell asleep in the shape of two swans. They went around the lake three times, and then flew to Newgrange, where they sang a song that put the people to sleep for three days and nights. She stayed with him thereafter.
(Paraphrase of an ?eighth-century story)

Bricriu's joke on the women of Ulster

Bricriu, lover of mischief, gave a great feast. Having set the chief men at each other's throats, he wondered how he could do the same to the women. Fedhelm of the youthful form came by with fifty women, the worse for drink. He greeted her, saying, 'Fedhelm of the Youthful Form, you are well-named, because of the perfection of your form, your wits and your ancestry, daughter of Conchobar, wife of Loeghaire the Victorious. If you come first into the banqueting hall this evening, you shall be the greatest in queenship over all the women of Ulster.' Flattered, Fedhelm strolled off across the fields with her women.

Next Lennabhair emerged, wife of Conall the Triumphant, with fifty women. Bricriu hailed her, punning, 'You are well named Lennabhair, being the *ban-lennán* (sweetheart) of all men for your brilliance and your fame. As your husband's courage surpasses that of other warriors, so do you surpass the other women of Ulster.' To her, too, he promised pre-eminence if she was first to enter the feasting hall. And so she and her women walked off into the fields.

Then Eimher passed by, wife of Cú Chulainn, and daughter of Forghall the Dexterous, with her fifty women. Bricriu praised her, saying, 'You are justly called Eimher of the Beautiful Hair, the rulers of Ireland admire you. As the sun outshines the stars, so do you outshine the other women of Ireland.' And to her, likewise, he made his promise of pre-eminence, before she and her women went for their walk.

Three fields distant from the hall, the three retinues, unaware that Bricriu had addressed each, began their stately approach ready for the feast. At first they walked in a dignified manner, but in the second field they began to hurry, hitching up their skirts. Soon the noise was louder than fifty chariots as the women thundered towards the hall. The men inside, fearing an attack, closed the doors. Eimher reached the door first, and shouted for it to be opened. The men rose, each intending that his wife should be first through the door, and so paramount queen of Ulster. Conall and Loeghaire each pulled a post from the wall, allowing their wives to squeeze in: but Cú Chulainn lifted the whole side of the palace up to let in Eimher, accompanied not only by her women, but by those of Conall and Loeghaire too, so that there was no comparison between her and the other women, as no man could compare to Cú Chulainn himself. Then he let the palace drop, and Bricriu and his queen were tumbled into the dunghill among the dogs.
(Paraphrase of part of *Bricriu's Feast*, eighth century)

THE PAGAN GODS OF IRELAND

'*There was over Ireland a famous king from the Tuatha Dé Danann [the People of the Goddess Danu], and Echu Ollathir was his name. Another name for him was the Dagda, for it was he who performed miracles and saw to the weather and the harvest, and that is why he was called the Dagda [the Good God].*'
The Wooing of Étaín; eighth century

The Irish literature is a source of considerable detail regarding the pagan gods. We find a universe populated by deities who can deceive mortals and shift their shapes (appearing as humans or animals), while mortals can visit the Other World. The gods were very near. For example, the Dagda or Good God was king of the Tuatha Dé Danaan, People of the Goddess Danu; these were believed to be early inhabitants of Ireland who, on the coming of the Gaels, retreated to live underground, especially in burial mounds (barrows). The Dagda, whose attributes were a mighty club and a magic cauldron, has a counterpart in Gaul known as Sucellos, characterized by a hammer and pot. One of the Dagda's consorts was the Morrigan, the Phantom Queen, one of a triad of war-goddesses who would appear on the battlefield as crows or ravens. The Morrigan was also associated with fertility, and had a daughter by the Dagda – the goddess Brigid.

Despite the appearance in the tales of the old gods and Druids (crucial players in the stories), there are very few references to pagan cult practice. One explanation might be that the tales were sanitized by the Christian Irish clergy who wrote them down. Whatever the truth, the stories do give an idea of how Celtic societies saw the universe.

FROM ST PATRICK TO THE VIKINGS

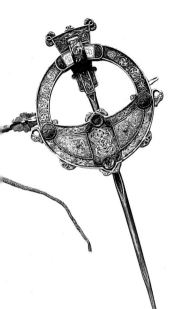

The 'Tara' brooch, from Bettystown, Co. Meath, eighth century AD. An artistic tour de force, it is made from gold, silver, copper, glass, enamel and amber.

AN ENGLISH DEBT TO IRELAND

'About this time [AD 664] there were in Ireland many nobles and lesser folk of the English who had left their country ... either for religious studies or for stricter discipline. Some soon devoted themselves to the monastic life, others preferring to travel and to study under different teachers. The Irish welcomed them all hospitably, asking for no payment, giving them food, books and instruction.'
Bede, *History of the English Church and People*, 3,27; eighth century

'Tara's mighty burgh perished at the death of her princes; with a multitude of venerable champions, the great height of Armagh abides.
'Rathcroghan, it has vanished with Ailill, offspring of victory; fair the sovereignty over princes that there is in the monastery of Clonmacnois...
'Emhain's burgh it hath vanished, save that the stones remain; the cemetery of the west of the world is multitudinous Glendalough.'
Aenghus; c. AD 800

ROMAN SOURCES of the fourth century mention people called *Scotti* among the barbarians attacking Britain. The Scotti eventually gave their name to modern Scotland, but originally they were from Ireland; the word derives from an Irish verb meaning 'to raid'. Like the later term 'Vikings', and the earlier Gallic *Gaesatae*, this was not a specific tribal name. The Scotti raided all along the western British coasts, one of their number – Niall Noígiallach (Niall of the Nine Hostages), who supposedly reigned at Tara and is one of the earliest undisputed Irish historical characters – even penetrating as far as the Isle of Wight.

Dynasts and missionaries, migrants and slaves

Niall's descendants, the Uí Néill, successfully invaded Ulster, and established a powerful dynasty – or more exactly two dynasties, one northern and one southern – which came to dominate much of Ireland. The appearance of such powerful dynasties reflects social change, with moves towards greater centralization of power. Roman

imports and influence were now extensive, including the fashion for burying the dead rather than cremating them, and literacy, which appeared with the Ogam script (see box). The most momentous import, however, was Christianity.

Missionaries from Britain or Gaul had probably crossed to Ireland by AD 400, hoping to convert the pagans. Their task may have been aided by the fact that there were already many Britons, including Christians, in Ireland: Niall's mother had a British name. Thousands of Romano-British slaves were brought back by the Scotti as booty. One of these was a sixteen-year-old youth who may have been called by the British names Magonus or Succetus, but who also took the Roman name *Patricius*. Destined to be remembered as the evangelist of Ireland, he is today revered as St Patrick.

Patrick entered a world in transition, possibly a major reason for his success. Ironically, this period of rapid change was encouraged, if not caused, by the opportunities arising from the *collapse* of Rome, in contrast to the earlier changes in areas like La Tène Gaul where the *arrival* of Rome on the scene had provided a catalyst.

A new power in the land: the church

According to legend, it was in 444 (in reality probably some decades later) that Patrick established his bishopric at the stronghold of Armagh, only a couple of

ST PATRICK

'I ask you; did I come to Ireland, except through God? ... I am bound, by the Holy Spirit, not to see anything more of my own kin. I ask you; is it my doing that I now extend this holy mercy to those very people who once took me captive, and who made such a havoc of the men and serving maids on my father's estate?'
St Patrick, *Letter to Coroticus*, 10; c. AD 470s?

Patrick was born into a wealthy family somewhere near Carlisle, in about AD 415. The son of a church deacon and decurion (town councillor), he described himself as a Roman and a Briton, and probably spoke British as his first language. At the age of sixteen, he was carried off to Ireland by a band of brigands, where he was enslaved for six years before he managed to escape on a merchant ship

bound for Gaul. He may have travelled in Brittany before eventually returning home. Here he was ordained and became bishop, but his real duty, he felt, lay in Ireland. Patrick returned to Ireland as a missionary in about 455, where he devoted himself to converting the pagan Irish to Christianity.

miles from Navan. Within one or two centuries the new monastic centres had become places of power; indeed, some wielded more authority than secular rulers, for the kings had to deal with touchy subordinates standing on their ancient privileges.

The development of the Irish Celtic church followed a unique pattern, revolving around monasteries rather than bishoprics, and evolving its own form of tonsure and its own method of calculating Easter. It also betrays strong but disguised continuity with pagan Ireland, aspects of the old religion being incorporated into Christian doctrine and practice to aid conversion. St Brigid, for example, probably developed from the goddess of the same name, and St Ann perhaps from the goddess Anu. But despite its peculiarly local flavour, the Irish church blossomed into the leading centre of scholarship in northwest Europe, with internationally renowned centres established for example at Clonmacnois and Glendalough. Students flocked to Irish monasteries, and Irish missionaries roamed the British Isles and Europe.

The golden age of Irish art

Looting by the Scotti in Britain, and later pastoral contacts between the Irish church and its counterparts on the British mainland, led to a remarkable flowering of art as well as religion. A new hybrid art appeared, to which the Irish, Anglo-Saxons and Picts all contributed. Exemplified by the magnificent Tara brooch, this Hiberno-Saxon style resulted from the fusion of the abstract patterns of late La Tène and the 'animal' art then common over much of Europe. (This animal style had evolved in the western Roman provinces and thence inspired the Germans, the Irish, the British and the Picts.) Artistic techniques then prevalent included Romano-Celtic enamelling, Roman *millefiore* glass and imitation of Roman faceted 'chip-carving' on metalwork.

A new class of craftsmen also arose during this period: the monks. These clerics were responsible for the spectacular illuminated manuscripts that appeared at this time (pp. 172–75).

The coming of the Norse

The Vikings first attacked the east coast of Britain in AD 789. Four years later, they

A tower at the great monastic site of Glendalough, Co. Wicklow.

plundered the largely Irish monastery of Lindisfarne, and in 795 they landed near Dublin. With the coming of the pagan Norse, the flowering of Ireland ended, and the long, tragic history of foreign interventions began.

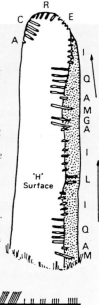

OGAM: THE FIRST IRISH WRITING

'Then Etarcomol's grave was made, and his tombstone set up, his name written in Ogam and they mourned him ...'
Táin, 1385–90

Ogam (or Ogham) was a unique Irish writing, thought to have been inspired by contact with Latin writing, and especially Roman numerals. Made of simple strokes, it was easily cut on stone or wood, along a central line – usually the edge of a slab. Messages carved on wood are mentioned in the Táin, but the surviving texts are mostly names on tombstones (another imported Roman idea). Exactly when Ogam first appeared is still unclear, but some time during the fourth century AD seems most likely: Ogam stones were erected during the fifth to seventh centuries. They are found mostly in southern Ireland and western parts of Britain where the Irish settled. In Britain the Ogam text is often accompanied by a Latin version.

X

THE CELTIC RENAISSANCE

*'Indeed, by this time, Britain had reached such a
standard of sophistication that it excelled all other
kingdoms in its general affluence, the richness of its
decorations, and the courteous behaviour of its
inhabitants.'*

Geoffrey of Monmouth on the reign of Arthur

THE HISTORY OF NORTHERN EUROPE in late Roman times
and the early medieval centuries was dominated
by massive folk-movements, the settlement of
Germans in the old Roman provinces, the terror of the
Asiatic Huns, and later the depredations of the Vikings.
No one knows what caused these vast movements, but
the remaining fragments of the Celtic world were also
caught up in the process, which laid the broad outlines
of the modern map of Europe.

In Britain this period is seen as a time of Celtic
resistance to Germanic invasion, in which the figure of
Arthur looms large. The collapse of Roman power led
to the re-emergence of heroic Celtic society in early
medieval Britain: it had persisted in the north, and
perhaps in the little-Romanized west, and now burst
forth anew. It was a time of danger and uncertainty: the
records of these centuries, fragmentary and obscure
though they are, depict a world of warfare. Yet the
archaeology of these so-called 'Dark Ages' shows that
remarkable developments were taking place, as new
contacts were made and new ideas spread. Among the
surviving Celts of the islands, who during these centuries
began to mould themselves into the modern nations we
know today, these interchanges resulted in flourishing
literatures, and the last, and some of the greatest,
treasures of La Tène-inspired art: in metalwork, and in
the fabulous illuminated manuscripts developed by the
triumphant new Irish church.

Initial page of St Mark's gospel from the Book of Kells.

THE WELSH AND THE ENGLISH

*'Welsh' is from the Old
English* wealas, *meaning
'strangers' or 'foreigners', used
of the native Britons.*

*The Britons came to call
themselves* Cymry *('fellow
countrymen'), which at first
included all British or early
Welsh-speaking areas (part of
northwestern England is still
called Cumbria). As the
British states collapsed or were
absorbed, the* Cymry *became
limited to the area of modern
Wales, or* Cymru.

*An enamelled escutcheon from
a bronze bowl found in the
early seventh-century tomb of a
king at Sutton Hoo, Suffolk. Its
place of manufacture is
uncertain but the pattern and
enamelling echo native British
traditions.*

*'The men went to Catraeth [?Catterick] in
column, raising the war-cry, a force with steeds
and blue armour and shields, javelins aloft and
keen lances, and bright mail-coats and swords ...
Seven times as many English they slew; in fight
they made women widows, and many a mother
with tears at her eyelids ... Mynyddawg I am
bitterly sad, I have lost too many of my true
kinsmen; of three hundred champions who set out
for Catraeth, but for one man none came back ...'*
The men of Manaw Gododdin in unsuccessful
war against the Northumbrian English, from *The
Gododdin*, attributed to Aneirin; about AD 600

It TOOK CENTURIES for the medieval nations
of Wales, Scotland and England to appear.
With hindsight the history of the fifth to
tenth centuries seems to be a story of the
gradual erosion of Celtic British territories
by waves of invaders. The collapse of the
Roman province left a political vacuum in
eastern Britain, in which those who had
the might seized power. The traditional
story focuses on the fifth-century figure of

Vortigern (whose name means something
like 'overlord'). Legend has it that he
invited Saxon mercenaries under the chieftains Hengist and Horsa to help defend
the land from other, mainly Germanic,
invaders. But the Saxons had other plans:
on arrival in the east of Britain they double-
crossed their hosts, seizing power and land.
The Saxon rebellion remains the metaphor
for the Germanic takeover of what was to
become the Land of the Angles and the
Saxons, England.

The pattern in the less Romanized west
of Britain and the free north was different.
Here a tangle of native kingdoms developed, great like that of the Picts, and small
like Elmet in west Yorkshire. But the
coasts of these lands too, were increasingly
threatened, by the Irish Scotti from the
west, and from the east the Germanic
Angles and Saxons (who became the English) and, later, the Scandinavian Vikings.

In the face of Anglo-Saxon military
expansion, the Britons appealed for help
from Gaul: 'the barbarians drive us to the
sea, the sea drives us back to the barbarians
...' The 'Dark Ages' are conventionally
seen as being characterized by the death,
destruction and dispossession of the British, and by the flight of many across the
sea to Armorica (henceforth known as
Brittany). But in fact the British Celts were
not simply victims: many were enthusiastic
participants in the social and military
chaos, insofar as their power permitted.
They attacked each other, some Britons
even allying themselves with Anglo-Saxon
rulers. The Irish raided Britain, but
Coroticus, probably king of Strathclyde,
counter-raided Ireland in the fifth century,
as recounted in one of St Patrick's few
surviving writings. In fact the Irish settlements in Britain, and the British conquest
of Armorica, may be seen as the last phase
of Celtic expansionism.

From British to Welsh

Numerous British-speaking kingdoms
arose from the Clyde to Cornwall, some
long-lived: Strathclyde was only absorbed
into Scotland in the eleventh century.
Others fell more quickly. Strathclyde's

eastern neighbour, Manaw Gododdin (earlier known as the kingdom of the Votadini), fell to the English, as did Elmet in the seventh century. In the long struggle against growing Anglo-Saxon power, the area ruled by British-speaking monarchs (whose language was evolving into Old Welsh) was gradually eroded, until only modern Wales was left. The details of British resistance to English expansionism are mostly lost, but one supreme figure remains: the semi-legendary Arthur (pp. 168–69).

Even the lands destined to become Wales were partly settled by Scotti from Ireland. Dyfed, ruled by an Irish dynasty, has many Ogam stones with additional Latin inscriptions. Gwynedd in northwest Wales is also the British form of an Irish dynastic name, the Féni, who were displaced from northwest Wales by the Gododdin, some of whom, under Cunedda, moved to Wales around the end of the Roman period (at the Romans' behest, or as another opportunistic migration). Most medieval Welsh royal houses traced their ancestry to the Féni.

While a unified English kingdom was developing, the Welsh kingdoms were also coming together under the so-called High Kings. A particularly prominent king was Hywel Dda (the Good), who codified Welsh law and by 950 had extended his power over almost all of Wales. But, threatened by the Norse, Hywel had to submit to English overlordship – a foretaste of future English domination.

Brittany

The conversion of Gallic Armorica into Brittany is all too often thought to have resulted purely from the arrival of British refugees from the English. In fact, Armorica

The surviving Celtic-speaking regions (shown in colour) in the post-Roman centuries.

was deliberately colonized during the first half of the fifth century by British mercenaries and princelings taking advantage of the chaos in a Gaul overrun by invaders.

The newcomers brought with them a dialect of British Celtic, which remained close to the developing Cornish language. They established petty kingdoms, populated by Gauls as well as immigrant and refugee British. By AD 450, much of the land north of the Loire was in British (soon called Breton) hands.

Breton rulers were often aggressive, fighting each other, raiding beyond their frontiers, and beating off Frankish (French) kings and marauding Danes alike. Their state, like that of emergent Wales and Scotland, was destined to have a long independent history.

BARDS OF THE WELSH
The bardic tradition of the Britons can be traced from the 'Dark Ages' to the seventeenth century. Among the few surviving very early works is the famous poem, The Gododdin, thought to have been written in what is now southeastern Scotland. The poet to whom it is attributed, Aneirin, and the equally celebrated Taliesin, were probably north Britons, but with the retreat of British independence into Wales they have been adopted as Welshmen in the modern sense.

The most famous group of Welsh tales is the Mabinogion, the name coined in recent times for a group of eleven tales, probably written down in the eleventh century but originating much earlier. The core of the work is the Four Branches of the Mabinogi, four tales probably deriving from an early epic about a Prince of Dyfed called Pryderi. Arthur appears in these and other fables included in the Mabinogion.

HOW ENGLISH ARE THE ENGLISH?

Many modern English people have Celtic blood, in that many of their ancestors were actually surviving Britons rather than immigrant Germans. This is particularly evident in western England, especially Cornwall, which retained some Celtic language until post-medieval times. But even in the east there is evidence that many Britons survived the Germanic

takeover, wars, plagues, and westward flight of many of their countrymen. Survival of British enclaves is detectable today in surviving place-names like Walton, 'settlement of the Britons'.

Some of the early Anglo-Saxon kingdoms may have had Celtic roots; they certainly had largely Celtic populations. Northumbria, one of the most powerful German kingdoms,

probably had a mostly native population. It has even been suggested that Cerdic, founder of the royal house of Wessex, may have been a Briton with the name Coraticus. These Britons were gradually absorbed and 'Germanized' by the Anglo-Saxons, rather more effectively and totally than their ancestors had been Romanized.

KING ARTHUR: FACT AND FICTION

*'Then Arthur fought against them in those days
with the kings of the Britons but he himself was
leader of battles [dux . . . bellorum].
The first battle was at the mouth of the river
called Glein.
The second, third, fourth and fifth upon another
river called Dubglas and is in the district Linnius.
The sixth battle upon the river which is called
Bassas.
The seventh battle was in the Caledonian wood,
that is Cat Coit Celidon.
The eighth battle was in Fort Guinnon . . .
The ninth battle was waged in the City of the
Legion.
The tenth battle he waged on the shore of the
river which is called Tribruit.
The eleventh battle took place on the mountain
which is called Agned.
The twelfth battle was on mount Badon, in
which nine hundred and sixty men fell in one day
from one charge, and no-one overthrew them
except himself alone.
And in all the battles he stood forth as victor . . .'*

'Nennius', *Historia Brittonum*, section 56; early
ninth century

*A medieval conception of the
battle between Arthur and
Mordred, from a Flemish
manuscript of the early
fourteenth century.*

IT IS WIDELY ACCEPTED that Arthur probably was a real person, but beyond that there is little agreement about who he was, what he did, or even where or when he lived. None of the early sources call him a king. He is described only as *dux bellorum*, 'leader of battles', perhaps a successful supra-tribal war-leader in the spirit of Vercingetorix and Caratacus, leading the combined forces of several British kingdoms against the invading Saxons. Variously seen as a Celtic war-chief, or a Romanized cavalry commander, Arthur could still also have been a petty king in his own right.

Arthur is traditionally associated with the British victory at the unlocated battlefield of Mons Badonicus (Mount Badon) in the decades around AD 500; this halted the Germanic advance for many years, but it is far from certain that Arthur was the commander. Consider, for instance, the writings of Gildas, a caustic monk whose

De excidio et conquistu Britanniae ('On the Ruin and Conquest of Britain') is one of the few documentary sources for the period. Gildas mentions that the Battle of Mount Badon took place in the year of his birth, and he should surely have known about Arthur – but he does not mention him. The *De excidio* is not a chronicle, but contains some historical material, often of dubious value, amidst biblical quotations and exhortations calling down the wrath of God on the sinful clergy and British princes. Not surprisingly, it lacks the sort of organized factual detail after which historians hunger.

The great Old Welsh poem *The Gododdin*, includes the lines, *gochone brein du ar uur/caer ceni bei ef Arthur*, 'he gorged black ravens [i.e. on the corpses of his slain enemies] on the rampart of the fortress, although he was not Arthur', suggesting that Arthur was already a renowned paragon of warlike courage in AD 600 (assuming of course that the poem is indeed that old, and that the lines are original). Certainly the name Arthur, or variations of it, suddenly appears among several royal houses in Britain about AD 600.

Another important source is the so-called 'History of the Britons', attributed to one Nennius. This ninth-century rag-bag of material assembled from earlier sources includes a list of Arthur's battles, and some very early annals mentioning Arthur as the victor of Badon. But while the details of his life and achievements still elude us, there can be no doubt about the importance of his role in subsequent popular and literary tradition.

Arthur in early medieval Celtic tales

Arthur features in a number of Welsh tales written down in the thirteenth and fourteenth centuries but probably earlier in composition; in these he appears to be much more a Celtic chief than the epitome of medieval chivalry he was already becoming in England and France. The tales include a raid on the Other World in an attempt to seize a magic cauldron, a story reworked by Breton poets and French authors into the quest for the Holy Grail. Arthur became a generic Celtic hero whose name became attached to adventures elsewhere attributed to others; Cú Chulainn (pp. 158–60), for instance, embarked on a very similar journey into the Other World, and

also features in a tale about beheading – clearly a prototype for the saga of Gawain and the Green Knight.

Medieval romances, Celtic echoes

Arthur became a folk-hero in westernmost Europe from Brittany to Scotland, a figure surrounded by myth and magic. Via Breton minstrels at Norman courts, his fame was carried to Italy by the early twelfth century; parents named their children after him, and in 1165, as far south as Otranto, he was depicted in a mosaic.

The real creator of the medieval King Arthur (and the converter of the British prophet Myrddin – previously unconnected with Arthur – into the king's wizard, Merlin) was Geoffrey of Monmouth, whose *History of the Kings of Britain*, published in about 1136–38, included much freely-invented material. It was hugely popular in the courts of feudal Europe.

Yet, distorted, reinterpreted and over-lain with medieval Christian sentiment as they are, the Arthurian romances do retain echoes of ancient, even prehistoric, themes and motifs. Perhaps the most striking is the story of the return by the dying king of his sword Excalibur to the Lady of the Lake, surely a memory of the Iron Age (and earlier) practice of sacrificing fine metalwork – not least swords – in rivers and pools (p. 94).

The dying Arthur instructs Bedivere to return his magic sword Excalibur to the Lady of the Lake. From an early fourteenth-century French manuscript.

EASTER ANNALS, IN 'NENNIUS'

Year 72 [AD 518]: 'The battle of Badon in which Arthur carried the cross of Our Lord Jesus Christ for three days and three nights on his shoulders and the Britons were the victors …'

Year 93 [AD 539]: 'The strife of Camlann, in which Arthur and Modred perished.'

THE PICTS AND THE SCOTS

(Above) Drawing of a recently discovered Pictish carving of a fierce-looking man with an axe. From Rhynie, Grampian.

POST-ROMAN BRITAIN consisted of a patchwork of minor states, the borders between them in almost constant flux. So while the kingdoms of England and Wales were developing in the south (pp. 166–67), the Picts and the Scots were contesting lands in the north that were eventually to be unified as the kingdom of Scotland.

The Picts

The Picts (from the Latin *Picti*, 'the painted ones', suggesting the survival of the British tradition of tattooing), are first mentioned in a Roman source of AD 297. They comprised a new tribal confederation north of the Forth/Clyde line, arising from the earlier Caledonii and others. The Picts are an enigmatic people, the least understood of all the cultures of the early medieval British Isles. A major reason for this mystery is the near-total obliteration of their culture, which surviving metalwork shows to have been artistically sophisticated. Their stone sculpture was the most accomplished in the British Isles at the time. They apparently spoke two languages, a dialect of British Celtic and a second, non-Indo-European tongue of unknown affinity and as yet undeciphered.

By the sixth century, they had formed a powerful kingdom (or sometimes two

kingdoms, a northern and a southern), but they faced continual pressure from the Scots in the west and the English to the south. At the Battle of Nechtansmere in AD 685, King Bridei was able to repulse the English, but the Picts eventually succumbed to the Scots. The appearance of the Vikings in the late eighth century was perhaps the final straw.

The Pagan Scots and Christian Irish in Britain

The presence of Ogam inscriptions and Irish dynasties in western coastal districts provide clear evidence that the Scotti estab-

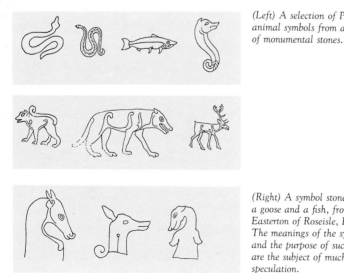

(Left) A selection of Pictish animal symbols from a variety of monumental stones.

(Right) A symbol stone bearing a goose and a fish, from Easterton of Roseisle, Elgin. The meanings of the symbols, and the purpose of such stones, are the subject of much speculation.

lished extensive settlements on British soil, of which ultimately the most important was the kingdom of Dalriada (below). The Irish roamed far inland. An Ogam stone has been found as far east as the Romano-British town of Calleva Atrebatum (Silchester).

Later the sword was followed by the Book: Irish raiders gave place to Irish priests, who had a profound effect on the history of the early medieval Celts, and indeed on the English and on continental Europe (pp. 172–73).

The Scots of Dalriada

Scotia ('Scot-land') was a term originally used of Ireland: it came to refer to northern Britain only from the eleventh century.

Modern Scotland's historical progenitor was the kingdom of Dalriada in Argyll. It was established, on land originally occupied by the Picts, by colonizers from the Irish kingdom of Dál Riada in Co. Antrim (perhaps in response to pressure from the Uí Néill). Probably settled before the end of the Roman occupation, Dalriada was traditionally supposed to have been founded by three sons of Erc. The descendants of one of the sons – Fergus – became kings of Scotland.

In the long struggle which ensued with the Picts, intermarriage took place as well as war: some Pictish kings may have been of Scots (that is, Irish immigrant) blood, while at times the Picts may have been overlords of Dalriada. In 843 a king of the Scots, Kenneth mac Alpin, seized the Pictish throne through a dynastic marriage (when the Picts were reeling from defeat by the Norse), uniting the two states into the single kingdom that developed into medieval and modern Scotland.

The triumph of the Scots of Dalriada meant that Irish Gaelic replaced earlier languages in northern Scotland, while a dialect of English (known, confusingly, as Scots) eventually came to predominate in southern Scotland. The Dalriadans may have deliberately suppressed Pictish history, but many aspects of Pictish culture (for example some state titles like *mormaer*, 'royal steward') nevertheless survived in medieval Scotland, as did many Pictish and imported Irish traditions. One of the most interesting is the practice of proclaiming rightful monarchs on special stones of consecration. Scottish kings were inaugur-

(Above) One of a pair of small silver plaques of unknown function from Norrie's Law, Fife.

(Left) The eighth-century Hilton of Cadboll stone, depicting a lively hunting scene. The border – a vine-scroll inhabited by birds – is unusual and suggests that the artist was familiar with metalwork or manuscripts ultimately of Classical inspiration.

ated on the Stone of Destiny, traditionally housed at the ancient Pictish centre of Scone. Stolen by the English in 1296, modern British monarchs are still crowned upon this stone: it is placed under the coronation throne in Westminster Abbey.

(Right) A silver object, probably the tip of a sword scabbard: part of a substantial hoard of bowls and other Pictish silverware of ninth-century date, buried on St Ninian's Isle.

171

SCHOLARS AND SAINTS, MISSIONARIES AND MANUSCRIPTS

'If you take the trouble to look very closely, and penetrate with your eyes to the secrets of the artistry, you will notice such intricacies, so delicate and subtle, so close together and well-knitted, so involved and bound together, and so fresh still in their colourings that you will not hesitate to declare that all these things must have been the result of the work, not of men, but of angels.'
Giraldus Cambrensis, on an illuminated gospel he saw in Kildare, Ireland; twelfth century

THE WORK OF PATRICK and other Christian missionaries was within a few generations rewarded by a great outpouring of Irish religious zeal. Irish hermit-monks sought salvation perched on remote rocks around the coasts of Ireland and Britain, while others roamed preaching the gospel to the Britons (i.e. the native Celts of the south), the Picts in the north, and the English (Germanic, Anglo-Saxon settlers).

Colum Cille, a prince of the royal house of the Uí Néill, moved to Dalriada, according to legend in flight from, or to atone for, his involvement in a great battle. Better known as St Columba, he settled on Iona in 563, and founded the famous monastery which became a chief centre of the Irish Celtic church. His piety did not extinguish the interest he had earlier shown in worldly affairs: on Iona he anointed Aidan as king of Dalriada, and gave sanctuary to the exiled Oswald, king of the English state of Northumbria. On recovering his throne in 634 Oswald asked Ireland for a bishop, and

(Above) The symbol of St Matthew from the Book of Durrow, *late seventh century.*

(Right) Detail of a carpet page from the Book of Durrow.

was sent another man called Aidan, who established the renowned monastery at Lindisfarne. These houses, and the monastic centres of Ireland itself, became sanctuaries of piety and learning in a Europe torn by war.

The great flowering of the Irish-centred Celtic church in the late seventh and eighth centuries engendered close cultural links between the Irish/Scots, the Picts and the English. One of the most visible results of this exchange was the production of the brilliant hybrid Hiberno-Saxon art of the illuminated manuscripts, a precious handful of which still survive today. While Ireland led the new cultural synthesis, the movement of people and ideas across the Irish Sea occurred in both directions, with some English settling in Ireland. Egbert, for instance, introduced the Roman way of calculating Easter to the Irish monastic houses, and sent the English Willibrord to convert the Frisians in 690. Conversely, other English holy men, such as St Cuthbert (died in 698), were deeply affected by the Irish monastic tradition.

Many Irish clergy (and others like Willibrord trained in the Irish manner) went to the continent as missionaries or, like St Gall who died in the Alps in 612, to seek solitude. The monastery of St Gall, established at his tomb in 720, became one of the most famed seats of learning in all Europe. Other individuals wandered great distances over many years. St Columbanus landed in Gaul in 590 with twelve disciples, founded a monastery at Luxeuil, but was forced out and eventually travelled as far as Italy, where he founded another abbey at Bobbio in 614. Such abbeys became places of scholarship and pilgrimage, or way stations for pilgrims including many Irish – crossing Europe to Rome. The monks of Ireland were famed throughout Europe for their piety, missionary zeal and artistic skill.

The work of angels: illuminated manuscripts

Referred to as 'the work of angels' by Giraldus Cambrensis in the twelfth century, the art of the illuminated manuscripts was a blend of Germanic, British/Pictish and above all Irish inspiration. These exquisite works were produced during the late seventh and eighth centuries by Irish artists – or others working in the Irish

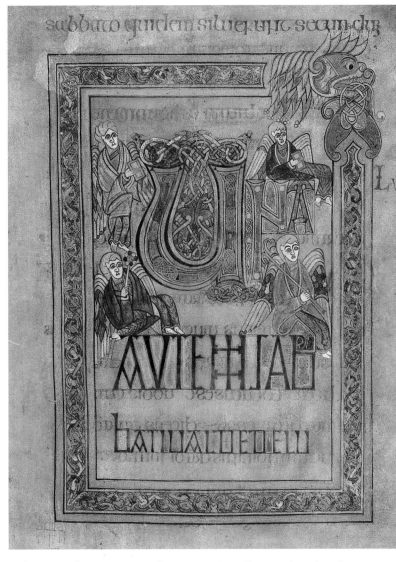

style – in the *scriptoria* of monasteries mostly of the Irish-dominated Celtic church, but often with the patronage of rich Anglo-Saxon kings.

The Irish-inspired manuscript style took time to develop. The dating of the manuscripts is actually very shaky, but an early example may be the elaborated initials in the *Cathach of St Columba* (possibly written by the saint himself), dating probably not much later than AD 600. The skill of the scribes was fully developed by about 680, when it is believed that the *Book of Durrow* was illuminated – arguably the earliest of the surviving masterpieces.

The *Lindisfarne Gospels* are thought to have been created in St Cuthbert's honour.

Ornamental text from the Gospel of St Luke, Book of Kells, about AD 800.

Apparently produced at Lindisfarne under Abbot Eadfrith, the *Gospels* were probably illuminated by an Anglian monk working in the Irish style (according to tradition Eadfrith himself, who is thought to have spent six years in Ireland before becoming bishop in 698). The Venerable Bede (673–735), monk and famed historian of the early English and their evangelization, will certainly have witnessed the creation of similar manuscripts at the Northumbrian double-monastery of Monkwearmouth and Jarrow. This was an Anglian centre connected to Rome rather than the Celtic

(Above) A detail of the Cathach of Columba, about AD 600, showing the early development of the decorative initial letter.

(Right) Here the initial letter has been fully developed to cover the whole page. From the beginning of St Luke's Gospel in the Lindisfarne Gospels, about AD 698.

A NOTE IN THE MARGIN
'Pleasant to me is the glittering of the sun today upon these margins, because it flickers so.'
A note in Irish by an unnamed scribe in a ninth-century manuscript

MIRACULOUS VOLUMES
'I have witnessed people bitten by snakes, on drinking water in which scrapings from the pages of Irish books have been soaked, by this cure [had] the spread of the poison halted and the inflammation relieved ...'
Bede, *History of the English Church and People*, 1,3; eighth century

church, but the Hiberno-Saxon style was the regional fashion at the time. Even among the Celtic and Anglo-Saxon monasteries on the continent, such as St Willibrord's foundation at Echternach, Insular art held sway.

The magnificent *Book of Kells* was probably made in Iona itself, and may be one of the last great examples: it was created shortly before the final Viking attack of 807 which drove the monks to Ireland. If these dates are correct, then the Golden Age of Hiberno-Saxon manuscript illumination lasted for little more than a century.

The artists and their art

The energy and loving skill put into the manuscripts compares favourably with the effort at that time expended on the finery of the Celtic kings. The Tara brooch is perhaps the most splendid example of personal adornment, sharing many stylistic features with the *Lindisfarne Gospels*. Celtic artisans habitually devoted wealth and flair to the manufacture of objects symbolizing the earthly and religious power of their kings. In many ways, the Christian monks, some of whom were drawn from the ranks of Irish craftsmen, continued this tradition, applying their talents to beautifying gospels and psalm-books, to the glory of God rather than that of mortal men.

Working with simple equipment, the artists were able to achieve stunning effects. The manuscript pages were of vellum – fine parchment prepared from the skins of calves or sheep: scores of animals must have been needed to produce a large Gospel book. The treated skins had a surface like very fine suede, perfect for ink and coloured pigments. Drawn, lettered and coloured with a variety of pens and brushes, they were laid out with rulers, compasses and assured free-hand lines. Each page was prepared separately, and the volumes bound in elaborate covers.

The manuscript style evolved over time, the enormous elaborate initial letters eventually coming to dominate the whole page. Embellished with scrollwork derived from La Tène pattern, with triskeles and trumpetlike shapes, or with interlace (especially of the ribbon-bodied, knotted monsters beloved of the contemporary Germanic world), the initials led into the elegant round letters of the text. Developing the late Latin half-uncial script, the

Celtic church created an exquisite *scriptura Scottica*, which was also adopted by the English and the Irish living on the continent.

Many pages are dominated by animal and human figures (symbols of the evangelists and portraits of saints), all highly stylized, some of the beasts being stylistically related to the 'heraldic' animals of the Pictish symbol stones. And ultimately there are 'carpet pages', which may have a cross embedded in the design, but which in essence consist of pure abstract decoration, great tangles of vivid pattern. All these are picked out in the most brilliant pigments.

The end of the tradition

The plundering Norse destroyed a vast wealth of manuscripts, and forced Columba's monastery on Iona to move to Kells in Ireland early in the ninth century. Viking depredations, the Norman invasions, the absorption of the Irish Church by Rome, and the arrival of the European monastic orders all contributed to the disappearance of this art by the twelfth century. The last vestiges of the long La Tène tradition were finally subsumed into the Romanesque style.

(Left) Calligraphic detail and a small decorative sketch from the Book of Kells.

Map of the important ecclesiastical centres and other sites.

(Below) Detail of animal interlace from a carpet page in the Book of Durrow. *Very similar patterns are found in Germanic art, for example on the royal jewellery from the Sutton Hoo ship burial in East Anglia.*

XI

TO MODERN TIMES

'You brave Irish heroes wherever you be,
I pray stand a moment and listen to me,
Your sons and fair daughters are now going away,
And thousands are sailing to Americay.'

Mid nineteenth-century ballad sung by the emigrant Irish

D URING THE MIDDLE AGES the surviving Celtic kingdoms fell one by one into the hands of their
more powerful neighbours, England and, in the
case of the Bretons, France. This led to the widespread
destruction of Celtic-speaking societies, pushing Celtic
tongues towards the precipice of extinction. The English,
for example, annexed Cornwall in Saxon times, leading,
by the eighteenth century, to the death of the Cornish
language.

The destruction of Welsh, Irish and particularly
Highland Scots societies in many ways echoed the
breakdown of Gaulish society through Romanization; it
also had familiar repercussions: the erosion of ancient
ties of obligation and the consequent collapse of the
economic and social order. There are close parallels
between England and Rome: intransigent members of
the old aristocracy, hostile to English rule, were once
more eliminated, while more receptive nobles were
assimilated. England imitated Rome's strategy for dealing
with the Gauls by coopting Highland manpower and its
dangerous military energy into the service of the imperial
British army, to fight foreign wars on distant frontiers.

These fundamental social and economic changes,
combined with the wider upheavals of the industrial
revolution, pushed the remaining Celtic peoples into
mass migration, to the new factory cities of Britain and
across the oceans, to America especially, in the biggest
and last of all the Celtic migrations.

But the exile of so many Celts from the old homelands
also coincided with an awakening to the Celtic past, and
growing consciousness of identity, leading, eventually,
to the reassertion of Celtic nationhood.

Immigrants on their way to a new life in the United States, 1906.

CELTS IN MEDIEVAL AND EARLY MODERN EUROPE

A VIEW OF THE WELSH

'These people are light and active, hardy rather than strong, and entirely bred up to the use of arms; for not only the nobles, but all the people are trained to war, and when the trumpet sounds the tribesman rushes as eagerly from his plough as the courtier from his court. They live more on flesh, milk, and cheese than bread, pay little attention to commerce, shipping, or manufactures, and devote their leisure to the chase and martial exercises. They earnestly study the defence of their country and their liberty. For these they fight, for these they undergo hardships, and for these they willingly sacrifice their lives. They esteem it a disgrace to die in bed, an honour to die on the field of battle.'

Giraldus Cambrensis; twelfth century

Muireadach's Cross, Monasterboice in Co. Louth, Ireland: a tenth-century masterpiece.

'The [Highlanders] delight in variegated garments, especially striped, and their favourite colours are purple and blue. Their ancestors wore plaids of many different colours, and numbers still retain this custom, but the majority ... prefer a dark brown, imitating nearly the leaves of the heather, that ... they may not be discovered ... Their weapons are, for the most part, a bow ... but a few carry swords or Lochaber axes. Instead of a trumpet they use a bagpipe. They are exceedingly fond of music ... Their songs are not inelegant, and, in general, celebrate the praises of brave men; their bards seldom choosing any other subject.'

George Buchanan; later sixteenth century

THE VIKINGS, although fearsome, did not threaten Irish society any more than Christianity had: despite the evangelical zeal of the missionaries, Ireland kept much of its earlier shape, with Gaelic-speaking lords, warriors, bards and learned men. The Norse settled as traders, building the first Irish towns, including Dublin. Irish kings, like Brian Boru, who beat the Vikings at Clontarf in 1014, sought to control them. From the twelfth century, the Norman-French lords who had recently conquered England established themselves in Ireland, bringing castles but, like the Norse, only limited change; many Normans became Gaelicized, even speaking Irish. English kings, following their enterprising barons across the Irish Sea, tried to assert themselves over Gaelic chief and Norman lord alike, but their power remained confined to a precarious area around Dublin.

The turning point came in the sixteenth century, when Henry VIII and Elizabeth I successfully enforced royal authority. The Irish chieftains now held their land not in their own right, but from the English monarch. Conflict was heightened by the Reformation, resulting in a Catholic Ireland dominated by a Protestant England. Loss of autonomy led to unsuccessful rebellions. The last real bid to maintain the old freedoms was made by Hugh O'Neill, Earl of Tyrone, who claimed descent from the Uí Néill. When he fled to France in 1607 his lands in Ulster were confiscated and extensively settled by Protestant Scots and English. This was part of a wider, long-term trend of dispossession, especially of Catholic (and therefore largely Gaelic-speaking) landowners.

A serious rising of the dispossessed Gaelic- and English-speaking Irish in 1641 resulted in atrocities against the Protestants, and the counter-horror of Cromwell's campaign which hardened Irish hatred for English rule. The modern pattern of two nations in Ireland, Celtic-Catholic and Protestant-British, was set by the deposed Catholic James II's siege of Londonderry, and the new Protestant King William III's victory over him at the Boyne in 1690. Dispossession, and penal laws against the religion of the native Catholic Irish, led to the demise of Celtic speech among the ruling classes. By 1714, only 7 per cent of Irish land was owned by Catholics. Following a disastrous uprising in 1798, Ireland was forcibly joined with Britain in 1801.

Wales

The Normans who conquered England in 1066 soon turned their attention to Wales, a struggle culminating in Edward I's destruction of the principality of Gwynedd in the 1270s. The last champion of Welsh independence, Owain Glyn Dŵr (Owen Glendower) led a ten-year-long revolt, finally suppressed in 1410. He then mysteriously vanished, later living in legend ready, like Arthur, to come again in Wales' time of need.

In 1485, the Anglo-Welsh Henry Tudor became king of England. Henry VII did not forget his Welsh roots, naming his eldest son Arthur. But King Arthur was not destined to reign again; the prince died young, succeeded by his younger brother, the thoroughly English Henry VIII. Under the Tudor dynasty Wales was politically united with England by Acts of Parliament from 1536 to 1543.

Much of Welsh native culture disappeared in the sixteenth century, with the abolition of Welsh law. The long tradition of professional bards lapsed by 1700, and the decline in local musical traditions was hastened by the spread of Methodism from 1660. The Welsh language was progressively, but far from completely, displaced by English.

(Left) Echoes of a pagan past on the walls of Clonfert cathedral, Co. Galway, Ireland. The stylized faces on this late-twelfth-century gable echo the severed heads of early Irish myth.

(Right) Irish soldiers serving on the continent, drawn by Albrecht Dürer in 1521. The wars of the Renaissance and early modern times provided many opportunities for Irish and Scottish exiles and soldiers of fortune.

Brittany

The squabbling petty kingdoms of Brittany were defeated by Clovis, King of the Franks (reigned 482–512), but he failed to impose taxes or government on them. Unified into one kingdom in the ninth century, Brittany became one of several largely autonomous principalities owing nominal allegiance to the French crown. Now a French medieval feudal state rather than a Celtic kingdom, it only lost its independence in 1488, union with France following in 1532.

The Highlanders

The clans of the Scottish Highlands and Islands remained a law unto themselves for 1,000 years, distinct from the Lowlanders in their Celtic language and way of life. Scottish kings tried in vain to control them, until the overthrow of the Royal House of Stuart with the expulsion of James II in 1688. Many Highlanders remained fiercely loyal to the exiled house, and it was this commitment to the Jacobite cause which ultimately brought about their downfall.

Rebellions followed the Union with England in 1707, culminating in the famous rising under Bonnie Prince Charlie in 1745 which led at last to the military occupation of the Highlands, and the smashing of clan power. The Forty-Five was followed by bloody reprisals, and something even more destructive: the banning of the traditional way of life – not least private war and raiding. This, together with the displace-

ment of some clan chiefs and the Anglicization of others, resulted in the collapse of the old social order: the autocratic chiefs no longer felt responsible for their clansmen. The fighting strength of the Gaelic-speaking clans was drained by the drafting of men in their thousands into the Highland regiments of the British army. Within a century, the old culture was dead.

(Left) The archetypal wild Highlander. Alistair Mhor Grant, at Castle Grant in 1714.

TO THE ENDS OF THE EARTH: THE NEW MIGRATIONS

(Right) Slum conditions in nineteenth-century New York: Mullen's Alley, 1888–89. Irish migrants faced terrible privations in their new lives, as well as the old.

'Farewell to the groves of Shillelagh and shamrock,
Farewell to the girls of old Ireland all around.
May their hearts be as merry as ever I would wish them,
When far away on the Ocean I'm bound.
'O my father is old and my mother's quite feeble,
to leave their own country it grieves their hearts sore.
O their tears in great drops down their cheeks they are rolling,
To think they must die upon a foreign shore ...'

Extracts from a nineteenth-century Irish migration song

(Below) The end of an ancient way of life. Abandoned house on the shores of Loch Hourn, with the bulk of Knoydart (the last part of the Scottish Highlands to be cleared) in the distance.

THE NINETEENTH CENTURY was a period of enormous social and economic upheaval, which affected the remaining Celtic lands as much as the rest of Europe. These areas became one of the main sources of emigration to the New World.

Scottish rebels had been sent as convicts to the Americas in the seventeenth and eighteenth centuries, and Welsh Quakers and Baptists also crossed the ocean, seeking religious freedom and a purer life. Now events conspired to turn the trickle of migrants into a flood.

Scotland: the Highland clearances

A devastating symptom of the collapse of the old Highland society after 1745 was the fact that chiefs now found the large populations in the glens a financial liability rather than a source of armed strength and prestige. The native lairds, and incoming English landowners, systematically evicted most of the Highland population between 1800 and 1850, turning the land over to profitable flocks of sheep. Those who did not take ship for the colonies migrated to the growing industrial slums of cities like Glasgow.

Ireland: starvation and emigration

The destruction of the old social order led to increasing distress among the mass of ordinary, Gaelic-speaking Irish, for the ruling classes in Ireland were even more callous and incompetent than their English counterparts. The country's problems were compounded by the vast population growth that took place in the early nine-

teenth-century – rising from five million in 1801 to eight million in 1840 – mostly of desperately poor families subsisting on potatoes. Disaster struck in 1845–47, when the potato blight brought mass starvation. The famine was an economic, more than a natural disaster, for the blight affected only potatoes: Ireland continued to export many other foods while those too poor to buy them perished. It is estimated that one million people died, and another million emigrated. It was the greatest single impetus to a longer-term mass migration from Ireland.

By 1940, about five million Irish had emigrated to America alone. Others, along with Welsh and Scots, went to Canada and Australasia, or to the growing industrial cities of Britain; the Liverpudlian accent today is detectably similar to that of Dublin.

THE CELTS TODAY

SINCE 1921, there has again been an independent Celtic state, the Irish Republic, where the speaking of a Celtic tongue has enormous cultural and political significance, as indeed it still has among many Scots, Welsh and Bretons, even if they now mostly speak the languages of their more powerful neighbours. Radio and television broadcasts in Welsh and Gaelic, and the popularity of events such as Pan-Celtic festivals, offer renewed hope for the survival of these languages – as a living link with the Celtic-speaking cultures of the Iron Age.

Today there are more people claiming some kind of Celtic identity than at any time in history, mostly descendants of the emigrants to the four corners of the world. Among some of these groups, old Celtic traditions survive as well as they do in the homelands. So Welsh-speakers still hold eisteddfodau in Patagonia, while in Canada – e.g. at Glencoe, Inverness County, Nova Scotia (New Scotland) – there are Gaelic-speakers who remember the deeds of ancestors born in the Scottish Highlands.

Celtic speech may still be in slow decline, but the contribution of Celtic-speaking peoples to European and world history is increasingly appreciated – and it is also clear that most of the people of Europe are likely to number Celtic speakers among their ancestors. The heritage of the Celts is not only around us: for many of us, it is also in our blood.

A Celtic might-have-been

With hindsight, it seems that the Roman destruction of most of the Celtic world was inevitable – but was it? There was a single moment when, if things had gone slightly differently, the history of the Celts, and ultimately of the entire world, would have followed quite another course.

In 390 BC the 'barbarian' Celtic Senones had the young city of Rome at their mercy (p. 34). Suppose that, instead of accepting ransom and withdrawing, they had destroyed the city, killing or enslaving its population (as the 'civilized' Romans had just done to Etruscan Veii). Without Rome – soon to develop unique skills in war and empire-building – Celtdom might still be a major power in continental Europe. Without Rome, we can imagine a Gallic urban civilization growing north of the Alps, forming a great Celtic-speaking medieval state in place of France. What then would have been the history of Europe, the Americas, or the rest of the world? Without Rome, this might have been a very different book – and in Celtic, instead of English.

Statue of the dying Cú Chulainn, a monument in the Dublin Post Office to commemorate the Easter Rising against British rule in 1916. It is remarkable that a strongly Catholic state like Ireland should choose a pagan symbol for a great national shrine: Celtic roots are deep indeed.

GLOSSARY

Anatolia Otherwise known as Asia Minor, this is the landmass roughly corresponding to modern Asiatic Turkey.

anthropomorphic In the form of a human being.

Asia Minor See **Anatolia**.

barrow See **tumulus**.

Brittany Westernmost France, the ancient Armorica, colonized by and renamed after Britons in the fifth century AD.

Celts From an uncertainly defined or located continental ethnic name, rendered in Greek as *Keltoi* and in Latin as *Celtae*, here defined as people speaking Celtic languages. See also **Gaul** and **Galatians**.

Celtiberians Celtic-speaking tribes of pre-Roman Spain.

Cisalpine Gaul 'Gaul this side of the Alps', the Roman name for the Celtic-occupied parts of northern Italy, centred on the Po Valley.

civitas (pl. civitates) A Latin term meaning city-state, also applied to the tribal states and peoples of areas like Celtic Gaul and Britain.

Classical world A shorthand collective term for the Greek, Roman, Etruscan and related civilizations.

crannog A settlement on an artificial island in a lake (in Britain or Ireland).

equestrian order The second rank of Roman citizens, after the senatorial order. Equestrians were often businessmen, and in imperial times had to possess property worth at least 400,000 sesterces. They filled many military and civil administrative posts under the emperors.

Galatians *Galatae* was a Greek term for continental Celts in general, and those who entered the Balkans in particular. From the third century BC, Galatia was a specific kingdom in central Turkey.

Gallia Comata Literally 'hairy Gaul', this term was used in the earlier first century BC to distinguish unconquered from conquered Gaul (*Gallia Transalpina*).

Gaul Romans called the Celts of France, the Alpine regions and northern Italy *Galli*. *Gallia* proper corresponded roughly to modern France.

Hallstatt culture The name now given to the archaeological 'culture' of the later Bronze and early Iron Ages of much of central Europe. Hallstatt in Austria was the site where this culture was first described.

inhumation Burial of the dead (as opposed to cremation).

Iron Age The term used by archaeologists to denote the latter phase of prehistory, after the Bronze Age and before the beginning of the historical period (which for much of Europe north of the Alps starts with the Roman conquest). Iron was the principal tool- and weapon-making metal during this period, which lasted from approximately the seventh to the first century BC in Gaul.

Ligurians The native people of the coastal areas from Marseilles to northwestern Italy. Their ethnic connections are obscure.

millefiore Literally 'a thousand flowers', this modern Italian term refers to the technique for making tiny patterns in glass by assembling bundles of coloured rods, heating and fusing them, and then stretching them into thin canes. Slices of the resulting canes contained the original pattern, greatly reduced, and could be inlaid into metalwork, etc.

oppidum Latin term for a town or urban agglomeration, by extension applied in documentary sources to some Celtic proto-towns and fortified sites. Used by many archaeologists to refer specifically to late Iron Age proto-towns on the Continent and in Britain.

procurator A Roman provincial official of equestrian rank. Mostly applied to financial officials.

Romanitas The (somewhat indefinable!) quality of being Roman.

Roman Iron Age This term refers to the period of the Roman empire's existence, but applies to areas *outside* the empire, for example northern Scotland, Ireland, free Germany etc.

senator A member of the senatorial order, the largely hereditary first rank of Roman citizens. Under the emperors, senators had to own property worth at least a million sesterces. The senate lost most of its power to the emperor, but remained important and prestigious. Membership was gained by election to junior state magistracies, and senior magistrates, provincial governors, generals and emperors were drawn from its ranks.

Scotti Irish raiders and settlers in late- and post-Roman Britain.

La Tène culture The name given to the archaeological culture typical of many parts of Europe and the British Isles, beginning in the fifth century BC. Characterized by a particular range of artifacts, and especially by the La Tène art style, it is commonly simply thought of as the material culture of the early Celts, although this is simplistic.

torc (torque) A neckring of metal. The name implies that it was twisted, although many were not. Typically thought of as items of Celtic jewellery, torcs were also worn by other peoples and were adopted as military decorations by the Romans.

Transalpine Gaul 'Gaul beyond the Alps' (in contrast to Cisalpine Gaul). A Roman designation which came to mean the Roman province conquered in the 120s BC.

tumulus A mound or barrow over a burial.

votive Given as an offering to the gods, literally in fulfilment of a vow.

GAZETTEER

The archaeology of the Celts is largely known through portable artifacts, scattered in many collections across the museums of Europe and beyond. The following list concentrates on the most important collections, but also gives a selection of less well-known sites and museums. (Please note, however, that there can be no guarantee that all the material possessed by a museum will be on display. Some of the material discussed in this book is yet to appear in permanent displays.)

AUSTRIA The site of **Hallstatt** itself is worth visiting: it features reconstructed tombs and access to some salt-workings. Most of the material from the site is held in the **Vienna** Naturhistorisches Museum (e.g. the scabbard with figures of soldiers, and textiles from the mines), although some of it (plus the Dürrnberg flagon) can be seen in the Museum Carolino Augusteum, **Salzburg**, along with other collections including blacksmith's tools. (Further material from Hallstatt is displayed in the British Museum, **London**.) The Vienna Naturhistorisches Museum also has items from ex-Yugoslavia (the Mihovo helmet) and Stradonice in Bohemia, while the **Hallein** Keltenmuseum houses material from the Dürrnberg salt-working centre and its cemetery. See also the Museum für Urgeschichte des Landes Niederösterreich at **Asparn** near Vienna. There are reconstructed prehistoric buildings at Asparn. The **Magdalensberg** trading settlement in the kingdom of Noricum is open to the public. Material from the site is in the Landesmuseum für Kärnten, **Klagenfurt**. The Manndersdorf Museum also contains rich cemetery material of the fourth and third centuries BC.

BELGIUM The Musées Royaux d'Art et d'Histoire in **Brussels** display Iron Age material including the Eigenbilzen gold drinking horn mount and vehicle fittings. The gold treasure from Frasnez-les-Buissenal is in the Metropolitan Museum of Art, **New York**. The Provinciaal Gallo-Romeins Museum, **Tongres** also houses interesting material.

BOSNIA The condition of the important **Sarajevo** Museum is unclear at the time of writing.

BULGARIA Vehicle fittings from the chariot grave at Mezek are in the Narodnija Archeologičeski Muzeji, **Sofia**. See also the archaeological museum in **Plovdiv**.

CROATIA The Arheolški Muzej in **Zagreb** holds jewellery and weapons.

CZECH REPUBLIC The Národní Múzeum, **Prague**, houses the Mšecké Žehrovice head, the hoard from the ancient hot spring at Duchcov, and material (including surgical instruments) from the *oppidum* at Stradonice. Glass bracelets and bronze waist-belts are also held here, plus objects from the Bohemian 'princely' burials at Chlum. The Maloměřice flagon mounts are in the Moravské Zemské Múzeum in **Brno**, Moravia, which also has collections of pottery and jewellery. Other museums holding La Tène material include the Muzeum husitského revolučniho hnuti at **Tábor**; the Hradní Muzeum in **Křivoklát**; and **Boskovice** Muzeum, which holds finds from the Staré Hradisko *oppidum*. The *oppidum* of **Závist** merits a visit, as does that at **Trisov** in the south, and **Staré Hradisko** in Moravia.

DENMARK The silver-gilt Gundestrup and bronze Rynkeby cauldrons are in the Danish Nationalmuzeet, **Copenhagen**, along with the Dejbjerg carts (found in a Jutland bog but argued by some to be of Celtic manufacture). The Brå cauldron is in the **Moesgaard** Forhistorisk Museum.

FRANCE In **Paris**, the Musée des Antiquités Nationales, St Germain-en-Laye, holds key collections including material from Alesia, a number of torcs (e.g. from Mailly-le-Camp), finds from La Gorge Meillet grave, the Amfreville helmet, the Euffigneix and Bouray statuettes, Gallo-Greek inscriptions, and material from Bibracte. The *Parc Asterix* Gallic theme-park north of Paris is also well worth a visit, especially for families.

In Brittany, at **Rennes**, the Musée de Bretagne has fairly good Iron Age collections. A small stone figure with a lyre, perhaps a bard, from Paule is on view in the Nouveau Musée at **St-Breuc**. The **Nantes** museum contains material from the rich late La Tène tomb from Châtillon-sur-Indre.

The Agris helmet is in the Musée des Beaux-Arts, **Angoulême**. **Rouen**'s museum holds collections including chariot burial material and some fine iron fire-dogs. The St Maur-en-Chausée warrior statuette belongs to the Musée Départmental de l'Oise, **Beauvais**, which has rich Iron Age collections. The Musée Municipal, **Epernay**, contains extensive collections of grave finds, arms, jewellery and ceramics, from the fifth century BC and after. At **Soissons** the Musée Saint Léger holds the three-faced Mercury relief. The **Châlons-sur-Marne** museum contains extensive collections, especially of La Tène cemetery finds, while the material from Gournay-sur-Aronde is displayed in the Musée Vivenel, **Compiègne**. At **Alesia**, traces of the pre-Roman site are overshadowed by interesting Gallo-Roman remains. There is no visible sign of Caesar's great siegeworks. There are good collections in **Troyes**. A visit to see the treasure of the Vix 'princess' in the Musée Archéologique, **Châtillon-sur-Seine**, can be combined with a trip to **Mont Lassois**, an impressive hill (although the earthworks of the Hallstatt hillfort are not readily detectable).

There are reliefs of Gallo-Roman life at a number of cities in France, such as in **Bourges** and **Metz**. **Dijon** museum holds early Roman period wooden figures from the source of the Seine. At **Mont Beuvray**, the ancient Bibracte, the Iron Age defences can still be seen. Finds from the old excavations are in Paris and Autun (Musée Rolin); Autun also boasts the impressive Temple of Janus, a Romano-Celtic temple. The Archeodrome, **Beaune**, contains a number of reconstructions of monuments, including a Hallstatt barrow, a section of Caesar's Alesia siegeworks, and a Romano-Celtic temple. **Chalon-sur-Saône** museum has recently been refurbished; it displays Iron Age metalwork and imported Roman amphorae. The Musée Déchelette, **Roanne**, holds La Tène pottery, as well as metal animal figurines and other objects. **Clermont-Ferrand** museum possesses early Gallo-Roman wooden statues, and a lead curse tablet in Gallic, from Chamalières. The Musée de la Civilisation Gallo-Romaine, **Lyons**, houses the Coligny calendar as well as remarkable collections representing the cosmopolitan life of the Roman city.

The site of the Saluvian capital of **Entremont** is well laid out, and lies close to **Aix-en-Provence** where the Musée Granet (which houses the sculpture and other finds from the site) has recently been renovated. In **Marseilles**, the Historical Museum near the old port includes a display on the Saluvian sanctuary at Roquepertuse, although the main collection from the site is in the Musée de la Vieille Charité, also in Marseilles. **Avignon**'s Musée Calvet possesses stone dedications to Gallic gods, while its Musée Lapidaire houses the warrior statues from Mondragon and Vachères, and other Gaulish pieces. The ancient religious centre of **Glanum**, near St Rémy-de-Provence, is a very picturesque site, with Graeco-Roman temples and public buildings around the ancient spring pool. There is a good new on-site museum. At **Nîmes**, the shape of the Iron Age and

Roman pool of the god Nemausus can be made out in the Jardin de la Fontaine. On the hill above stands the Tour Magne, probably of pre-Roman origin. **Ambrussum**, an *oppidum* site close to the motorway between Nîmes and Montpellier, is well sign-posted and worth a detour. At **Enserune**, the site of the proto-town is supplemented by an on-site museum which holds collections from the cemetery and the settlement. The museum at **Millau** has an excellent display of Samian pottery from the kilns at La Graufesenque, which can themselves be seen. There are also very important collections in the Musée Saint-Raymond at **Toulouse** (e.g. gold jewellery).

GERMANY The Schwarzenbach cup and grave assemblage is in **Berlin**, in the Antikenmuseum der Staatlichen Museen Preussischer Kulturbesitz, which also houses the Canosa helmet from Italy. **Cologne** contains many monuments of the Roman period, as well as the important Römisches-Germanisches Museum. The Waldalgesheim tomb assemblage, the Niederzier gold hoard and the decorated stone pillar from Pfalzfeld are in the Rheinisches Landesmuseum, **Bonn**. The imperial city of **Trier**, capital of the Belgic Treveri, is also home to a Rheinisches Landesmuseum, where the early La Tène material from the Weisskirchen princely tomb and other finds are displayed. There are many Roman sites in the Moselle region, for example the villa at **Nennig**. The collections of the Mittelrheinisches Landesmuseum at **Mainz** include La Tène jewellery. The jewellery and other objects from the Reinheim grave are in the Landesmuseum für Vor- und Frühgeschichte, **Saarbrücken**. At **Stuttgart**, the Württembergisches Landesmuseum contains collections from the Asperg region, including the Hochdorf and Kleinaspergle burials, goldwork from Bad Cannstatt, the Hirschlanden warrior statue, and gold from barrows around the Heuneburg. It also possesses wooden figures from the sanctuary site at Fellbach-Schmiden. At **Asperg** itself the setting of the Hallstatt fort and the Kleinaspergle barrow can still be seen. The objects from the 'surgeon's grave' at München-Obermenzing and material from the *oppidum* of Manching are housed in the Prähistorische Staatssammlung, **Munich**.

GREAT BRITAIN *Scotland* In **Edinburgh**, the National Museums of Scotland contain the Torrs pony cap, the Deskford *carnyx*, the Traprain Law late Roman treasure, St Ninian's Isle hoard, Norrie's Law pendants and other Pictish treasures.

A Scottish hillfort site worth visiting is **the Chesters** at Haddington. There are well-preserved brochs on Shetland at Jarlshof, **Clickhimin** and **Broch of Mousa**, while on the mainland, good examples may be seen at **Dún Trodden** and **Dún Telve** in Gleann Beag, near Glenelg. To reach the latter it is necessary to pass close by the Bernera barracks on the Sound of Sleat, a British military outpost built in 1723 in an attempt to control the Highland clans.

Sections of the **Antonine Wall** are visible as earthworks. One of the best parts to visit is around Rough Castle fort. There are a number of other Roman forts which are worth seeing, e.g. **Ardoch** in Perthshire.

England In northern England, many parts of **Hadrian's Wall** remain intact, although there are fewer obvious traces of the native population. In **Newcastle upon Tyne**, the University Museum of Antiquities and the Society of Antiquaries contain some Iron Age material and important collections relating to the Roman military occupation. At the large Brigantian site of **Stanwick** a section of the earthwork defences has been reconstructed. **Liverpool** Museum contains some important items of La Tène metalwork. **Hull** Museum possesses good new displays of Iron Age and Romano-British archaeology, including reconstructed chariot burials and dioramas. The Castle Museum in **Norwich** has important prehistoric collections, including part

of the Snettisham goldwork, while in **Cambridge**, the University Museum of Archaeology and Ethnology holds La Tène metalwork. **Colchester** Castle Museum contains finds from the Iron Age *oppidum* and the Roman city, including traces of the Boudican revolt. The castle stands on the podium of the Temple of Claudius. See also **Chelmsford** Museum. At Verulamium (**St Albans**) there are extensive visible Romano-British remains; the newly refurbished Verulamium Museum tells the story of the Iron Age and the Romano-British town.

The British Museum in **London** holds one of the world's finest collections of British masterpieces, including the Waterloo helmet; the Battersea, Chertsea and Witham shields; the Kirkburn sword; the Snettisham hoards (some of which are in Norwich Castle Museum); the Holcombe and Desborough mirrors; and extensive displays of weapons, pottery, coins and grave material from Britain and Gaul (including both the Hallstatt and La Tène 'type-sites'). It also houses the Basse-Yutz flagons, items from the Somme-Bionne chariot grave, and Classical imports from the fifth to first centuries BC, including Roman amphorae in the reconstructed late Iron Age grave from Welwyn Garden City. On display too is extensive material from Roman Britain and Gaul, including the tomb of Classicianus, and the Mildenhall and other hoards. The British Library holds the Lindisfarne Gospels, while the Museum of London possesses some important Iron Age metalwork and fine displays relating to the Roman city.

At **Silchester**, the site of the late Iron Age *oppidum* lies beneath the clearly visible Roman city walls. See also **Reading** Museum. In Hampshire, **Butser** Ancient Farm near Petersfield is open to the public for much of the year; it displays Iron Age agricultural techniques, crops and livestock, and also has impressive reconstructions of roundhouses. **Fishbourne** Roman Palace, perhaps the residence of King Cogidubnus, is on the outskirts of the Iron Age settlement and Roman town of **Chichester**. **Portchester Castle** is not far away.

The hillfort of **Danebury**, Hampshire, is a pleasant site to visit, especially in conjunction with a trip to the Museum of the Iron Age in nearby Andover, which houses a fine display of the Danebury excavations. The Iron Age forts on **Hambledon Hill** and **Hod Hill** are impressive, the latter complete with an invasion-period Roman fort in the corner. **Maiden Castle** is one of the most spectacular prehistoric sites in Britain. Finds from the excavations are in nearby **Dorchester** Museum.

The Ashmolean Museum, **Oxford**, has Iron Age collections, including the Little Wittenham sword. The **Bagendon Dykes** are near to the Roman town of Corinium (**Cirencester**), and the Corinium Museum. See also **Gloucester** City Museum. The **Glastonbury** lake villages are now illustrated through a new interpretation centre in the Somerset Levels. **Tintagel**, with its spurious Arthurian connections, has a British monastery of the fifth to eighth centuries AD.

Wales The National Museum of Wales in **Cardiff** houses the finds from Llyn Cerrig Bach in Anglesey, as well as other extensive collections from prehistoric to post-medieval times, including the Capel Garmon fire-dog, and many early Christian stone monuments. Welsh hillforts that merit a visit include the **Breiddin** in Powys; Moel-y-Gaer, **Rhosesmor** in Clwyd; or **Dinas Emrys**, Gwynedd – an Iron Age fort with 'Arthurian' period occupation. There is also the reconstructed Iron Age village at **Castell Henllys**.

HUNGARY The Magyar Nemzeti Múzeum, **Budapest**, contains swords, spears, jewellery (including gold torcs), and pottery from all over Hungary. There is cemetery material in the Damjanich János Múzeum, **Szolnok**. Collections may also be found in other museums, for example in **Esztergom, Keszthely, Pécs, Sopron, Székesfehérvár** and **Szombathely**.

IRELAND (Eire and Northern Ireland) The National Museum of Ireland in **Dublin** boasts a rich collection of antiquities from prehistoric to post-medieval times, including the Broighter hoard, Clonmacnois torc, Loughnashade trumpets and much other metalwork. It also contains wooden items like the Clonoura shield, plus Ogham stones and early Christian treasures such as the eighth-century AD Ardagh Chalice. Trinity College, Dublin, houses the Book of Kells and Book of Durrow.

It is worth visiting the evocative earthworks of the royal site of **Tara**, Co. Meath.

Navan fort lies close to **Armagh** in Northern Ireland. The cathedral church of St Patrick in the historic city of Armagh is well worth seeing, as is the library, which houses the Tanderagee 'idol'. The archaeology galleries of the Ulster Museum in **Belfast** display swords, scabbards, horse-harnesses and other items such as the wood-and-bronze tankard from Carrickfergus.

Glendalough provides good examples of early ecclesiastical architecture, including 'St Kevin's kitchen' and a fine round tower. **Cork** Public Museum possesses the bronze 'Cork horns', perhaps a religious headdress. The Rock of **Cashel** in Tipperary – the ancient royal centre of Munster – is crowned by a ruined medieval cathedral. Reconstructions of a ringfort, a crannog and other early Irish buildings may be found at the Craggaunowen Project, near **Quin** in Co. Limerick. The Hunt Museum at the University of **Limerick** is also part of the Project.

Do not miss **Dún Aengus** on Inishmore in the Aran Islands, Co. Galway: it is one of the most spectacular sites anywhere in the Celtic world. There are important Celtic crosses at a number of sites including **Clonmacnois**, **Durrow** and **Monasterboice**. Ireland also has a number of pre-Christian, La Tène-decorated stones, of which the most famous is at **Turoe**, Co. Galway. The British Museum in **London** displays some objects of Irish origin, including a scabbard from the River Bann, an Ogham stone, the Coleraine treasure (silver looted from late Roman Britain), and medieval material, both Celtic and Viking.

ITALY At **Ancona**, the Museo Nazionale delle Marche has extensive collections, especially from the Montefortino and Filottrano cemeteries. In **Bologna**, see the Museo Civico Archeologico and Museo Civico L. Fantini (where the Civitalba relief and important grave finds – e.g. from Monte Bibele – are kept). Other notable centres are at **Como** (housing the Bormio relief and other extensive collections, including a vehicle and other finds from the Ca' Morta cemetery), **Brescia** (contains the Manerbio silver *phalerae*), **Bergamo**, **Milan**, **Modena**, and **Padua** (where the chariot relief is held). The museum in **Turin** houses Celtic metalwork, grave-goods and other treasures.

LUXEMBOURG Treveran grave groups of the early Roman period from Göblingen-Nospelt are in the Musée National d'Histoire et d'Art, which also holds material from the **Titelburg** site (itself worth a visit). The Musée Luxembourgeois at **Arlon** contains a Gallo-Roman relief with market and agricultural scenes.

NETHERLANDS Holland was largely outside the Celtic world, but La Tène material has been found there, e.g. the enamelled bronze mirror now held in the Provinciaal Museum, **Nijmegen**. The new 'Archeon', currently under construction at **Alphen aan den Rijn**, will include reconstructed 'Celtic' fields, prehistoric buildings in the local regional style and a Roman fort.

POLAND Finds from the middle La Tène site at Iwanowice near Cracow are in the Muzeum Archeologyczne, **Warsaw**.

PORTUGAL In **Lisbon**, the Museu Nacional de Arqueologia possesses hoard material, vessels, bracelets and brooches, as well as torcs (such as those from Vilas Boas and Paradela do Rio).

RUMANIA The Muzeul Naţional de Istorie, **Bucharest**, holds the Ciumeşti warrior grave and other items from the same cemetery. See also the museums at **Cluj**, **Secuieni** and **Sibiu**.

SERBIA The Muzej Grada Beograda, **Belgrade**, contains pottery and jewellery. There are Celtic coins in the Narodni Muzej. **Novi Sad** Museum contains material from Gomolava, the settlement of the Celtic Scordisci.

SLOVAKIA The Slovenské Národné Muzeum, **Bratislava**, has finds from the **Bratislava-Devín** *oppidum*, which is itself worth seeing. Other museums at **Komárno**, **Košice** and **Michalovce** contain La Tène material.

SLOVENIA The Narodni Muzej, **Ljubljana**, contains La Tène coins, swords and a helmet.

SPAIN The spectacular city of **Numantia** is a must for visitors, while the excellent new Museo Numantino at **Soria** possesses many artifacts from the site, as does the Museo Arqueológico Nacional, **Madrid** (including the wolf's head trumpet). The latter possesses the most extensive collection of metalwork in Spain – including coins, torcs and other jewellery – plus sculpture and ceramics. In **Avila**, the Museo di Avila contains metalwork and grave goods. Much of the best figural sculpture of the period is in **Jaén**'s Museo Provincial, and in the Museo at **Burgos**. A number of other Spanish museums display putatively Celtic material, for example **Salamanca**, **Saragossa** and **Asturias**. The Museo Provincial in **Lugo** owns gold torcs, while in **Barcelona**, the Museo Arqueológico displays swords.

SWITZERLAND Material from **La Tène** itself is displayed in a number of museums, including the Musée Schwab, **Biel**; the Schweizerisches Landesmuseum, **Zurich** (which also houses the Erstfeld gold hoard); the Musée d'Art et d'Histoire, **Geneva** (e.g. a leather-worker's toolkit); and the Musée Cantonal d'Archéologie, **Neuchâtel** (e.g. some of the swords and toilet sets, and a cauldron).

The Historisches Museum, **Basel**, contains major groups of material from the Gasfabrik site and the Münsterhügel *oppidum*. In **Berne**, the Bernisches Historisches Museum has extensive collections of weapons and votive deposits, grave material (including the key Münsingen-Rain cemetery) and finds from the Bern-Engehalbinsel *oppidum* (of which the defences may still be seen) and the Port-Nidau votive material (arms etc.).

At **Lausanne**, the Musée Cantonal d'Archéologie contains tomb-groups, arms, jewellery and other finds from St-Sulpice.

TURKEY In Turkey itself there is as yet nothing to see of the Galatians. The famous reliefs from Pergamon depicting captured Galatian arms are in **Berlin** (Pergamonmuseum), as are all three known Galatian La Tène brooches from Turkey (two in the Museum für Vor- und Frühgeschichte, the other in the Antikenmuseum der Staatlichen Museen Preussischer Kulturbesitz). The famous Dying Gaul can be seen in the Capitoline Museums, **Rome**, while the statue of the Gaul committing suicide beside his dead wife is in the Museo Nazionale, Rome. Other copies of statues of Galatians from the original Pergamon victory monument are in **Naples**, **Paris** and **Venice**.

UKRAINE At **Užhgorod**, the Oblasnij Muzej possesses metalwork, including swords, of La Tène affinity.

FURTHER READING

A vast range of literature in a great many languages has been written on the Celts. The following selection concentrates mainly on titles in English, but readers seeking foreign-language and more specialist books and papers are referred to the bibliographies of the books listed below. There are also several specialist journals, such as the *Proceedings of the Prehistoric Society* and *Gallia Préhistoire*, where many new discoveries are published.

General books on the Iron Age Celts and their world
Chapter 1: Who Were the Celts?
An enormous collection of papers on the Celtic world was assembled for the book which accompanied the great Venice exhibition of Celtic archaeology: Kruta, V., Frey, O., Raftery, B. and Szabó, M. (eds), *The Celts* (Thames and Hudson, London/Rizzoli, New York 1991). This contains information on almost every conceivable aspect of Celtic life, as well as a comprehensive and multilingual bibliography.

An excellent introduction to the methods of archaeology and theoretical developments is Renfrew, C. and Bahn, P., *Archaeology: Theories, Methods and Practice* (Thames and Hudson, London and New York 1991).

To pursue themes such as prestige goods economies, and the idea of state development arising from rivalry and interplay between groups of communities ('peer-polity interaction'), the reader is referred, for example, to Collis, J., *The European Iron Age* (Batsford, London 1984 – very much an archaeological view, discussing the Hallstatt and La Tène cultures in their wider European context). See also Cunliffe, B., *Greeks, Romans and Barbarians* (Batsford, London 1988), and Champion, T. and Champion, S., 'Peer polity interaction in the European Iron Age', in Renfrew, C. and Cherry, J., *Peer polity interaction and sociopolitical change*, pp. 59–68 (Cambridge University Press, Cambridge 1986).

On the question of the origins of the Celtic languages, see: Renfrew, C., *Archaeology and Language* (Penguin, Harmondsworth/Cambridge University Press, New York 1987, especially Chapter 9 on the 'ethnogenesis' of the Celts). Mallory, J.P., *In Search of the Indo-Europeans: Language, Archaeology and Myth* (Thames and Hudson, London and New York 1989) presents an alternative view.

The following discuss the question of modern conceptualizations of the Celts: Piggott, S., *Ancient Britons and the Antiquarian Imagination: Ideas from the Renaissance to the Regency* (Thames and Hudson, London and New York 1989); Trevor-Roper, H., 'The Invention of Tradition: The Highland Tradition of Scotland', in Hobsbawm, E. and Ranger, T. (eds), *The Invention of Tradition*, pp. 15–41 (Cambridge University Press, Cambridge 1983); Morgan, P., 'From a Death to a View: The Hunt for the Welsh Past in the Romantic Period', in Hobsbawm, E. and Ranger, T. (eds), *The Invention of Tradition*, pp. 43–100 (Cambridge University Press, Cambridge 1983); Chapman, M., *The Celts: the construction of a myth* (Macmillan Press, Basingstoke/St Martin's Press, New York 1992); and Merriman, N., 'Value and motivation in prehistory: the evidence for "Celtic spirit"', in Hodder, I. (ed.), *The Archaeology of Contextual Meanings*, pp. 111–16 (Cambridge University Press, Cambridge 1987).
Other references
Cunliffe, B., *The Celtic World*, Constable, London 1992 (reissue of original 1979 edn).
Filip, J., *Celtic Civilization and its Heritage*, Collet, Wellingborough/Academia, Prague 1977.
Powell, T. G. E., *The Celts*, Thames and Hudson, London and New York 1980 (new edn).
Eluère, C., *The Celts: First Masters of Europe*, Thames and Hudson, London/Abrams, New York 1993.
Chadwick, N., *The Celts*, Penguin, Harmondsworth and New York 1971.
Ross, A., *Pagan Celtic Britain*, Constable, London 1992 (new edn).

Chapter 2: The Earliest Celts
Here are some examples of specific works on important discoveries: Joffroy, R., *Le Trésor de Vix (Cote D'Or)* (Presses Universitaires, Paris 1954); Biel, J., *Der Keltenfürst von Hochdorf* (Konrad Theiss, Stuttgart 1985); Vouga, P., *La Tène* (Karl W. Hiersemann, Leipzig 1923).

Chapter 3: The Celtic Lands
Much information on this topic is also available in the general works cited above. Kruta et al, *The Celts* (op. cit.), is a good place to start.
Other references
Rigby, V., 'The Iron Age: continuity or invasion?', in Longworth, I. and Cherry, J., *Archaeology in Britain since 1945*, pp. 52–72, British Museum Publications, London 1986.
Cunliffe, B., *Iron Age Communities in Britain*, Routledge, London and New York 1991 (3rd edn).
Cunliffe, B., *Danebury: Anatomy of an Iron Age Hillfort*, Batsford/English Heritage, London 1993 (rev. edn).
Sharples, N., *Maiden Castle*, Batsford, London 1991.
Collis, J. (ed.), *The Iron Age in Britain: a review*, University of Sheffield, Sheffield 1977.
Cunliffe, B., *Hengistbury Head, Dorset. Volume 1: The Prehistoric and Roman Settlement, 3500 BC–AD 500*. Oxford University Committee for Archaeology, Oxford 1987.
Niblett, R., 'A Catuvellaunian chieftain's burial from St Albans', *Antiquity* 66: 917–29, 1992.
Parfitt, K., *Iron Age burials from Mill Hill, Deal in Kent*, Antiquaries Research Report, forthcoming.
Macready, S. and Thompson, F.H. (eds), *Cross-Channel Trade between Gaul and Britain in the Pre-Roman Iron Age*, Society of Antiquaries, London 1984.
Roymans, N., *Tribal Societies in Northern Gaul: an Anthropological Perspective*, Cingula 12, Universiteit van Amsterdam, Amsterdam 1990.
Collis, J., *Oppida: Earliest Towns North of the Alps*, University of Sheffield, Sheffield 1984.
Jenö, F. (ed.), *The Celts in Central Europe*, Székesfehérvár 1975.
Mitchell, S., *Anatolia. Volume 1: The Celts and the Impact of Roman Rule*, Oxford University Press, Oxford 1993.

Chapter 4: The Patterns of Life
Reynolds, P., *Ancient farming*, Shire Archaeology, Aylesbury 1987.
Ehrenberg, M., *Women in Prehistory*, pp. 142–71, British Museum Publications, London 1989.
Ross, A., *The Pagan Celts*, Batsford, London 1986.
Nash, D., *Coinage in the Celtic World*, Seaby, London 1987.
Cunliffe, B., 'Pits, preconceptions and propitiation in the British Iron Age', *Oxford Journal of Archaeology* 11: 69–83, 1992.

Chapter 5: The Celts at War
For the most extensive, detailed and vivid account of ancient Celtic armies at war, read Caesar's *Gallic War*.

Still the best widely available illustrated introduction is in Connolly, P., *Greece and Rome at War*, pp. 113–26 (Macdonald, London 1981).

For the ceremonial Chertsey shield, see: Stead, I., 'Many more Iron Age shields from Britain', *Antiquaries Journal* (forthcoming).

Other references
Ritchie, W. and Ritchie, J., *Celtic Warriors*, Shire Archaeology 41, Aylesbury 1985.
Pleiner, R., *The Celtic Sword*, Oxford University Press, Oxford 1993.

Chapter 6: Gods and the Afterlife
Piggott, S., *The Druids*, Thames and Hudson, London and New York 1985.
Green, M., *The Gods of the Celts*, Alan Sutton, Gloucester 1986.
Mac Cana, P., *Celtic Mythology*, Newnes, Middlesex 1983.
Green, M., *Dictionary of Celtic Myth and Legend*, Thames and Hudson, London and New York 1992.
Brunaux, J.L., *The Celtic Gauls: Gods, Rites and Sanctuaries*, Seaby, London 1987.
Brothwell, D., *The Bogman and the Archaeology of People*, British Museum Publications, London 1986.
Stead, I.M., Bourke, J.B. and Brothwell, D.R., *Lindow Man: the Body in the Bog*, British Museum Publications, London 1986.
Stead, I.M., *The Arras Culture*, Yorkshire Philosophical Society, York 1979.
Stead, I.M., *Iron Age Cemeteries in East Yorkshire*, English Heritage, London 1991.
Bradley, R., *The Passage of Arms: an archaeological analysis of prehistoric hoards and votive deposits*, Cambridge University Press, Cambridge and New York 1990.
Woodward, A., *Shrines and Sacrifice*, Batsford/English Heritage, London 1992.

Chapter 7: La Tène Art and Technology
Megaw, R. and Megaw, V., *Celtic Art from its Beginnings to the Book of Kells*, Thames and Hudson, London and New York 1989.
Stead, I.M, *Celtic Art*, British Museum Publications, London 1985.
Jacobsthal, P., *Early Celtic Art*, Clarendon Press, Oxford 1944 (reprinted 1969).
Brailsford, J., *Early Celtic Masterpieces from Britain in the British Museum*, British Museum Publications, London 1975.
Megaw, J.V.S. and Megaw, M.R., *The Basse-Yutz Find: Masterpiece of Celtic Art*, Thames and Hudson, London and New York 1990.
Stead, I.M., *The Battersea Shield*, British Museum Publications, London 1985.
Stead, I.M., 'The Snettisham Treasure: Excavations in 1990', *Antiquity* 65: 447–65, 1991.
Millett, M. and McGrail, S., 'The Archaeology of the Hasholme logboat', *Archaeological Journal* 144: 69–155, 1987.
McGrail, S., 'Boats and boatmanship in the late prehistoric southern North Sea and Channel region', in McGrail, S. (ed.), *Maritime Celts, Frisians and Saxons*', CBA Research Report 71, pp. 32–48, 1990.

Chapter 8: The Celts and the Classical World
Rankin, H.D., *Celts and the Classical World*, Croom Helm, London 1987.
Blagg, T. and Millett, M. (eds), *The Early Roman Empire in the West*, Oxbow, Oxford 1990.
Goudineau, C., *César et la Gaule*, Errance, Paris 1991.
Brogan, O., *Roman Gaul*, Bell, London 1953.
Drinkwater, J., *Roman Gaul*, Croom Helm, London 1983.
King, A. C., *Roman Gaul and Germany*, British Museum Publications, London 1990.
MacKendrick, P., *Roman France*, Bell, London 1971.
Wightman, E., *Gallia Belgica*, Batsford, London 1985.
Rivet, A.L.F., *Gallia Narbonensis*, Batsford, London 1988.
Bromwich, J., *The Roman remains of southern France*, Routledge, London and New York 1993.

Siva, H., *Ausonius of Bordeaux*, Routledge, London and New York 1993.
Frere, S., *Britannia*, Routledge and Kegan Paul, London 1987.
Millett, M., *The Romanization of Britain*, Cambridge University Press, Cambridge 1990.
Potter, T. and Johns, C., *Roman Britain*, British Museum Press, London 1992.
de la Bédoyère, G., *Roman towns in Britain*, Batsford/English Heritage, London 1992.
Hingley, R., *Rural settlement in Roman Britain*, Seaby, London 1989.
Thomas, C., *Christianity in Roman Britain to AD 500*, Batsford, London 1981.

Chapter 9: The Celts of Ireland
Harbison, P., *Pre-Christian Ireland: from the first settlers to the early Celts*, Thames and Hudson, London and New York 1988.
Ryan, M. (ed.), *The Illustrated Archaeology of Ireland*, Country House, Dublin/Batsford, London 1991.
O'Kelly, M., *Early Ireland*, Cambridge University Press, Cambridge 1989.
Raftery, B., *La Tène in Ireland: problems of origin and chronology*, Marburg 1984.
Raftery, B., *A Catalogue of Irish Iron Age Antiquities*, Marburg 1983.
Raftery, B., *Pagan Celtic Ireland*, Thames and Hudson, London and New York 1994.
Gantz, J., *Early Irish Myths and Sagas*, Penguin, Harmondsworth 1981.
O'Rahilly, C., *Táin Bó Cúailnge*, Dublin Institute for Advanced Studies, Dublin 1976.

Chapters 10 and 11: The Medieval Celtic World and Beyond
Thomas, C., *Celtic Britain*, Thames and Hudson, London and New York 1986.
Alcock, L., *Arthur's Britain*, Penguin, Harmondsworth 1971/St Martin's Press, New York 1972.
Morris, J., *The Age of Arthur: a History of the British Isles from 350 to 650*, Weidenfeld and Nicolson, 1975 (rev. edn).
Jackson, K.H., *A Celtic Miscellany*, Routledge 1951.
Henderson, G., *From Durrow to Kells: the Insular Gospel Books, 650–800*, Thames and Hudson, London and New York 1987.
Nordenfalk, C., *Celtic and Anglo-Saxon painting*, Chatto and Windus, London 1977.
Redknap, M., *The Christian Celts: Treasures of Late Celtic Wales*, National Museum of Wales, Cardiff 1991.
Ritchie, A., *Picts*, HMSO, Edinburgh 1989.
Ritchie, A. and Breeze, D., *Invaders of Scotland*, HMSO, Edinburgh, no date.
Ritchie, G. and Ritchie, A., *Scotland: Archaeology and Early History*, Edinburgh University Press, Edinburgh 1991 (original edition, Thames and Hudson 1981).
Laing, L. and Laing, J., *The Picts and Scots*, Alan Sutton, Gloucester and Dover, USA 1993.
Hanson, W. and Slater, A., *Scottish Archaeology: New Perceptions*, Aberdeen University Press, Aberdeen 1991.
Edwards, N., *The Archaeology of Early Medieval Ireland*, Batsford, London 1990.
Williams, G., *When was Wales?* Penguin, Harmondsworth 1985.
Prebble, J., *The Lion in the North*, Penguin, Harmondsworth 1981 (an excellent concise history of Scotland).
Galliou, P. and Jones, M., *The Bretons*, Blackwell, Oxford and Cambridge, Mass. 1991.
Sheehy, J., *The Rediscovery of Ireland's Past: the Celtic Revival 1830–1930*, Thames and Hudson, London and New York 1980.

ACKNOWLEDGMENTS

Sources of texts and illustrations

The quotations from Classical authors are translations from books in the Loeb Classical Library unless otherwise indicated:

Aelian, *On the Characteristics of Animals*, tr. A.F. Schofield, 1959
Ammianus Marcellinus, tr. J.C. Rolfe, 1935
Appian, *Roman History*, tr. H. White, 1912
Athenaeus, *Deipnosophistae*, tr. C.B. Gulick, 1928
Ausonius, *Letters* and *The Moselle*, tr. H. White, 1949
Caesar, *Gallic War*, tr. H. Edwards, 1917
Cassius Dio, *Roman History*, tr. E. Cary, 1914
Catullus, tr. F.W. Cornish, 1913
Cicero, *Pro Fonteio*, tr. N.H. Watts, 1953
Diodorus Siculus, *Historical Library*, tr. C.H. Oldfather, 1933
Herodotus, *Histories*, tr. A.D. Godley, 1920
Livy, *History of Rome*, tr. B.O. Foster, 1924
Pausanias, *Description of Greece*, tr. W.H.S. Jones and H.A. Ormerod, 1926
Pliny, *Natural History*, tr. H. Rackham, 1938
Polybius, *The Histories*, tr. W.R. Paton, 1922
Strabo, *Geography*, tr. H.L. Jones, 1917
Tacitus, *Annals*, tr. J. Jackson 1931; *Agricola*, tr. Mattingly, Penguin Classics

Later Celtic and medieval texts:

Extracts from Celtic myths: Sliabh gCua, p. 158; Mael Mhuru, p. 158; Edain the fairy, p. 159; May-time, p. 160; Goddodin at Catraeth, p. 166; Note in the margin, p. 174: all from K.H. Jackson, *Celtic Miscellany*, Routledge 1951
Extracts from the *Táin*, pp. 153, 158–60: from *Táin Bó Cúailnge*, tr. C. O'Rahilly, Dublin 1976
St Patrick's letter, p. 162: tr. C. Thomas, in C. Thomas, *Christianity in Roman Britain to AD 500*, Batsford 1981
Geoffrey of Monmouth, p. 165: Geoffrey of Monmouth, *The History of the Kings of Britain*, tr. L. Thorpe, Penguin 1966
Nennius, p. 168: L. Alcock, *Arthur's Britain*, Penguin 1971
Extracts from Giraldus Cambrensis, pp. 172, 178: *Gerald of Wales: The History and Topography of Ireland*, tr. J.J. O'Meara, London 1982
Extract from Bede, p. 174: *History of the English Church and People*, tr. L. Sherley-Price, Penguin 1968

Buchanan on the Highlanders, p. 178: J. Prebble, *The Lion in the North*, Penguin 1981
Traditional Irish ballad, p. 177: D. Bellingham, *An Introduction to Celtic Mythology*, Apple Press 1990

Illustration credits

t = top, a = above, b = below, c = centre, l = left, r = right
The photographs and drawings on the following pages are all by Simon James: 8l, 9a, 9b, 10ac, 10c, 15b, 22ar, 25a, 25b, 26t, 26a, 26cr, 27c, 28a, 28bl, 40, 41b, 45b, 47bl, 47bc, 50–51, 53, 54r, 55a, 55c, 55bl, 56b, 57l, 57c, 57r, 58a, 58bl, 58br, 60a, 60b, 61l, 62a, 62b, 63b, 64c, 64r, 66, 68a, 70a, 75l, 75r, 76ar, 77b, 78, 79al, 79ac, 79bl, 81, 82r, 83a, 89r, 92r, 100bl, 101bl, 101br, 103r, 106r, 107bl, 110lc, 111a, 111b, 112l, 115br, 116–117, 124, 125a, 126a, 127a, 129ac, 129br, 130l, 131, 134, 135l, 135r, 137b, 138a, 138b, 139a, 140l, 142a, 142b, 143a, 145al, 145br, 149ar, 149b, 150bl, 150br, 151a, 156b, 163a, 180l, 181
The drawings on the following pages are by Annick Petersen: 16b–17b, 21, 22c, 23r, 24, 29, 35, 36b, 39, 43b, 44a, 44b, 48, 56a, 59a, 59b, 61r, 69c, 79ar, 83b, 85a, 93, 100a, 102a, 102b, 106bl, 107ar, 119, 121a, 123a, 125b, 126b, 127b, 128, 129al, 129bl, 132l, 137a, 139b, 147b, 151bl, 155, 156a, 158 (ornamental border), 167, 175c

Other credits:

Title-page Musée des Antiquités Nationales, St Germain-en-Laye. 6–7 Museo Nazionale Archeologico delle Marche, Ancona; photo Piero Baguzzi. 8r From Goscinny and Uderzo, *Asterix ac Anrheg Cesar (The Gift of Caesar)*, 1981, © 1993 Les Editions Albert René/Goscinny-Uderzo. 10al, 10ar, 11 British Museum. 13 After V. Kruta et al. (eds), *The Celts*, Thames and Hudson 1991. 14r Society of Antiquaries, London; photo Simon James. 15a From Vouga, *La Tène*, 1923; photo Simon James. 16a–17a Line drawings by Simon James, Geoff Penna. 18–19 Society of Antiquaries, London; photo Simon James. 20r Württembergisches Landesmuseum, Stuttgart. 22al Editions Errance; painting Mark Taraskoff. 22b Musée Archéologique, Châtillon-sur-Seine. 23l Musée Archéologique, Châtillon-sur-Seine; photo Piero Baguzzi. 26b, 27a, 27b, 28br From J. Biel, *Der Keltenfürst von Hochdorf*, Konrad Theiss 1985. 30a Württembergisches Landesmuseum, Stuttgart. 30b Peter A. Clayton. 31l British Museum; photo Erich Lessing. 31r Musée des Antiquités Nationales, St Germain-en-Laye. 32–33 Bologna Museum; photo Leonard von Matt. 34 Staatliche Museen, Berlin. 36al From M.-R. Sauter, *Switzerland*, Thames and Hudson 1976, fig. 58. 36ar Landesmuseum, Zürich. 37 British Museum. 38 Rosmarie Pierer. 41a Staatliche Museen, Berlin. 42, 43a British Museum. 45a Jean Roubier. 46 Musée des Antiquités Nationales, St Germain-en-Laye; photo RMN. 47a, 47br British Museum. 49a Drawing Stephen Conlin, from Mallory, *Navan Fort*, 1985. 49b Crown copyright. 54l After J.L. Brunaux. 55br Musée Historique d'Orléanais, Orleans. 64l Mšecké Žebrovice National Museum, Prague. 65 Painting Peter Connolly. 67 Cardiff City Council. 68b Society of Antiquaries, London; photo Simon James. 69tl, 69al, 69ar L'Univers des Formes – La Photothèque, Paris. 70b Drawing Mrs Margaret Scott. 72–73 British Museum. 74 G. Loeffel. 76al From Vouga, *La Tène*, 1923; photo Simon James. 76bl Painting Peter Connolly. 76br Ralph Jackson. 77a Painting Peter Connolly. 79br British Museum. 80 Painting Peter Connolly. 82l Centre Camille Jullian, CNRS Clichés Chéné. 84 Painting Peter Connolly. 84b–85b Drawing Ian Bott. 86–87 Institut Pédagogique National, Paris. 88l Musée des Antiquités Nationales, St Germain-en-Laye; photo Giraudon. 88r Württembergisches Landesmuseum, Stuttgart. 89l Musée des Antiquités Nationales, St Germain-en-Laye; photo Giraudon. 90 Peter Horne. 91 From William Stukeley, 1740. 92l Musée Borély, Marseilles. 94, 95a From C. Eluère, *The Celts*, Thames and Hudson 1993. 95b National Museum, Copenhagen. 96, 97a, 97b British Museum. 98 British Library. 99a Danebury Trust 99b Musée des Antiquités Nationales, St Germain-en-Laye; photo Giraudon. 100br British Museum; drawing Steve Crummy. 101a Painting Peter Connolly. 103l Werner Forman. 104–105 Musée de la Société Archéologique et Historiques de la Charente, Angoulême. 106al British Museum. 107al Staatliche Museen, Berlin. 107br Romanisches Germanisches Zentralmuseum, Mainz. 108 British Museum. 109al, 109ac 19th-c book; photo Simon James. 109ar British Museum. 109bl Rheinishes Landesmuseum; photo L'Univers des Formes – La Photothèque. 109br Werner Forman. 110al

Drawing Simon Driver. 110lb National Museum of Wales, Cardiff. 110c Moravian Museum, Brno. 110r After V. Kruta et al. (eds), Thames and Hudson 1991, p. 377. 112r, 113a British Museum; drawings Steve Crummy. 113b British Museum. 114a From Vouga, *La Tène*, 1923; photo Simon James. 114b, 115a British Museum. 115c, 115bl Hull City Museum. 121b After V. Kruta et al. (eds), *The Celts*, Thames and Hudson 1991, p. 421. 122 Musée du Louvre, Paris; photo Giraudon. 123b Museo Nazionale, Ludovisi Collection; photo Leonard von Matt. 129ar Bibliothèque Nationale, Paris. 130r Royal Commission for Historic Monuments (England). 132r Simon James/Steve Trow. 133 From Stuart Piggott, 'An Ancient Briton in North Africa', *Antiquity* XLII, 1968. 136a Jean Roubier. 136b Anderson. 140r British Museum. 141l, 141r, 143bl, 143br Peter Horne. 144l Rheinisches Landesmuseum, Bonn. 144r Thames and Hudson. 145ar Dr Grahame Soffe. 146 A.C.L., Brussels. 147a R. Agache, Service des Fouilles. 148a, 148b Peter Horne. 149al Provinzialmuseum, Trier. 150a British Museum; drawing Steve Crummy. 151br British Museum. 152–153 Irish Tourist Board. 154a British Museum. 154bl After Paul-Marie Duval, *Les Celtes*, 1977. 154br National Museum of Ireland, Dublin. 157 Cambridge University Collection of Air Photographs. 162 National Museum of Ireland, Dublin. 163b Drawings Charles Thomas. 164–165 The Board of Trinity College, Dublin. 166 British Museum. 168 Koninklijke Bibliotheek, The Hague. 169 British Library, London. 170a Drawing Geoff Penna. 170bl Drawings Charles Thomas. 170br From Nora K. Chadwick, *Celtic Britain*, Thames and Hudson 1963, fig. 26. 171al Crown copyright. 171ar British Museum. 171b Senatus Academicus, University of Aberdeen. 172l, 172r, 173 The Board of Trinity College, Dublin. 174a Royal Irish Academy, Dublin. 174b British Library, London. 175a, 175b Drawings Peter Bridgewater. 176–177 Library of Congress, Washington, D.C.; photo Edwin Levick. 178 Photo Centrehurst Ltd. 179al Belzeaux-Zodiaque. 179ar Bildarchiv Preussischer Kulturbesitz. 179b Private collection. 180r Museum of the City of New York.

INDEX